D1518918

First in the Homes of His Countrymen

Lydia Mattice Brandt

First in the Homes of His Countrymen

George Washington's Mount Vernon in the American Imagination

★ ★ ★ ★ ★ ★ ★ ★ ★

University of Virginia Press

Charlottesville & London

University of Virginia Press

© 2016 by the Rector and Visitors of the University of Virginia

Printed in the United States of America on acid-free paper

First published 2016

9 8 7 6 5 4 3 2 1

Library of Congress Cataloging-in-Publication Data
Names: Brandt, Lydia Mattice, author.
Title: First in the homes of his countrymen : George Washington's Mount
    Vernon in the American imagination / Lydia Mattice Brandt.
Description: Charlottesville : University of Virginia Press, 2016. | Includes
    bibliographical references and index.
Identifiers: LCCN 2016023613| ISBN 9780813939254 (cloth : alk. paper) |
    ISBN 9780813939261 (ebook)
Subjects: LCSH: Mount Vernon (Va. : Estate) | Nationalism and collective
    memory—United States. | Nationalism and architecture—United States.
    | National monuments—Social aspects—United States.
Classification: LCC E312.5 .B76 2016 | DDC 973.4/1092—dc23
LC record available at https://lccn.loc.gov/2016023613

Title page spread: West facade and dependencies of Mount Vernon, Virginia,
1735–87 (photograph 2008).

Cover art: Postcard view of Mt. Vernon Motor Lodge in Winter Park, Florida.

For the Richards:
Rick Brandt
Richard Martin Brandt
Richard Guy Wilson

Contents

Acknowledgments

Although my name is the only one on the cover, this book is the result of the love, enthusiasm, and humor of so many people I've had the great pleasure of knowing over the last decade. The Mount Vernon Ladies' Association made the single-greatest outside monetary and intellectual contributions to this project. The timing of the opening of the Fred W. Smith National Library for the Study of George Washington could not have been better for my research on Mount Vernon's image and preservation. The result was a partnership that strengthened the book exponentially and kept me going when the final draft seemed far away. The board offered encouragement and, through an inaugural fellowship at the library, crucial access and monetary support. The individuals who make up Mount Vernon's impressive staff and scholarly community became my colleagues. In the library, Douglas Bradburn, Stephen McLeod, Mark Santangelo, and their staff took care of all the details to make sure that every minute of my time at Mount Vernon was productive. The other fellows, especially John Sprinkle and Jon Taylor, provided invaluable hints, advice, and outlets for sharing my ideas. Research comrade Ann Bay became a great friend and colleague over many hours in the library's vault. Carol Borchert Cadou, Dean Norton, Thomas Rhinehart, and Mary Thompson shared their expertise and patiently answered my questions. Organizational wizard Dawn Bonner made the preparation of more than half of the book's images both a breeze and a pleasure.

I am enormously grateful to Susan P. Schoelwer and former Mount Vernon employees Esther White and Dennis Pogue; each made significant suggestions that greatly improved the final manuscript. Finally, Adam Erby was a constant sounding board and editor in the last year of the book's preparation. His insights and vast knowledge of all things Mount Vernon had a tremendous impact on the book. My confidence in this final document is especially indebted to these individuals' generous commentary, although all of its errors are entirely mine.

Funding for earlier phases of research for this project came from the Mellon Foundation and the University of Virginia Faculty Senate. The College of Arts and Sciences and the School of Visual Art and Design at the University of South Carolina provided additional funding for research and for the book's images and production. I am grateful for the financial support of each of these institutions, as well as the individuals who ensured that I received it.

Certain individuals have seen this long-standing project from its beginning. Richard Guy Wilson has been its most steadfast supporter. His tip on a "funny little building" at the World's Columbian Exposition started the whole thing off; his insistence that being the "Mount Vernon Lady" was a pretty good thing kept it going. Daniel Bluestone, Edward Lengel, Maurie D. McInnis, and Louis P. Nelson all remained supportive of the project, and their words of wisdom still rang true in the final phases of editing. I first encountered Scott Casper while he was a fellow at the University of Virginia in 2006 and am grateful for all of his suggestions for the project since. The members and attendees of a decade of annual meetings of the Southeast Chapter of the Society of Architectural Historians (SESAH) provided invaluable feedback on bits and pieces; the annual questioning of "When will this be a book?!" helped to sustain my confidence. My editor at the University of Virginia Press, Boyd Zenner, expressed interest in this work in its early stages and ushered it into its final form.

My devoted friends Amanda Bird, Amanda Das, Caitlin Fitzgerald, Philip Mills Herrington, Emilie Johnson, and Elizabeth Milnarik productively distracted me from writing and research over the past ten years. They are still always eager to drive out of their way to see "a Mount Vernon" and regularly drop new ones in my e-mail inbox. To Philip I am especially grateful; he gave me close notes on each phase of the manuscript, suggested many of its most intriguing examples, and provided me with essential commiseration throughout the publication process. The journey of this book would not have been as fun or as interesting without Philip.

From my earliest years, the Brandt and Page families encouraged my interests in writing, reading, dead presidents, and off-the-beaten-path "historic" sites.

Pretty much anything with a sign qualified, and questions were always answered with patience and interest. My mother, Joyce, and my brother, Austin, have long weathered the tedious explanations about what I do all day with good humor. My grandmother, Eva Page, has provided endless love and support. The three people who would have most enjoyed reading this book, my grandfather Richard Martin Brandt, my grandmother Mattice Fritz Brandt, and my father, Rick Brandt, never had the chance. But I like to think that they would have found all the right parts funny.

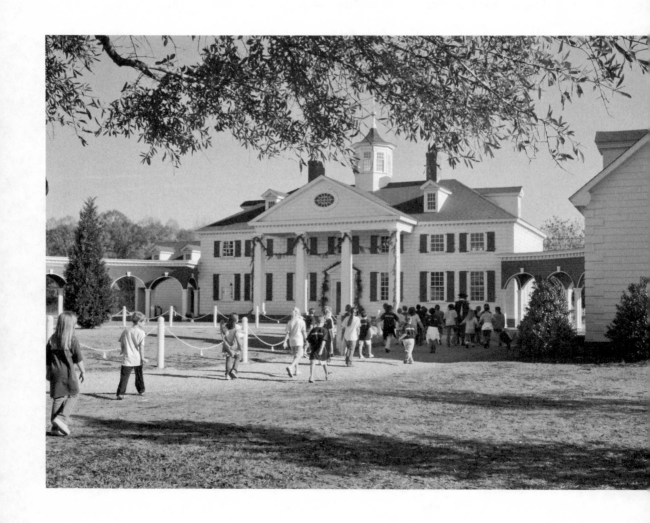

★ Introduction

M OUNT VERNON stands atop a hill in Montevallo, Alabama. "Washington Hall" is the focal point of the 183-acre campus of the "American Village." It reproduces the distinctive three-part composition, color scheme, rusticated (faux stone) siding, and cupola of George Washington's iconic Virginia plantation house. The building's interior boasts a version of the "New Room," Mount Vernon's largest and most elaborate space, as well as the principal chamber of Philadelphia's Independence Hall. The White House's Oval Office occupies one of its two connected service buildings (or dependencies), complete with Ronald Reagan's beloved jellybeans and the Resolute desk preferred by John F. Kennedy and other twentieth-century presidents. A bronze copy of Jean-Antoine Houdon's eighteenth-century marble sculpture *Washington* stands atop a pedestal in the building's soaring central hall.

Since the American Village opened in 1999, replicas of a number of other Colonial American buildings have joined Washington Hall on the Alabama campus. Beyond its commanding facade stand copies of the first presidential residence in Philadelphia, Williamsburg's courthouse and Bruton Parish Church, Carpenter's Hall (host of the first Constitutional Congress), a building housing a version of the White House's East Room, and the Old North Bridge in Concord, Massachusetts (the site of the first battle of the Revolutionary War). Fund-raising is currently under way for a full-scale replica of Independence Hall. The site's owner, the public-private partnership American Village Citizenship Trust, believes that these buildings "symbolize the principles of the new Republic."[1]

But why copy Mount Vernon at the end of the twentieth century, hundreds of miles away from Virginia? Why reimagine the building's architectural features and interior spaces alongside other historic places, melding different moments

Fig. 1. Washington Hall, Mike Hamrick (architect) and Tom Walker (founder and CEO), American Village, Montevallo, Alabama, 1996.

and individuals from the nation's past? Of all of the country's historic structures, why should Mount Vernon be at the center of a make-believe eighteenth-century America?

As old as the nation itself, Mount Vernon's image has been replicated more often and in a greater variety of ways than any other American building. Washington Hall is just one of countless examples of the appropriated image of Mount Vernon. Even before Washington's death, Americans used the building as they began to define the new republic. In the centuries that followed, Americans molded it to relate the past to a continually changing present. At the American Village, the building acts as a stage on which visiting schoolchildren and costumed interpreters reenact pivotal moments in American history.[2] Through architecture and programming, the site aims to reverse the growing "national amnesia" of American history and civics.[3] By casting students and visitors in the roles of historic decision makers, the immersive experience seeks to engage and inspire present and future citizens to "take on what has been called the most important office in our land, that of citizen."[4] Through a copy of Mount Vernon, the American Village intends to effect change in the present.

The American Village's architect, Mike Hamrick, and founder, Tom Walker, chose Mount Vernon as the model for the American Village's most commanding structure because they believed that visitors would immediately recognize and revere it. They found it to be the most emblematic American building and, therefore, the most obvious prototype for their "beacon of liberty."[5] Inextricably connected to the country's earliest national hero, Mount Vernon is indeed among the United States' most iconic structures. In the more than two hundred years since Washington's death, it has also become the most imitated American building. Its rusticated white walls, three-part composition, and cupola efficiently convey "history!" and "America!" to the masses on an astonishing range of building types.

The American Village Citizenship Trust also chose Mount Vernon because it was easy to manipulate, both ideologically and architecturally. Americans have used Mount Vernon to represent many different ideas over the past two centuries, priming it for adaptation at the American Village. Although the American Village does not declare allegiance to any political party, it does offer a very particular view of the country's past. Its approach presents an originalist interpretation of the Founding era in which its documents (namely the Constitution and Declaration of Independence) are read literally.[6] It promotes the country's early history as an exceptional event in human history. The spaces of Washington Hall draw a straight line between the leadership of George Washington, successive presidents and historic actors, and the site's contemporary visitors. As part of the American Village Citizenship Trust's belief that past sacrifices should serve as direct lessons for present-day political activism, Washington Hall is a place where eighteenth-century spaces and actions inspire twenty-first-century Alabamans.

This book looks to explain how and why Mount Vernon became a fitting model for a site like the American Village. How did Americans come to know what the house looked like? How did it develop into one of the country's most popular historic tourist destinations? Why did people choose it as the model for private houses, world's fair pavilions, dining halls, college dormitories, and funeral homes? Most importantly, what does Mount Vernon mean? Surveying more than two hundred years, this book balances a history of Washington's plantation house after the death of its illustrious owner with the development of its memory in popular visual culture and architecture. It explores Mount Vernon's starring role in Americans' attempts to relate the material past to the present and explains the process by which this single house became an internationally recognizable icon.

Resting on theories of collective memory, this study assumes that a society's understandings of its past are consciously and continuously reconstructed.[7] A community's position on past events and their meanings is the result of contemporary circumstances: we craft our memories based on how we want to remember them, selectively forgetting or emphasizing aspects in order to make them more relevant to ourselves in the present. Each successive generation of Americans has cast Mount Vernon in its own image, manipulating its significance to suit the needs of a particular moment.

Mount Vernon's flexibility was well established within decades of George Washington's death in 1799. It became a recognizable symbol that could be adjusted to signify many different (and sometimes contradictory) things. Its beauty was something to aspire to, but its simplicity made it attainable. It was both southern and American: evoking a particular regional identity as a Virginia plantation, it could also represent the entire nation as the home of its first president. Associated with the almost universally revered figure of Washington, it was an inclusive symbol. As a plantation operated by enslaved African Americans, it also carried unmistakably hierarchical connotations. Beyond these politically and socially charged meanings, Mount Vernon's image could simply communicate a vague connection to the past. Such a wide range of ambiguous possibilities for Mount Vernon's meaning ensured its popularity and longevity as a national symbol for many—but not all—Americans.

Social and technological change constantly offered new opportunities for expressing these varying interpretations of Mount Vernon. A surge of patriotism and lament over Washington's death prompted a number of printed views of the house at the turn of the nineteenth century, making its appearance known to a wider population than ever. Improvements in transportation facilitated public visitation after the Mount Vernon Ladies' Association (MVLA) opened the house as a public shrine in the mid-nineteenth century. The rise of American consumer culture created untold new businesses in the twentieth century, and many borrowed Mount Vernon's trademark architectural features for their buildings; its cupola, piazza, and other Colonial-era details signaled timeless tradition along the fast-paced roadside. Each of these new methods created additional ways for Americans to get to know Mount Vernon, broadening the collective memory of the building. The more ubiquitous Mount Vernon's image became, the more potential it stored for connecting America's past and present.

The building's broad appeal relied heavily on its early preservation and transformation into a tourist destination. People could actively engage with Mount Vernon because it survived, it was accessible, and Washington's life there was easy to imagine. The Mount Vernon Ladies' Association, the United States' first national women's historic preservation organization, transformed Mount Vernon from a working plantation into the country's premier house museum. Most accounts of historic preservation in the United States rightly applaud the MVLA's pioneering purchase of the property in 1859 but stop their analysis of the organization's impact there.[8] Over 150 years, the MVLA established the house museum as a genre and worked to define Mount Vernon and George Washington for the

American people. This study chronicles the MVLA's changing interpretation of Mount Vernon from the organization's purchase of the building through the early 1980s. In the process, a secondary story of the development of historic preservation in America emerges and offers a compelling argument for the importance of the MVLA beyond its founding moment.

This book charts the increasingly complicated dialogue between Mount Vernon as overseen by the MVLA and the house's image in popular visual culture. The organization spent much of the twentieth century fighting what it believed to be the commercialization and exploitation of Mount Vernon's image. But the gulf between the MVLA's interpretation of Washington's home and a 1939 advertising campaign for Mount Vernon Brand Straight Rye Whiskey, for example, was not as great as the Association wanted to believe. Both used Washington's house to project a particular brand of early America; both hoped the historic house's image would appeal to people in the present. Unlike the MVLA's meticulously researched narrative offered through the actual architecture, interiors, and landscape of Mount Vernon, the advertisements were unconcerned with authenticity. They relied on a mere glimpse of the house in order to convey an idea quickly and to a wide audience. Regardless of their differences, one could not exist without the other: the MVLA depended on the wide appeal of Mount Vernon to keep its charge relevant, while the commercial imagination needed a body of source material on which to draw. Despite its attempts to fully control Mount Vernon's memory, the MVLA discovered that its control extended no further than its own gates.

The Mount Vernon Ladies' Association's careful preservation and publicity not only guaranteed the building's cultural staying power but also facilitated the most popular means of remembering it: replication. Retelling history through architecture is a particularly effective means for making connections between the past and present. Buildings are conspicuous, costly, and lasting. Choosing to mimic an existing structure can impress a tangible link to the past upon a large audience for a very long time. From world's fair pavilions and private homes in the 1890s to the American Village one hundred years later, full-scale reproduction became the primary means by which Americans remembered Mount Vernon over the course of the twentieth century. All the while, the MVLA's study, documentation, and restoration primed Mount Vernon for widespread adaptation.

Honed by a century of prints, pilgrims, and the MVLA's preservation efforts, Mount Vernon was an obvious choice for anyone looking to copy a historic building in the wake of the revival craze of the nineteenth century. The range of building types and methods by which Americans adapted Mount Vernon's architecture grew steadily over the course of the twentieth century; each "replica" encouraged more replication. The fidelity of each to its model varied considerably, depending on the purpose, knowledge, and budget of its builder. In their increasing ubiquity, these variations on Mount Vernon took on lives of their own; their relationships to Mount Vernon became less clearly defined. By the mid-twentieth century, replicas copied replicas without referring back to the original model. As the MVLA took Mount Vernon ever-closer to what it believed was its eighteenth-century state, the replicas ventured further away from the original. This ongoing exchange between the replicas and the metamorphosis of Mount Vernon as a house museum demonstrates the importance of historic preservation for popular architecture and the potential impact of public history on American culture more broadly.

To tell the story of the phenomenon of replicating Mount Vernon's image, this study analyzes specific examples and situates them in larger cultural movements. Rather than theorize the idea and the role of reproduction in modern society, it tracks the processes of *how* and *why* something becomes reproducible.[9] Relying upon archival sources wherever possible, this book considers the contributions of individual examples to a collective memory of the past as well as the impact of the larger cultural impulse to replicate.

This study follows a roughly chronological narrative, pausing to more thoroughly explore moments in which Mount Vernon's memory was particularly fractured or dense. From advertising and architecture to print culture and popular literature, it draws on a wide range of sources to touch upon every genre of American visual culture that Mount Vernon has permeated. Throughout, the book builds on the popular memory of George Washington thoroughly explored by other scholars.[10] But while Mount Vernon's image is inextricably connected to how Americans have chosen to remember Washington, the significance of its architecture should also be recognized in its own right. As national symbols, both Washington and

Mount Vernon are accessible enough to be configured in a range of ways. As a physical and architectural object, Mount Vernon offers different possibilities for manipulation. Washington's long shadow lingers beneath the piazza of each replica of Mount Vernon, but the building has also established meanings and adaptations that are relatively independent of his memory.

Chapter 1 surveys the prints, paintings, published stories, and pilgrimage accounts that made Mount Vernon recognizable and determined its significance over the first half of the nineteenth century. As Washington's beloved home and the setting for his architectural, agricultural, and horticultural experimentation, Mount Vernon represented George Washington's relinquishment of executive power and joy in domestic tranquility.[11] As the sanctuary sacrificed by Washington during his public service and one regained only after he gave up command, Mount Vernon became integral to early Americans' beliefs about what made the general an ideal leader. By the middle of the nineteenth century, the house's image was a central component to many Americans' desire to see Washington as a relatable, humanized figure rather than a marble demigod.

The rising public interest in Mount Vernon among nineteenth-century Americans culminated in the unprecedented national fund-raising and publicity campaigns for the purchase of the house by the Mount Vernon Ladies' Association of the Union. Chapter 2 charts the rise of the MVLA and its purchase of Mount Vernon in 1859 amid intense public scrutiny. By casting Mount Vernon as a politically neutral symbol and its members as representative of a politically disenfranchised gender, the organization united the nation around the preservation of Mount Vernon on the eve of the Civil War. In the process of turning Mount Vernon into the country's first furnished house museum over the following thirty years, the organization solidified the building's iconic status and offered a simulated eighteenth-century Mount Vernon as the best way to remember the life of the great hero.

Chapter 3 argues that by making Mount Vernon more accessible, the MVLA facilitated a new way of remembering it: replication. At the turn of the twentieth century, Americans felt free to manipulate the house's image and began to copy it in full scale and in an ever-increasing range of building types. Early versions relied heavily on Mount Vernon's image as a gracious and hospitable southern planation, but later adaptations saw other possibilities for Mount Vernon's meaning. Over the first three decades of the twentieth century, replicating Mount Vernon's architecture became an easy and very public way for individuals and groups to connect past and present.

The Great Depression, the rise of historic tourism, enthusiasm for Colonial Revival goods, and the bicentennial of George Washington's birth boosted Mount Vernon's popularity in the 1930s.[12] Chapter 4 focuses on this decade before World War II to argue that as the house's architecture became more democratized through a proliferation of copies, the MVLA's interpretation and narrative of the building's architectural and historical significance grew more academic. Whereas in previous decades different political groups and factions had manipulated Mount Vernon to fit a variety of versions of the past, the house's memory was remarkably consistent in the 1930s: it was *the* example of American domesticity and good taste, fit and ready for imitation.

Chapter 5 examines the widening divide between Mount Vernon's popular image and preservation over the second half of the twentieth century. Whereas its architecture appeared on more buildings than ever along America's roadsides, the Mount Vernon Ladies' Association struggled to keep Mount Vernon relevant. The period's marked social and cultural changes challenged the organization to interpret Washington and his house in more inclusive ways at the same time that funeral homes and motels cherry-picked from the building's iconic architectural features without considering the building's connection to slavery or even history at all. Mount Vernon's image at once became more hollow and charged than it had ever been before.

The American Village's Washington Hall obviously lacks the gravitas of Mount Vernon. But it does radiate a certain power. In its evocation of George Washington's iconic home, it draws upon hundreds of years of reverence and enthusiasm for this single building and its role in American history. It makes clear that Americans still find the 250-year-old house relevant and rich enough to host diverse views of the country's past, present, and future.

1 ★ Prints and Pilgrimage

1790s–1850s

ARLY AMERICANS LOVED MOUNT VERNON because George Washington did.[1] He wrote in 1790: "I had rather be at Mount Vernon with a friend or two about me, than to be attended at the seat of government by the officers of state and the representatives of every power in Europe."[2] Mount Vernon was central to the creation of Washington's celebrity, both as imagined by his contemporaries and fashioned by the man himself. The plantation's distinctive house and prosperous agricultural operations bolstered the dedicated republican's overwhelmingly positive public image. Mount Vernon signified his personal sacrifices and the place to which he selflessly returned once he relinquished power. It offered Washington refuge throughout his career as a public servant. To the new nation, it afforded a glimpse of the private man behind the civic hero.

The large amount of information about the house available around the time of Washington's death in 1799 ensured its centrality to his fame. Early nineteenth-century Americans saw it in various forms of visual media and read about it in ubiquitous descriptions, poems, and eulogies. Many traveled to Virginia to see it for themselves. Even Washington had acknowledged the public's interest in his house, writing: "I have no objection to any sober & orderly person's gratifying their curiosity in viewing the buildings, Gardens &ca. about Mount Vernon."[3] After his death and burial at the plantation in 1799, it became a site of pilgrimage and one of the country's first historic tourist destinations.

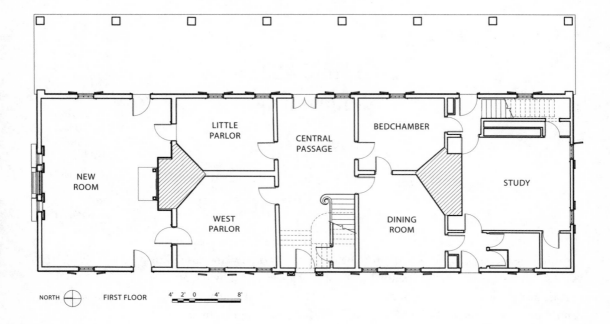

LITTLE PARLOR

CENTRAL PASSAGE

BEDCHAMBER

NEW ROOM

STUDY

WEST PARLOR

DINING ROOM

NORTH ⊕   FIRST FLOOR   4' 2' 0   4'   8'

Fig. 2. Plan of the first floor of Mount Vernon, Virginia, 1735–87 (with current interpretation of room use).

As Mount Vernon grew more accessible and its image more visible over the first half of the nineteenth century, its meaning became more pliable. Just as generations shaped Washington to suit their own image, so too did they mold Mount Vernon to fit their ideas of the past. Its ambiguities ensured its flexibility, creating a memory that was densely woven: it was both patrician and republican, relatable and idealized, a private house and public shrine. By the eve of the Civil War, the recognizable and pliable Mount Vernon had become an important national symbol in its own right.

Picturing Mount Vernon, 1790s–1810s

Washington and his house on the Potomac River were intrinsically connected long before the public found them inseparable. Much like many of his peers in England and in the colonies, Washington found pleasure in redesigning the house

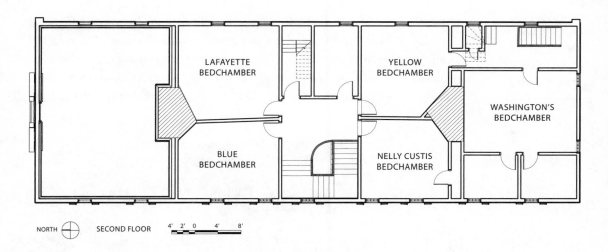

LAFAYETTE
BEDCHAMBER

YELLOW
BEDCHAMBER

WASHINGTON'S
BEDCHAMBER

BLUE
BEDCHAMBER

NELLY CUSTIS
BEDCHAMBER

NORTH   SECOND FLOOR   4' 2' 0   4'   8'

and immediately adjacent landscape over his lifetime and used it as a means of communicating his social status. He carefully directed alterations to better accommodate its occupants and their changing needs, as well as to convey his own perceptions of self.[4] Beginning with a one-and-a-half-story dwelling with eight rooms and a central hall built by his father in 1735, Washington expanded the house to two-and-a-half stories and twenty-one rooms over the next forty years. At 11,028 square feet, it was one of the largest houses in Colonial Virginia by the time it was completed in the 1780s.

Mount Vernon was not only big in size but was also distinctive in its architecture. Washington borrowed some of its features from pattern books and invented others. No aspect of the building's aesthetics was left unconsidered; he was conscious of how the house communicated his taste and character to his peers and the increasingly interested public.[5] Like many of his contemporaries, Washington organized his house as a three-part composition in the vein of the

Fig. 3. Plan of the second floor of Mount Vernon, Virginia, 1735–87 (with current interpretation of room use).

sixteenth-century Italian architect Andrea Palladio. Curved covered walkways connected Mount Vernon's long central block to two dependencies facing each other across a carriage circle on the house's west side. The main block was balanced rather than symmetrical, belying the building's multiple construction phases. A high hipped roof with wooden shingles boldly painted red, gabled dormers, and two brick chimneys dominated the mansion's mass. A cupola and floating pediment in the approximate center of the long facade focused and organized its irregularities. Washington coordinated the parallel, connected service buildings (a servant's hall to the north and a kitchen to the south) with the main

Fig. 4. West facade and dependencies of Mount Vernon, Virginia, 1735–87 (photograph 2008).

block using similar dormers and materials. All three of the buildings' clapboards underwent a "rustication" process to imitate the appearance and texture of stone: workmen grooved and beveled the pine panels, varnished them and painted them white, and then threw tan-colored sand onto their wet surfaces.[6] Green shutters adorned the large, double-sash windows. This impressive ensemble looked out over a landscape of Washington's own design. Beyond the carriage circle, serpentine pathways wound in and out of groves alongside a wide bowling green. Lanes of coordinated service buildings extended north and south from the carriage circle, balanced with a walled garden on each side. Samuel Vaughan, a British merchant and friend of Washington's, accurately captured the symmetrical and considered composition in a presentation drawing in 1787.[7]

Perched on a hill, the house's long, two-story piazza and dramatic view of the Potomac River defined its east side. Just as Washington used the pediment to focus and bring the illusion of symmetry to the long west facade, he devised a novel piazza for the building's east side. With eight square columns and a slate floor, the porch provided an ideal place to enjoy the view of the wide river stretching north and south below the house. Brick ha-ha walls ran parallel to the Potomac down the hill, keeping animals out without spoiling the vista.

By the last years of the eighteenth century, the building's idiosyncrasies ensured its easy recognizability. Even before Washington's 1799 death and especially in the decade following, printed views and published accounts established what the building looked like for those who could not visit it for themselves. These visual and verbal descriptions also codified what was important about the building to Washington's biography and American architecture more generally.

The genesis of most early printed views of Mount Vernon was a pair of small paintings by the enterprising portrait artist and engraver Edward Savage.[8] After visiting Washington's home over Christmas of 1789, Savage painted small oil pictures of the house's two facades in 1790–91.[9] His painting of the west side carefully documented the asymmetry of the window placement, position of the cupola, and the distinctive dove-of-peace weathervane, as well as the bowling green's weighted chain railing. He angled his view of the east facade to maximize the visibility of that side's most recognizable architectural features: beyond the piazza, river vista, ha-ha walls, and outbuildings along the north service lane, the

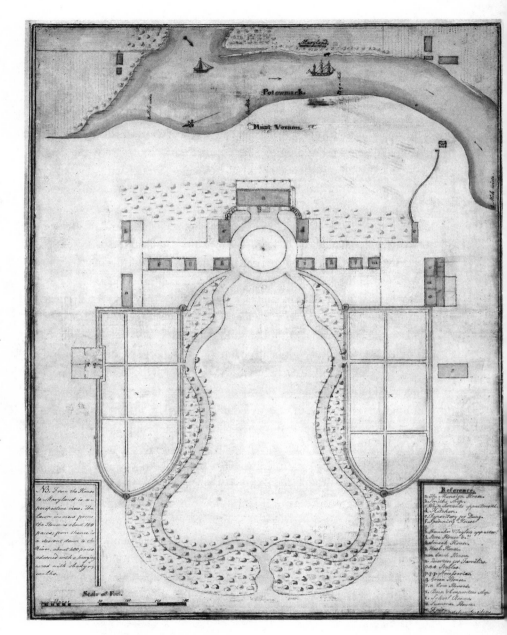

Fig. 5. Samuel Vaughan, presentation drawing of the Mount Vernon landscape, ink and watercolor, 1787.

view also featured the large Venetian window that George Washington copied from Batty Langley's pattern book, *The City and Country Builder's and Workman's Treasury of Designs,* for the north side.[10] To add veracity to his depiction, Savage titled this view *A North-East View of Mount Vernon, Painted on the Spot.*[11]

Although Savage most likely intended to make prints from the pictures, he never did. Instead, he exhibited the paintings in his galleries in New York, Philadelphia, and Boston into the early nineteenth century.[12] He probably hung them in his Philadelphia gallery when he opened it on George Washington's birthday in 1796, perhaps alongside his recently finished *The Washington Family.*[13] The publicly exhibited paintings of Mount Vernon provided opportunities for those who could not travel to Virginia to see it in vivid detail. As Savage's reputation grew with his immensely successful prints of *The Washington Family,* the pictures of Mount Vernon confirmed his direct experience with the hero.[14]

Savage's pair of Mount Vernon pictures provided valuable visual material for artists looking to capitalize on Washington's popularity in the years just before and after his December 1799 death. They established the conventions that other

Fig. 6. View from the northeast of Mount Vernon, Virginia, 1735–87 (photograph 2008). Note the New Room's distinctive Venetian window.

artists would rely upon when depicting Mount Vernon: emphasis on the Potomac River; a vantage point highlighting the Venetian window and piazza on the east side; and a slightly oblique perspective of the west facade allowing for a view of the parallel connected outbuildings. Either Savage or another artist copied the pair at least once in oil, while others adapted the image for inexpensive, mass-market prints.[15] Printed images of American buildings were relatively rare at the turn of the eighteenth century, but enterprising engravers produced a number of images of Mount Vernon. Prints of both facades of the building established its main features in the public's imagination, illustrating the increasing number of visitors' descriptions and patriotic odes published in popular magazines.

Most likely after seeing Savage's pictures on display in Philadelphia, David Edwin used the artist's take on Mount Vernon in his 1800 print of the apotheosis of Washington.[16] Draped in classical garb and crowned with a laurel wreath by a winged putto, the hero gestured to Mount Vernon as he ascended to heaven.[17]

The long, low profile and particular angle of Edwin's depiction of the east facade was unmistakably based on Savage's picture. The rest of the print borrowed from a transparency by Rembrandt Peale.[18] It is easy to imagine Edwin sketching the painting of Mount Vernon in Savage's gallery and deciding later to insert it into a larger composition.

George Isham Parkyns issued a print in 1799 that relied on Savage's painting of the west front of the house.[19] One of only a few views produced out of a contemplated series of twenty-four, Parkyns's image reversed Savage's painting.[20] He also pushed the house farther back into the picture plane in order to make room for a road curving gracefully southward to the Potomac River beyond (punctuated by a boat with raised sails). The print established the principal architectural features of the west side of the building for a potentially broader audience than Savage's painting.

Fig. 8. George Isham Parkyns, *Mount Vernon*, aquatint, 1799. The print reverses Edward Savage's 1790–91 painting.

Parkyns also emphasized the importance of the Potomac River to the plantation. The result is a view that is impossible to see in person; Parkyns took license with reality in order to include this feature. Waterways were essential components in many pictured American scenes, providing the artist with an easy way to create spatial depth while celebrating America's profitable natural resources.[21] Including the Potomac River in a print of Mount Vernon also situated the house in its precise geographic location. When Parkyns issued his view in 1799, Pierre Charles L'Enfant's elaborate plan for the District of Columbia was only just under way a few miles upriver. Parkyns's exaggerated view visually connected the plantation with the new seat of the federal government, evoking Mount Vernon's potentially national significance.

Coinciding with the swelling demand for mass-produced goods, Mount Vernon's image manifested in objects beyond printed views. The transition of prints and paintings of the house to ceramics and banjo clocks are just two examples of the translation of images across media in the first two decades of the eighteenth century. These items created more opportunities for Americans to encounter Mount Vernon in their everyday lives.

Around 1805, Chinese export porcelain teawares began to appear with a central medallion featuring Savage's distinctive depiction of Mount Vernon. His careful portrayal of the east facade and the landscape's principal features were clearly visible in the diminutive, hand-painted scenes.[22] Like many other porcelains produced in China for a Western market, an enterprising broker likely provided a sketch to the manufacturer, who then copied the scene directly.[23] The unknown merchant who commissioned the wares might have hailed from Philadelphia or Boston, where he could have seen and copied the picture in Savage's galleries.[24] Although scenes of American buildings and landscapes were relatively rare on Chinese export porcelain at the turn of the century, the Mount Vernon pattern was produced with at least five different borders.[25]

Chinese export porcelain was expensive and often custom-designed, pushing it out of the reach of most early Americans. English-made transfer ware was a more affordable choice for consumers looking to show their patriotism on household goods, especially after trade routes reopened after the War of 1812.[26] English-made transfer wares featuring a view of Mount Vernon by the English engraver,

landscape designer, and sometime architect William Birch were available by the 1810s.[27] Based on a print of the house's east facade that Birch first published in 1804 and then included in his *Country Seats of the United States* in 1808, such ceramics were more widely available than Chinese export porcelain.[28] The mass-produced transfer ware indicated the breadth of the public's interest in Mount Vernon in the decade after Washington's death (or at least the British manufacturers' perception of the demand).

Mount Vernon's visage also migrated to a new and uniquely American form: the banjo clock. Shaped like the musical instrument after which it was named, banjo clocks usually had rounded heads featuring the timepiece's face and long throats ending in boxes housing suspended pendulums. Clock makers covered the surfaces of the clocks' necks and rectangular boxes with glass paintings that mimicked the techniques and subjects of popular engravings.[29] A banjo clock made by Lemuel Curtis in Concord, Massachusetts, circa 1815, for example, was among the second generation of the patented form. A faithful, reverse copy of an 1800 print by the artist Alexander Robertson and the engraver Francis Jukes of the east side of Mount Vernon graced the clock's box. Washington's house continued to appear on banjo clocks in the following decade, often embellished with eagles, American flags, or other flourishes typical of the Federal period.[30]

Published descriptions supplemented the available images of Mount Vernon, expanding attention to the well-appointed interiors and weaving the building and landscape's aesthetic attributes into accounts of Washington's character and biography. In David Humphrey's very early attempt at a Washington biography in the 1780s, he described the "lofty Portico," "pleasantly situated" site, and the *"tout ensemble"* of the coordinated mansion and outbuildings. He also hinted at Washington's interests as a gentleman architect: "The Mansion House itself, though much embellished by yet not perfectly satisfactory to the chaste taste of the present Possessor, appears venerable & convenient." Humphreys made sure to mention "the superb banqueting [*sic*] room," referring to the double-height, multipurpose "New Room" with the large Venetian window that Washington began adding onto the north side of the building in the late 1770s.[31]

Usually printed in popular magazines, such tellings were often compilations of multiple sources; like the printed views, the verbal descriptions were frequently reconfigured in new contexts. Humphreys's account of Mount Vernon, for example, was reprinted in part in Jedidiah Morse's *Geographies* in 1789 and as a section of a more lengthy biographical account by Thomas Condie in the *Philadelphia Monthly Magazine* in 1798. Morse and Condie both elaborated upon the life Washington led at Mount Vernon, specifying his disciplined and "industrious" daily routine and the many dignitaries who came to visit him there.[32] The account George Isham Parkyns wrote to accompany his 1799 print also borrowed liberally from Humphreys's account. He erroneously specified that General Lafayette presented the Washingtons with the mantel then in the New Room, an inaccuracy that reporters and visitors perpetuated well into the nineteenth century (the mantel was a gift from Samuel Vaughan).[33]

As visual and verbal descriptions of Mount Vernon became increasingly available in the years just before and after Washington's death, Americans shaped its role in national symbolism and in Washington's mythology. There were very few other buildings with such patriotic resonance, making room for Mount Vernon to operate somewhere between a public and private building and to offer an example of a distinctly American architecture. Until construction began on the White House and U.S. Capitol in the mid-1790s, most major public buildings in the United States were associated with Colonial governments. Even Independence Hall, the location of the country's ideological founding, had been constructed as the seat for Colonial Pennsylvania's legislature.[34] Images and descriptions revealed not only what Mount Vernon looked like, therefore, but also what it could mean to the recently united states. In determining Mount Vernon's symbolic role, newly minted citizens navigated its potential ambiguity. Its "simple" architecture balanced Washington's republican values as well as his patrician aspirations, making it the home of both an ideal democratic leader and a social elite.

William Birch was one of many who regarded Mount Vernon for both its architectural merits and its associations with Washington. He included an engraving of the east facade in his 1808 *Country Seats of the United States* as a fine example of the nascent fine arts in America.[35] He described Mount Vernon as "hallowed," its site as "dignified," and the piazza and New Room as "proofs of the legitimacy of the General's taste."[36] Placing it alongside neoclassical suburban residences outside of Philadelphia and Baltimore, Birch separated Mount Vernon from its agricultural operation to admire it as a refined "American Country Residence" akin to the villas of classical Rome or the English countryside.[37]

In addition to Mount Vernon's elegance, most published descriptions of its architecture also praised its "simplicity." An early biography of Washington, published in the *American Museum* in 1792, proclaimed that the house was "elegant, though simple, and of a pleasing aspect."[38] In the description accompanying his print, George Isham Parkyns said Mount Vernon was "simple and unadorned," with "an air of convenience and grandeur." An explanation of the Jukes and Robertson print went so far as to say that the house was "extremely plain, and has nothing, except extreme neatness, to recommend it to attention."[39] The admirable restraint implicit in descriptors such as "neat," "plain," and "simple" reinforced Americans' desire to identify Mount Vernon as a specifically eighteenth-century building, inextricably connected to Washington and the Revolutionary period.[40] Pieced together over forty years, the house did have a distinctly eighteenth-century feel; the entire ensemble was less academic in its neoclassicism than more recent elite dwellings.

For many, the supposed simplicity of Mount Vernon's architecture confirmed Washington's disinterest in authority; it differentiated him from European monarchs and Mount Vernon from their palaces. The house was a stage for tales of the supposedly humble and industrious life Washington chose to live there. Shortly after describing the house as "venerable and convenient," the early biographer David Humphreys wrote: "The virtuous simplicity which distinguishes the private life of General Washington, though less known than the dazzling splendor of his military achievements is not less edifying in example, or worthy the attention of his countrymen."[41] In a 1789 ode, Samuel Knox described Mount Vernon as Washington's "rural dome" before emphasizing the difference between Washington and other world leaders: "No Alexander's mad career / No Caesar's dictatorial reign / No daz'ling pomp that sceptres wear / Thy soul with thirst of pow'r could stain."[42]

The first president's relationship with his house became a key component in one of the most common tropes used by his contemporaries to express his fitness for leadership: the comparison between Washington and the legendary Roman statesman Cincinnatus. The antique hero exemplified the ideal of virtuous citizenship in the classical republic; he left his farm to fight for Rome, fought valiantly and achieved victory, and then relinquished military power in order to return to work on his farm. Early Americans venerated the Roman for sacrificing his private life and for voluntarily surrendering the sword of command.[43] Likewise, Americans celebrated Washington for leaving his family and business at Mount Vernon to serve the nation as commander in chief of the Continental Army and as president, and for publicly relinquishing both positions in 1783 and 1797, respectively.[44] Washington's deference to the democratic process and his very public retreats to Mount Vernon provided an example for a new kind of citizenship and quieted debates about whether the federal government was merely replacing George III with the tall, graceful Virginian.[45]

Without Mount Vernon, the comparison to Cincinnatus would not work. The public had to understand the private world Washington left and returned to in order to appreciate his sacrifice. Historians typically focus on Jean-Antoine Houdon's *George Washington,* a life-size marble sculpture commissioned for the Virginia State Capitol Building in 1788–92, as the epitome of the artistic representation of Washington as Cincinnatus.[46] Combining a portrayal of Washington in his contemporary military uniform with allegorical classical attributes, the work symbolized his renunciation of military power (represented by a sword and cloak) to the U.S. government (the fasces on which he rests his hand) in favor of life on his farm (a plow at his feet).[47]

Easily distributed images and descriptions were even more important in the establishment of the metaphor than Houdon's singular sculpture. The connection between Washington, Cincinnatus, and Mount Vernon was made again and again in published and oral eulogies, for example. In his eulogy for Washington given just weeks after the general's death, Thomas Paine proclaimed: "We might behold the majestic Cincinnatus, who, like thee, in the vigour [*sic*] of Roman heroism, could return from the conquest of his country's enemies, to his humble Mount Vernon beyond the Tyber."[48] John James Barralet's 1799 print *General Washington's Resignation* depicted "the American Cincinnatus" at the moment of his resignation from the presidency.[49] Like Houdon's sculpture, the engraving combined allegory with contemporary representations of Washington. With his armor and sword laid at his feet, Washington handed over his authority to the seated classical figure "America." As he descended the steps, Washington gestured to "a beautiful landscape, representing Mount Vernon, in front of which were seen oxen harnessed to the plough."[50] Borrowing from a 1798 print by Isaac Weld, Barralet was sure to include the house's cupola, piazza, and river view so that his audience would recognize the building as Mount Vernon.[51] The brief treatment of the features suggests that Barralet could depend on his audience needing only these few visual cues to recognize the house. In the foreground, symbols of the new republic (shield, eagle, and motto "E Pluribus Unum"), peace (olive branches), and plenty (cornucopia) indicated that Washington's disinterestedness in power ensured both peace and prosperity for the nation. For an eighteenth-century audience, Mount Vernon's appearance in this print was an explicit acknowledgment of the house's role in his refusal to be a despot. Even Washington

GENERAL WASHINGTON'S

RESIGNATION.

Fig. 10. Alexander Lawson after John James Barralet, *General Washington's Resignation,* engraving, frontispiece to *Philadelphia Magazine and Review* (January 1799).

promoted the Cincinnatus myth in his design of Mount Vernon. When planning the New Room at the end of the Revolution, he chose a decorative program featuring farm implements for the delicate neoclassical stuccowork on the ceiling.

Pilgrimaging to Mount Vernon, 1810s–1850s

Upon Washington's death at Mount Vernon on December 14, 1799, and his subsequent burial on the plantation, the house took on additional meanings in American culture: as Washington became the nation's sacred figure, it became both a reliquary for his remains and a relic in itself. For both reasons, Mount Vernon developed into a pilgrimage site for those seeking to understand the first president and America's short but storied past. It became ever more important as Washington's mythological status grew, a process perpetuated by the passing of the Revolutionary War generation in the 1810s, the return of General Lafayette for a national tour in 1824, and the centennial of the hero's birth in 1832.[52] Popular literature, images, and tourism allowed Americans who had not lived during Washington's lifetime to imagine the man in the shade of the trees he planted and the piazza he designed. These various media further codified visual and verbal descriptions.

Echoing apotheosis images such as Edwin's that cast Washington as a demigod, early nineteenth-century writers spoke of Washington as a divine figure and of Mount Vernon as a sacred place.[53] In eulogies, speakers compared it to Eden, and newspapers often referred to it as the "American Mecca." Patriotic tourists continually described their trips to see the house in religious terms: "Mt. Vernon is sacred in the eyes of Americans; it is the spot to which many a pilgrim wends his way, anxious to drop a tear at the tomb of the Father of his country."[54] A reporter for the *National Register* described the "hallowed" mount and pushed beyond the comparison of Washington with Cincinnatus to one with Jesus Christ: "From this tranquil spot he was again summoned to give form, solidity and coherence to the rising republic; and after eight years of unparalleled prosperity, he retired again to this consecrated asylum, to die amidst this his paternal shades, and this is the spot where *he is now awaiting the day of resurrection*."[55]

By the second quarter of the nineteenth century, average Americans could pilgrimage to the plantation more easily than ever before. With more disposable income and free time and continually improving transportation networks, Americans were traveling in greater numbers by the 1830s. "Sacred" sites like Washington's home provided destinations that helped to define secular American culture and identity in a similar way temples had for ancient societies.[56] Mount Vernon's Washington-designed picturesque landscape, already commemorated in prints and published descriptions, was also a draw for the distinguished visitor looking to emulate European Grand Tours.[57] New guidebooks and popular magazines defined Mount Vernon as a tourist destination, while steamboat technology made the house easier to reach and the journey far more pleasant than the laborious land route used by the majority of earlier travelers.[58]

In the first four decades of the nineteenth century, reporters, dignitaries, and pilgrims published their accounts of visits to Mount Vernon in popular magazines and newspapers across the country. These explanations standardized tourists' experiences and provided a sense of what they could expect; much like earlier reports, they were often reprinted without attribution. Some descriptions even began with recognition of the repetitive nature of pilgrimage accounts: "So much has been written by others respecting that venerated spot, that the subject has become a good degree hackneyed."[59] Most visitors provided virtually identical remarks on travel conditions (either by road or river), the house and immediate landscape, and the tomb. Many commented on the outbuildings, enslaved inhabitants, and recounted poems or other sentimentalities.[60] The cumulative effect of these corroborating reports was the creation of a consistent narrative of the most important aspects of Mount Vernon's landscape.

Depending on whether or not visitors could provide a letter of introduction, they were granted entrance to the house itself. Mount Vernon's owner-occupants following George and Martha Washington, Washington's nephew Bushrod Washington and then Bushrod's nephew John Augustine Washington II and his wife, Jane Charlotte Washington, systematized the visitor's experience by effectively operating the house as a museum for those with the proper credentials.[61] They lived upstairs and used Washington's study as a dining room (the kitchen in the south dependency was still operational), leaving most of the first floor and the few intact Washington-era objects to curiosity seekers. Enslaved African Americans provided informal tours of the house and grounds, with some claiming to have known or been owned by Washington in order to create a living link between the general and his world.[62] This codified pilgrimage route would become central to the interpretation of the house by the Mount Vernon Ladies' Association in decades to come.

Two remarkably similar descriptions of the house written twenty years apart, one under Bushrod Washington's tenure and one under Jane Charlotte Washington's, give a sense of the increasingly standardized Mount Vernon tourist experience. In 1824, a "gentleman travelling in Virginia" recounted:

> Taking with me an introduction to Judge Washington, and others, I was with great cordiality welcomed. . . . The whole structure has lately undergone a thorough repair, and has in every respect the same appearance as when the General died, except a small portion which the Judge has built at the south end. . . . The hall of the celebrated Seat is long with a great variety of elegant prints. The first thing, however, which caught my eye, was a huge mapine iron key, which has screamed in the affrighted ear of thousands, as they passed the threshold of the Bastile [sic] . . . [La]Fayette sent this monstrous key to Gen. Washington, and it now hangs in the very spot where he placed it. There are four public rooms in this establishment, two sitting rooms, a dining room, and a drawing room. The Judge has recently converted the General's study into another dining room. The General's library is in good order, and contains a very handsome collection of books.[63]

A visitor to the house in 1846 similarly described his tour of the mansion:

> Mrs. [Jane Charlotte] Washington, a lady venerable in years and worth, received us in the library of the General, a sacred room, which has been preserved as nearly as possible in the state in which he left it. Here were several family pictures, and various memorials of the great man: the original bust by Houdon placed over the door by Washington's own hand, and never since

removed. . . . In the family dining room were several beautiful engravings that had been presented to the General; in a private parlour was the key of the Bastile [sic] given to Washington by La Fayette after its memorable destruction, and several paintings that possessed peculiar interest from the fact that they connected their possessor with events that they illustrated. We were now introduced into the great dining room that the General was obliged to erect at the North end of his mansion to enable him to entertain the numerous guests that thronged his house after he retired from the Presidency.[64]

Written twenty years apart, these two descriptions are notable for a number of reasons. Each discussed the similarities (or differences) between Washington's household and that of his successors, suggesting that the visitors had some previous knowledge of the house and that they were interested in the authenticity of the architecture, the function of the rooms, and the items within them. Both visitors seem to have been granted access to all of the rooms on the first floor, including Washington's study. An intensely private space when Washington lived in the mansion, the study was an essential part of Mount Vernon as a shrine. Visitors came to see the personal items Washington consulted while planning Revolutionary battles and writing his Farewell Address. Finally, both descriptions are careful to include the key to the Bastille prison in Paris, one of the few objects owned by Washington left in situ since his lifetime. Given to Washington by Lafayette, it gave Mount Vernon authority as a pilgrimage site. Mentioned in almost every account of the house from the first half of the nineteenth century, the Bastille key in particular reinforced the international importance of Washington and his role as a public figure.

Shifts in the content of printed images of Mount Vernon also reflected the rising number of pilgrims to the plantation. Peppered with fashionable (and well-behaved) Americans, prints testified to the transformation of Mount Vernon into a tourist destination in the decades preceding the Civil War. Two very similar prints typical of the period, engraved in 1853 and 1856 by C. H. Wells and Currier & Ives, respectively, featured tourists looking at the house and grounds. Both showed the east side of the house from approximately the same angle as had Birch and Jukes and Robertson, yet with a much tighter view. The building's most

Fig. 11. *Great Hall at Mount Vernon, from the S. E. End (Built by Washington),* wood engraving, frontispiece to *Godey's Lady's Book* (July 1849). The print's angle and line weight emphasize the Bastille key (center left, hanging between the two doors), the room's principal Washington-related object.

iconic architectural features were all visible, but the landscape was treated much more briefly. People came to see the house where Washington lived and in which he died; the landscape was merely a setting for it.

In addition to continuing to make Mount Vernon's exterior recognizable to a wide audience, images produced in the second quarter of the nineteenth century also portrayed the interiors and articles of furniture most often mentioned in visitors' published accounts. The vantage point of an engraving of the central passage published in *Godey's Lady's Book* in 1849 looked from the east end of the space to the west, ensuring the inclusion of the famous Bastille key in between two doors. A view of the New Room also published in *Godey's* in 1849 skewed the space's perspective in order to exhibit as much of the ceiling's elaborate stuccowork as possible without sacrificing the window and fireplace on the side-walls. Both prints arranged the figures to direct the viewer's attention directly at these distinctive features: a man looks to the Bastille key in the passage, while a gesturing woman in a bonnet looks up at the ceiling in the New Room. Such detailed illustrations reinforced the most important aspects of the interior and confirmed that it was accessible to contemporary visitors.

The Softer Side of Washington, 1810s–1850s

The public's interest in Mount Vernon over the first half of the nineteenth century both drove and was fueled by a shift in the ways in which Americans saw George Washington. Access to it—either through published accounts, prints, or pilgrimages—allowed for a closer look at Washington's private world. Over the decades following Washington's death, his image gradually became more relatable than the stoic classical figure depicted in Houdon's sculpture and Barralet's print. With the passing of the Revolutionary War generation in the 1810s, an approachable version of the paragon became even more important; Washington had to be more human if he were to serve as an example for Americans who never knew him alive. After the emergence of Andrew Jackson and his new kind of "everyman" celebrity, the public especially desired a more accessible Washington than the cold marble figure of previous decades.[65]

In the trail of the domestic reform movements inspired by the Second Great Awakening, Americans were increasingly interested in Washington's domestic life at Mount Vernon. While the public had previously regarded Mount Vernon as evidence of Washington's impeccable character (the Cincinnatus comparison being the best example), by midcentury many Americans believed that the house had played a more active role in shaping the hero. As the industrializing country grappled with defining what it meant to be a democracy, domestic space became a repository for the values many hoped would be the driving forces for society. From design to functionality, architecture received unprecedented attention in popular and scientific literature to ensure that Americans lived in the most efficient and moral homes possible.[66] As the most famous and revered of all the nation's citizens and houses, Washington and Mount Vernon were naturally sought as prime examples for the ideal American and his home. An 1838 course of reading lessons "selected with reference to their moral influence of the hearts and lives of the young," for example, was titled *The Mount Vernon Reader*.[67] Its authors explained that they selected the name "in the hope that this work may contribute something to extend, among the rising generation of our land, those feelings of piety, philanthropy, and patriotism" that Washington had so perfectly embodied at Mount Vernon.[68]

Images and descriptions of Mount Vernon and its relationship to Washington shifted to exhibit this new emphasis. By the second quarter of the nineteenth century, depictions of Washington's domestic life enlivened the more academic classical metaphors established just twenty years earlier.[69] Beginning with Mason Locke Weems's oft-repeated tall tales about the childhood hero's encounter with a cherry tree, a growing cadre of biographies helped to humanize Washington.[70] Popular images of the first president increasingly started to depict him as a private man just as his biographies did; his childhood, marriage, death, and daily life at Mount Vernon emerged as popular subjects for prints, paintings, and book illustrations.

Two series of paintings, one by John Gadsby Chapman in the 1830s and the other by Junius Brutus Stearns in the 1850s, told the story of Washington's life. Both artists engraved, printed, and distributed the works widely; they intended the images to reach large audiences. Mount Vernon featured prominently in both, attesting to the importance of the building to the public's understanding of Washington's biography by the second quarter of the nineteenth century. Using very different narrative strategies, Chapman and Stearns communicated the importance of Mount Vernon not only to Washington's life but also to the ways in which contemporary Americans remembered him. Both artists treated Mount Vernon more briefly than the late eighteenth-century images that carefully detailed architectural and landscape features. As Americans became more familiar with Mount Vernon, the artists were able to assume that their audiences could quickly recognize it without including all of the specific visual signifiers so central to earlier views.

The Virginia-born and Italian-trained artist John Gadsby Chapman painted a series of landscapes central to the first president's biography in the 1830s.[71] Among the sites Chapman chose were Washington's birthplace, his childhood homestead, his mother's house in Fredericksburg, the bedchamber in which he died, and his tomb.[72] A picture of Yorktown is the only one in the cycle to refer directly to Washington's political or military career. Chapman painted the exterior of Mount Vernon from a variety of viewpoints, including from the Potomac River and from the northeast. He showed the Washington pictures at the National Academy of Design in the summer of 1835 as well as in his own New York studio, and used them as sources for a number of engravings.[73]

Most conspicuously, Chapman's images did not feature Washington or any other discernible historical figure. A sense of absence defined the small, sentimental pictures; Washington was clearly missing. In the intimate painting of Washington's bedroom at Mount Vernon, for example, sunlight streamed through an open window, a blanket laid across a chair with a book on a nearby table, and the bed's muslin summer curtains were drawn back to reveal the pillows on which the great hero rested his head. It was as if Washington had just left the room. The sole reliance on a physical or architectural setting to carry emotional, or at least patriotic, gravitas spoke to the public's visceral connection with Mount Vernon by the 1830s. The scene was a fantasy, however; the furniture in the Mount Vernon bedchamber had long been removed to Arlington House, the nearby home of Washington's beloved step-grandson, George Washington Parke Custis. Chapman reconstructed the space in order to help his contemporaries imagine what it would have looked like during Washington's lifetime. He banked on his audience's desire to better understand the hero through the intimate things he touched and spaces he inhabited.

Chapman's views of Mount Vernon were vastly different from those that preceded them; few followed the established conventions, and most featured spaces or views never considered by earlier artists. They became immediately popular, flooding the market for Washington- and Mount Vernon–related images through a variety of venues. Chapman's print renditions of his exterior paintings of Mount Vernon appeared in popular magazines, illustrating the growing number of pilgrims' accounts of the hallowed site. In general, these depictions were far tighter in composition than earlier images, focusing closely on the building rather than the surrounding picturesque landscape or Potomac River. An engraving of Chapman's painting of the house from the southeast, an angle that actually denied the view of the river so central to earlier prints, made the house itself the sole subject of the picture. Published in the *Family Magazine* as part of a series entitled "Residences of the Presidents," the image deemphasized the landscape and provided the visual interest of a small porch added onto the south side in 1822. Chapman was perhaps the first to depict the house from this tighter angle, yet it quickly became a new standard type.[74]

Junius Brutus Stearns similarly ignored previous neoclassical images of Washington in his own biographical painting cycle, completed between 1851 and 1856. Unlike Chapman's series, Stearns's explicitly covered all aspects of Washington's life: his marriage, death, and work as a soldier, statesman, and farmer. His works were also explicitly narrative history paintings; they are far more conventional than Chapman's evocatively empty landscapes. Four of the compositions became wildly popular after they were published as lithographs in 1853–54.[75] Stearns's first painting in the series, *The Marriage of Washington,* responded to the trend in contemporary biographies to compare Washington's wedding and marriage to Martha Custis to those of other well-to-do Americans. When Stearns engraved the painting, he appropriately retitled the image *Life of George Washington—The Citizen,* as if to confirm that what made Washington a legitimate and contributing member of society was his commitment to family.[76] Besides humanizing the hero, the painting's focus on Washington's marriage to the young widow Martha Custis supported contemporary Americans' belief that he ascribed to their idea of the Christian home.[77]

Stearns's painting *Washington as a Farmer, at Mount Vernon* positioned this newly domesticated George Washington back in the Cincinnatus metaphor with a more narrative bent. The image clearly implied the connection to the ancient Roman: Washington inspected the ongoing harvest surrounded by his overseer, slaves, and grandchildren with Mount Vernon in the distance. By 1851, there was no need for Stearns to compare the hero to Cincinnatus explicitly or to employ classical allegory; he could depend on the audience to make the connection and to recognize Mount Vernon. Playing with flowers in the corner of the picture, the young Nelly and George Washington Parke Custis encouraged the vision of Mount Vernon as a home and sentimentalized Washington as a grandfather. The well-dressed, hardworking, and smiling slaves verified the house as a working plantation and further suggested Washington as a benevolent master.[78] The inclusion of Martha Washington and her grandchildren in Stearns's paintings suggested the love and family values behind Washington's character and peopled Mount Vernon with women and children; it made the mansion a home rather than merely an expression of Washington's political fitness.

Spurred by the public's exposure to the house, descriptions of Mount Vernon in Washington biographies also shifted. John Frost's 1848 description of George and Martha's marriage, for example, humanized the house in a way previous biographies had not: "In that hallowed retreat, [Martha Washington] was found entering into the plans of Washington, sharing his confidence, and making his household happy. . . . During his absence [from Mount Vernon] she made the most strenuous efforts to discharge the added weight of care, and to endure, with changeless trust in Heaven, continual anxiety for the safety of one so inexpressibly dear."[79] Mount Vernon had signified Washington's Cincinnatus-like sacrifices for decades. By the mid-nineteenth century, it also suggested the family he left behind. They, too, had made a patriotic sacrifice; they gave up their patriarch so that their country might have one.[80]

Memorializing Washington, 1820s–1850s

With a growing number of opportunities to imagine George Washington's private life at Mount Vernon in the first half of the nineteenth century, discussions mounted over the house's future and its potential role as a public monument. Suggestions for the federal or Virginia state government's purchase of the house cropped up repeatedly, often prompted by major events such as Lafayette's visit in 1824 or the centennial of Washington's birth in 1832. Since Washington's death, the American public increasingly felt it had the right to see the house whenever and on whatever terms it desired. A visitor wrote in 1822: "The fame of General Washington is the property of the nation, and individuals appear to consider the mansion and lands which formerly belonged to him, so far public property as to entitle them to run through them and round them without regard to the convenience of the present proprietor."[81] The deteriorating conditions of the plantation's buildings and landscape under the care of Washington's successors drew progressively more vehement calls for public ownership.

When Washington died in 1799, public discussion over Mount Vernon's future

had centered almost entirely on whether or not it should remain the resting place for the first president's bones. Before her death, Martha Washington had consented to the reinternment of her husband's body in an appropriate monument in the new Capitol. Accordingly, the building was planned and constructed with a crypt. In 1816, the Virginia legislature proposed to build a new monument for Washington's remains in Richmond. Neither idea came to fruition, and Washington's body remained at Mount Vernon.[82]

George Washington was buried in his family's hillside tomb, located south of the house. Washington recognized in his will that the structure was in bad shape

Fig. 12. Claude Régnier after a painting by Junius Brutus Stearns, *Life of George Washington— The Farmer,* hand-colored lithograph printed by Lemerciere, Paris, 1853.

and specified that he wished to be reburied as soon as a new, larger vault could be built in a different location.[83] Visitors in the first quarter of the nineteenth century almost always remarked upon the modest, and even dilapidated, burial site. A visitor wrote in 1813: "The father of our country sleeps unnoticed, almost unremembered. No insignia distinguish[es] him from the lowest individual of the family. No sculpted stone; no monumental brass, will tell the future wanderer where the Veteran lies."[84] To some, the unpretentious tomb seemed an appropriate place to remember the Cincinnatus-like leader: "I was better pleased, than to have seen it crowded with pillars and statuary of every kind. The simplicity of the place gives it an imposing air, and the mind is left free to expatiate on the actions of this accomplished hero."[85] At the highly publicized visit by the Marquis de Lafayette to the tomb in 1824, George Washington Parke Custis proclaimed that the tomb should not be considered a monument in itself, as Washington would forever be immortalized in the "freedom and happiness of his country."[86]

Most visitors, however, decried the state of the tomb. Pilgrims' accounts published in popular magazines called it a "humble show" and a "stain," insisting that it was an embarrassment to the entire country.[87] Prints of its rotten wooden door and compromised brick walls, including one based on a painting by John Gadsby Chapman, often illustrated pilgrims' disappointed accounts or featured prominently in Washington biographies. Spurred by an increasing number of disparaging accounts in the 1820s and 1830s, the publicity following Lafayette's visit, and an attempt by a grave robber to steal bones from the tomb, the family built a new vault at the location specified in Washington's will and relocated his remains there in 1831.[88] Soon after, they constructed a brick Gothic Revival enclosure.[89]

As it became increasingly clear that Washington's body would remain at Mount Vernon, conversations about the future of the property shifted to ownership of the site.[90] The Washington family tired of the constant stream of visitors; they publicly complained of the pilgrims' often unruly or disrespectful behavior, and Bushrod Washington was notoriously cranky about allowing unannounced visitors to access the property.[91] As more people learned about Mount Vernon's condition, the public began to chastise the family more vehemently for its inability to maintain the plantation as the wealthier Washington had left it. After the construction of the new tomb, descriptions shifted to lament the condition

of the entire plantation; one visitor remarked in 1838 of the "painful air of desola-
tion over the whole."[92] Unlike descriptions from the first quarter of the century
that began with discussions of quiet reverence at the tomb or lofty accounts of
Washington's impeccable character, later reports started with comments on poor
road conditions, idle slaves, and badly needed repairs.[93]

With no comparable precedent in the United States to look to, people began to
call for a public entity to rescue Mount Vernon from its demise and to preserve it
as a public monument. A decade before the Mount Vernon Ladies' Association's
ultimate purchase of the property, a newspaper correspondent for the *Liberator*
wrote in 1849: "We do not believe that any person ever visited this hallowed spot,
without going away with the conviction that the purchase of it should be made
by Congress. . . . It is disreputable that it should longer remain in its present
state."[94] One observer, writing in the *Ladies' Companion* in 1840, claimed that
the "hallowed" grounds of Mount Vernon "form[ed] a link between the 'Father
of his country' who is gone, and his People who remain to revere his memory."[95]
Many writing about the property in the decade following the completion of the
new tomb agreed that, as his retreat during life and his final resting place, it was
Washington's "true monument."[96]

Ideas for the logistics of transforming Mount Vernon into a public shrine
varied. One recurring theme was to make the property a version of Westminster Abbey, where it could be the depository of the monuments and remains of
American heroes like Washington.[97] Others called specifically for the house to be
returned to its original condition, as if Washington had only left it momentarily.[98]
Regardless of the particulars, Americans largely agreed by the 1840s that Mount
Vernon needed to be out of private hands and more accessible.

With the realization that Washington's remains would never be transferred to
the capital city, various campaigns to create permanent monuments to the first
president began in Washington, D.C. Two independent efforts attempted to fulfill
the promise made for a sculptural commemoration of Washington in L'Enfant's
original plan for the city: the federal government commissioned a large-scale
sculpture of Washington for the Capitol Rotunda, while local politicians and no-
tables initiated a major private monument to him. Ignoring the consensus of the
popular literature, prints, and discussions of Mount Vernon's preservation that

focused on Washington as a relatable domestic figure, the Washington Monument and Horatio Greenough's colossal sculpture *Washington* failed to appeal to popular taste. Both monuments denied the public's voracious appetite for the "real" Washington, reverting instead to classical representations of an infallible demigod.

After decades of discussion about a sculpture of Washington for the U.S. Capitol, the government commissioned Horatio Greenough for a statue commemorating the 1832 centennial of his birth.[99] As the first American sculptor to attempt a portrait of Washington in stone, Greenough tried to create a timeless image that would both elevate the artistic taste of his countrymen and represent the greatness of their most important hero. Based on the famed statue of Zeus by the ancient Greek sculptor Phidias, Greenough clad his Washington in a toga and sandals. With chest exposed, the figure sat on a throne decorated with classical allegories representing the founding of the republic. A sheathed sword recalled well-established imagery of Washington's multiple resignations; he was made godlike by his willingness to relinquish power. Although critics praised Greenough's colossal sculpture as evoking the "moral sublime" upon its unveiling in 1841, the public hated it.[100] It ignored contemporary preferences for images of a mortal Washington, returning instead to the classical allegory popular at the turn of the century.[101] As one reviewer put it: "People *are* disappointed. They expected something better—something American in its character—something like Washington as he lived—either as a general, statesman, or farmer."[102] As Congressman Leonard Jarvis said simply: "It is not *our* Washington."[103]

Also inspired by the centennial of Washington's birth, a group of D.C. residents and politicians (led by the Washington biographer and Supreme Court justice John Marshall) formed the Washington National Monument Society. By 1845, they had chosen a design by Robert Mills that they believed "harmoniously blended durability, simplicity, and grandeur."[104] Mills's monument featured a 500-foot obelisk (intended to be the tallest structure in the world) encircled by a 100-foot-high, circular colonnade. Scenes from Washington's career decorated each side of the obelisk's shaft. The "National Pantheon" below boasted history paintings, statues of the signers of the Declaration of Independence and other Revolutionary War heroes, and both a colossal Washington and a sculptural representation of the first president leading a charge in a chariot.[105] Despite their apparent love for all things Washington, Americans were not interested in the Society's proposed national monument. In the first three years after the Society's founding, it collected just twenty-eight thousand dollars. By the 1848 cornerstone-laying more than a decade later, it had raised only eighty-seven thousand dollars of the $1 million goal.

There were many reasons for the Washington Monument's failure, including the group's political leanings amid mounting sectionalism and its initial restriction of individual donations to one dollar.[106] The slow timeline of the monument (beginning with discussions in the 1780s) must also have contributed to the public's lack of faith in the project. The design itself, however, was surely the most significant reason for the memorial's failure. On the heels of criticism for Greenough's *Washington,* discussions over the Washington Monument were quick to point out the elaborate plan's lack of relevance to the modest and domestic Washington with whom Americans had come to identify. A critic wrote of Mills's design: "A simple obelisk, as an expression of aspiring thought, is well enough; but to surround its base with Grecian architecture, detracts from the dignity of the one and ruins the beauty of the other. Neither is in keeping with the character of Washington."[107] In response to such criticism and the high price tag for the Mills design, the Society proceeded with construction of the obelisk only, and by the outbreak of the Civil War, only 176 feet of the shaft had been completed. Much like the enthroned *Washington,* the grandiosity of the monument project was just too out-of-sync with mid-nineteenth-century Americans' preference for remembering the first president as a farmer and family man; to many, it seemed inappropriate to remember a man revered for his humility with the tallest structure in the world.

Over the first half of the nineteenth century, Americans transitioned from understanding Mount Vernon as an essential part of Washington's biography to a national symbol in its own right. Mount Vernon's deep connection to Washington's private life ensured a strong foundation for popular ideas of the house as both a shrine and as a home lived in by a relatable family. Printmakers, painters, and writers idealized its architecture and landscape, normalizing and venerating what would otherwise be regarded as an idiosyncratic old building. As national monuments to Washington failed to inspire in the 1830s and 1840s, Americans remained interested in Mount Vernon and concerned with its future. Unlike a colossal obelisk or classical sculpture, it reminded people that Washington had been human. In imaginings of Washington's life on the Potomac, both he and his house were examples to be emulated.

2 ★ "Keep It the Home of Washington!"

THE MOUNT VERNON LADIES' ASSOCIATION OF THE UNION, 1854–1890

As the public's imagination of Mount Vernon grew more vivid, people became increasingly concerned about its fate; its sagging piazza and the crumbling tomb inspired many to declare the place a "burning shame."[1] Outcry lambasted everyone from the owner, John Augustine Washington III, for not adequately maintaining Mount Vernon to the state and federal governments for refusing to purchase it for the public. As the nation divided, the present condition and questionable future of Mount Vernon became a metaphor for the fractured union.

In 1858, the painter Thomas Prichard Rossiter verbalized the nation's anxiety over the future of Mount Vernon: "The soul sickens to witness the dilapidation and utter neglect, the want of ordinary thrift, to say nothing of the veneration which permits the elements to work this ceaseless havoc, with no apparent effort made to arrest their ravages." And yet Rossiter glimpsed hope around the corner. The Mount Vernon Ladies' Association of the Union was in the process of purchasing the house: "At last, the women of the land—God bless them!—having waited and hoped in vain for a recognition of the sanctity of Mount Vernon, moved with feminine zeal and loyalty to the noble dead, have combined, organized, and purchased the property, to transmit the guardianship of the tomb from daughter to daughter, and make the spot from this time onward a shrine for coming generations. Rescued from decay, the question of most importance is, what shall be done with the tomb, mansion, and domain?"[2] Rossiter's feelings about what would happen to Mount Vernon, shared by many of his fellow Americans, were complicated. He felt responsibility for the place and knew *something* needed to happen. He was hopeful about the group of women who had stepped up to take charge; they seemed to be so capable, especially when contrasted against politicians unwilling to compromise. And yet, he was uneasy about what would occur next. There was no precedent for a national shrine of Mount Vernon's symbolic magnitude, nor had a group of American women ever taken on a task as publicly meaningful as the preservation of Washington's home.

Amid public scrutiny and without any workable models, the Mount Vernon Ladies' Association of the Union (MVLA) sought to purchase Washington's house and to "preserve" it on behalf of the American people. Upon its initial founding in the early 1850s, the group's goals appeared simple: to prevent the physical deterioration of the one-hundred-year-old house and to open it to the public.

Fig. 13. The Grand Council of the Mount Vernon Ladies' Association of the Union in front of Mount Vernon in 1873. Nancy Halsted is standing in the back, to the left of the bust of Washington; Ann Pamela Cunningham is seated directly next to the bust; Margaret Sweat is seated just below the bust; and Philoclea Eve is at the far right.

The realities of forming a politically neutral, national organization during the politically divisive 1850s were far more complicated; the same sectional conflict that made Mount Vernon an especially powerful symbol of unity threatened to torpedo the women's efforts to transform it into a museum. The Association's board focused on convincing the public that it was uniquely positioned to care for Washington's revered domestic sanctuary and that it would keep the shrine outside of the political fray.[3] Using a shrewd variety of strategies, the MVLA completed a nationwide capital campaign to purchase Mount Vernon in 1859 and kept it politically neutral through the harrowing war that followed. At the moment of the country's deepest division, the Association succeeded in creating a national shrine to Washington that represented a unified America.

Only after the house and the Association emerged from the Civil War was the MVLA able to consider how it would interpret the site. Beginning with limited resources and no comparable examples at which to look, the MVLA's board and employees struggled over the 1870s and 1880s to re-create Mount Vernon's late eighteenth-century appearance. With trial and error came confidence, and by the 1890s, the MVLA had finally realized the nation's first exhibit of in situ simulated historic interiors.[4] In the process, it codified preservation practices still used by curators today, assured the public that it could be trusted with the site, and made the home Washington loved a truly national monument.

A National Organization for a National Shrine, 1854–1860

Although historians have rightly credited the MVLA as the first national women's preservation organization, the group and its ideas did not emerge out of thin air. In the first half of the nineteenth century, middle- and upper-class white women were involved in many different reform and benevolent efforts. Many Americans believed such women to be society's rightful moral guardians, whether they were organizing to promote abolition or temperance. As keepers of the domestic sphere, white women could effect positive and sweeping change even when locked out of the political system.[5] That women established the country's first permanent house museum with in situ simulated interiors, therefore, is not all that surprising: nineteenth-century American society largely entrusted women with the domestic sphere. The public did not immediately trust the MVLA with Mount Vernon, however; it took considerable effort in the face of tremendous scrutiny for the Association to convince the country that it stood outside of sectional politics—and that it would keep Mount Vernon and Washington's memories neutral.

The Mount Vernon Ladies' Association began with a single woman: Ann Pamela Cunningham. The unmarried Cunningham was educated, highly intelligent, and singularly obstinate. Her ever-worsening invalidism often kept her confined at her family's South Carolina plantation or under her doctor's care in Philadelphia.[6] Upon the suggestion of her mother, she became impassioned over the state of Mount Vernon. In the *Charleston Mercury* in December 1853 (and subsequently reprinted in papers across the country), the thirty-seven-year-old published an appeal that dramatically forecast the "noise and smoke, and the busy hum of men" that threatened to destroy "all sanctity and repose" of Washington's house and tomb. She posited that male politicians were too busy with "degeneracy" in the halls of Congress to save the house for the nation. Remaining anonymous behind the moniker "A Southern Matron," Cunningham called on the "Ladies of the South!": "Should we appeal to or through your Senators and Representatives? . . . No! it is to *you,* mothers and daughters of the South, that the appeal can be made with a hopeful confidence! It is woman's office to be a vestal, and even a fire of liberty may need the care of her devotion and the purity of her guardianship. Your hearts are fresh, reverential, and elevated by lively sensibilities and elevating purposes."[7] Despite her rather visceral admonishment of male politicians, Cunningham initially planned for southern women to act as intermediaries for the purchase of the house: after raising the money to buy Mount Vernon, they would hand it over to the U.S. president or the governor of Virginia. There were no other examples of museums run by women in the United States, and Cunningham likely could not imagine any other outcomes.

In this first public call to arms, Cunningham clarified what the future MVLA would use as a central argument for its fitness to own and operate Washington's home: women's gender made them uniquely qualified to act as Mount Vernon's "vestals." She believed that only women—who operated outside of the political sphere—could preserve Mount Vernon as a national monument and that their unfettered patriotism could protect the nation's shrine from commercial development and political wrangling.[8] The federal government's failure to pass a bill to purchase Mount Vernon just weeks after the publication of Cunningham's call to arms confirmed the inability of politicians to put aside their differences for the good of Washington's memory; debates over the bill were rife with sectional division.[9]

In newspapers all over the country, women echoed Ann Pamela Cunningham's belief that their gender made them the rightful saviors of Mount Vernon and reinforced the house's importance to Washington's legacy. An Alabama woman wrote passionately in the *Mobile Tribune:* "To rescue the home of Washington from spoliation is the peculiar business of a woman. At the sick bed, at the grave, she has power; here is the grave of one to whom she, equally with the other sex, owes a debt of eternal gratitude. To save it from harm, is her duty particularly."[10] A Philadelphia woman asked readers in that city's *Evening Bulletin* to join the "Southern Matron," reminding them that because the politicians neglected "to protect the home and hallowed remains of him who braved *his* life that *they* might enjoy the blessings of freedom—then, is it not a fitting time that the women, possessing the spirit of their revolutionary mothers, should fearlessly show to the world that by *them,* at least, Washington is 'praised, wept, and honored in the land he loved!'"[11] Cunningham capitalized on the immediate positive response to her appeal and by the spring of 1854 had formed a three-tiered organization of southern women. With her at the helm and committees at the state and local levels, women across the region began to collect funds "to secure and hallow the 'home and grave' of the immortal Father of our Country."[12]

Cunningham soon found that organizing such a large group of women was easier said than done. Prompted by a series of misunderstandings, the Virginia state committee erroneously declared itself the governing body of the organization raising money for Washington's home. This revealed chaos within Cunningham's effort and led some to question the movement's motives to acquire Mount Vernon for ownership by the State of Virginia, unintentionally politicizing it.[13] Her initial limitation of her appeal to "Ladies of the South!" further undermined Cunningham's attempts to convince the public that female stewards would keep Mount Vernon outside of the mounting sectionalism.

In response to this public relations crisis, Cunningham re-formed the "Ladies' Mount Vernon Association" and strategically dubbed its governing board the "Mount Vernon Central Committee *of the Union*" with herself at the helm in the summer of 1855.[14] The newly formalized organization explained its national scope in *Godey's Lady's Book:* "We neither desire nor intend sectionality. . . . [W]e hope to see the master minds, from the remotest sections of our country, gathered within the folds of this 'glorious enterprise.'"[15] Cunningham was careful to explain that women from "Maine to Texas" would oversee the purchase of Mount Vernon.[16] Within weeks, new state committees formed in "the four corners of the Union" according to Cunningham's revised plan.[17] In March 1856, the Virginia state legislature passed a bill officially chartering the organization.[18]

With a national fund-raising campaign under way, Cunningham was finally explicit about *why* she and her compatriots were fighting to save Mount Vernon. Her initial public appeals had assumed that the house's connection to Washington was an obvious reason to secure its future. The Association's narrative of the house and its importance was clearly and logically rooted in the images and stories popularized in the preceding decades: the Association held that Washington was a national hero, Mount Vernon played a determining role in his exemplary character, and the memories of both had the potential to effect great change in the present. Cunningham wrote in an appeal published in the *Southern Literary Messenger:* "If ever in the future period of our national history, the Union should be in serious danger, political storms rocking it to its base, or rendering it in twain, there will be such a moral grandeur (perhaps an assuaging influence we cannot now estimate) in the *mere fact* that the tomb of Washington rests secure under the flag of his native state, *enshrined* in the devotional reverence of the wives, mothers and daughters of the Union as will be *felt* over the civilized world, making glad every elevated and patriotic heart!"[19] Only after the nascent association had expanded to a national scope could Cunningham convincingly claim that its actions to preserve Mount Vernon and to ensure its impact on contemporary life were without political motivation.

Despite the claim of neutrality, Cunningham and her allies hoped that their preservation of Mount Vernon would have a real effect on contemporary politics and public life. The influential editor of *Godey's,* Sarah J. Hale, echoed the

Association's sentiment about the power of Mount Vernon as a *national* symbol: "Washington's fame belongs to his whole country—his name is the holy cement of our Union."[20] By promoting union, Cunningham and her compatriots were advocating a political position, even if it was far from radical.

The plan remained for the group to limit itself to a custodial role: the MVLA would turn the deed over to Washington's "native state" of Virginia once the Association raised the purchase money. Cunningham claimed that "in becoming Virginia's," Mount Vernon would become the property of "the *patriots* in our land," but the proposed arrangement certainly undermined the national image of the Association she was working so hard to establish. Some states understandably objected to raising money for Virginia to own Washington's home.[21] But the agreement was necessary to circumvent a significant roadblock: its owner, John Augustine Washington III, refused to sell to the Association. Since 1854, he had publicly insisted that the preservation of Washington's home by women would "commemorate the degeneracy of myself and the men of our land." He proclaimed that he would rather give Mount Vernon away to the state or federal government than "be subject to the mortification of receiving these offerings of patriotism from the mothers, wives, and daughters of Virginia."[22] Holding the property in trust for the State of Virginia was the only circumstance under which the Association could imagine John Augustine Washington agreeing to sell to it, even if the circumstance complicated its wish to be perceived as a national organization.

Undermined by the campaign's initially southern slant and Washington's public refusal to sell to a group of women, the Association reenergized its campaign in 1856.[23] It found its most important publicity tool in an alliance with Edward Everett, the nationally esteemed former secretary of state, president of Harvard University, minister to Great Britain, and Massachusetts state senator.[24] Everett gave his lecture "The Character of Washington" 129 times to benefit the organization over the next five years. Besides raising one-quarter of the two-hundred-thousand-dollar purchase price, the effort gave the organization much-needed continuity and confidence.[25]

Everett's speech reinforced the MVLA's claim that the house had played an active role in the formation of Washington's "well-balanced" character. In an elaborate comparison between the "modest private mansion" of Mount Vernon and the despotic, "monumental pile" of the luxurious and aristocratic Blenheim Palace in England, Everett harkened back to decades of comparisons between Washington and Cincinnatus. He insisted that Mount Vernon's lack of grandeur was a lasting reminder of the hero's fitness for republican leadership: "From beneath that humble roof went forth the intrepid and unselfish warrior,—the magistrate who knew no glory but the country's good; to that he returned happiest when his work was done. There he lived in noble simplicity; there he died in glory and peace."[26] Everett's speech also reminded audiences across the country that Mount Vernon was part of Washington's legacy as a unifier, bolstering the MVLA's narrative for the power of the place and its owner as national symbols. He concluded by cautioning that the dissolution of the union would be an injustice to Washington's personal sacrifices and legacy.[27] The allegiance of the northern statesman with the women's organization also reinforced the group's supposed lack of sectional affiliation: his participation proved that even though the MVLA began as a southern effort, it had ardent northern allies.

Disentangling the Association's campaign from politics became increasingly important against the backdrop of the Kansas-Nebraska Act and the *Dred Scott* decision in the mid-1850s. Debates among Virginia state legislators dragged the board and its individual members into political debates, vilifying the women and their efforts and embroiling the supposedly neutral campaign in nasty public arguments in widely read newspapers.[28] Ann Pamela Cunningham responded by attempting to legitimize and formalize the national scope of the organization once again in January 1858 with an official constitution and by-laws. The constitution of the "Ladies' Mount Vernon Association of the Union" finally set her in the supreme position as "regent," with the power to nominate "vice-regents . . . from each State in the Union" to serve on a "Grand Council." Consisting of representatives from each state, the newly specified board of vice regents finally ensured that the Association's central governing body would represent the entire nation's interests; Cunningham now had a structure by which she would evenly distribute power among representatives from across the country. The choice of the terms "regent" and "vice regent" distanced the female officers from the positions usually held by men in business and American politics. With newspaper editors printing prejudiced comments like, "To our ear there is something harsh and unpleasant in the sound of *Mrs.* President and *Miss* Secretary," it is likely that the Association thought these terms more fitting to its self-identification as a women's organization guided by domestic sympathies rather than politics.[29] With "Union" in its title and nationwide representation written into its constitution, the MVLA of 1858 was a far cry from the loosely organized southern group Cunningham had organized four years earlier.[30]

The Association's perseverance after John Augustine Washington's initial refusal to sell, its continual reorganization and active revision of its public image, and the fact that it had eighteen thousand dollars in hand finally changed Washington's mind by the spring of 1858.[31] Disillusioned by the state and federal governments' sectional debates over Mount Vernon and convinced that the Association was his only serious buyer, Washington entered into a binding contract to sell to the MVLA directly. It was clear to both parties that neither the state nor the federal government was in a place to care for the property, and both were eager for a solution.[32] Washington wrote to Cunningham in a letter published in the *Richmond Enquirer* that "the women of the land will be the safest—as they will certainly be the purest—guardians of a national shrine."[33] The "purity" of which Washington spoke harkened back to the image of "vestals" that Cunningham had evoked in her initial appeal. Whether or not he actually believed the Association was, in fact, politically neutral, he cited this as a reason to trust it with his ancestors' property. After a series of payments amounting to a total of two hundred thousand dollars (plus interest), the Mount Vernon Ladies' Association of the Union would own Mount Vernon independently.[34]

With Washington publicly willing to sell and its organizational structure finally solidified, the MVLA initiated an unprecedented national publicity and fund-raising campaign, pioneering many strategies now standard in nonprofit development. The Association began its own newsletter, the *Mount Vernon Record,* in July 1858. Distributed to those who gave money to the MVLA between 1858 and 1860, the Association used the monthly *Record* to rally support; to legitimize its cause; and to confirm its identity as a selfless, national organization. With some northern newspapers refusing to publish its appeals, the MVLA could no longer count on local or national publications to present its cause without bias;

the *Record* was a means for the organization to control its message.[35] It reassured the public that the MVLA represented Americans from all over by printing the names and hometowns of individual donors from across the country and appeals by vice regents to their respective states.[36] The Association reprinted articles from newspapers from coast to coast praising the organization and explicitly corrected errors in reports published elsewhere.[37] Articles recounting the biographies of Washington and assorted Revolutionary-era individuals, anecdotes about Mount Vernon and other places related to Washington, and reviews of history books reminded readers of the historical importance of the place.[38] Most issues were illustrated, though the *Record* remarkably never published a picture of Mount Vernon itself.[39] Perhaps this was an indication of the Association's confidence that its public already knew what the building looked like. In the end, the *Record* was an important factor in how the Association was able to raise the money to buy Mount Vernon.[40]

The Association also continued to establish and strengthen strategic alliances with publications and individuals outside of the organization who acted as spokespeople for the MVLA. These relationships ensured positive publicity in a range of venues and legitimized its commitment to Mount Vernon and political neutrality. Edward Everett (who was still engaged with giving orations for the Association's benefit) arranged to publish a year's worth of weekly articles in the *New York Ledger* in exchange for the paper's bequest of ten thousand dollars toward the purchase of Mount Vernon in 1858–59.[41] The Association's relationship with *Godey's* editor Sarah J. Hale proved to be especially fruitful in the final year and a half of fund-raising.[42] Besides republishing the Association's various announcements and appeals, Hale wrote a number of editorials encouraging readers to donate money to the MVLA and to organize picnics and other fund-raising events to benefit the cause.[43]

By 1858, the MVLA had also aligned itself with the popular historian, engraver, magazine editor, and George Washington enthusiast Benson J. Lossing.[44] Earlier in the decade, Lossing had published the acclaimed *Pictorial Field-Book of the Revolution,* an enormous, two-volume undertaking that was part travelogue and part history of the events, places, people, and relics important to the nation's founding.[45] While doing research for *Pictorial Field-Book* and other publications,

Lossing became acquainted with Arlington House and its owner, George Washington Parke Custis. There Lossing heard stories about Custis's childhood at Mount Vernon and studied his collection of Washington memorabilia.[46] Mary Hamilton (vice regent, New York) saw Lossing's potential as an advocate for the MVLA's campaign and involved him and his wife in the cause. The couple raised a substantial sum for the campaign, and Lossing served on the New York State committee's "Advisory Committee of Gentlemen."[47]

Far outstripping these contributions, Benson Lossing's publications about Mount Vernon were absolutely critical to keeping Mount Vernon in the public eye in the MVLA's final years of fund-raising for the house's purchase. In addition to publishing articles in New York newspapers and *Harper's* at the behest of the Association, Lossing released a book-length history of Mount Vernon in 1859: *Mount Vernon and Its Associations, Historical, Biographical, and Pictorial.*[48] Tapped by a New York publisher to capitalize on the publicity surrounding the MVLA's pending purchase of Mount Vernon, Lossing built on his previous research to produce what is most likely the first monograph on an American building.[49] Despite its status as a "gift book" written years before the development of the scholarly study of American design, *Mount Vernon and Its Associations* did treat the architecture of Mount Vernon as significant in its own right. In typical nineteenth-century fashion, Lossing intertwined stories of the objects and events at Mount Vernon with anecdotes from Washington's biography. He established a basic chronology for the construction of the building and gave full credit to Washington as a designer: "Washington was his own architect, and drew every plan and specification for the workmen with his own hand."[50]

In addition to stories about Washington's daily life at Mount Vernon and details about the building's architecture, Lossing featured more than 139 engravings of the house, its immediate landscape, and its relics. Many were "spirited and faithful" sketches of individual Washington-related items he had made during previous visits to Arlington House.[51] Lossing's drawings of these "relics" carefully and often quite faithfully recorded their details, while his descriptions attempted to provide their provenances. In both word and image, *Mount Vernon and Its Associations* effectively repopulated Mount Vernon with objects that had not been in the building for years.[52] Well-timed with the Association's campaign

Fig. 14. Benson Lossing's depiction of Nelly Custis's harpsichord in *Mount Vernon and Its Associations* (1859). He drew the instrument while it was still at Arlington House. It was the first relic to return to Mount Vernon under the MVLA's ownership and soon after became the focus of the little parlor.

and providing such "intimate knowledge of the home of Washington," Lossing's book helped to peak—and satiate—the public's interest in Mount Vernon.[53]

As the MVLA got closer to making the final payments to John Augustine Washington, the focus of its publicity began to narrow from the general preservation of Mount Vernon—its purchase and maintenance—to define exactly *how* the organization intended to turn it into a public shrine. In the months before the MVLA took ownership of the house in the winter of 1859, it laid out the deceptively simple strategy that continues to guide its efforts in the twenty-first century.[54] In July, the banner line of the *Mount Vernon Record* shifted from the phrase "Devoted to the Purchase of the Home and Grave of Washington" to "Devoted to the Purchase and Restoration of Washington's Home."[55] The concept of "restoration" of American architecture was essentially unheard of in 1859. European architects were currently embroiled in a debate that distinguished conservation (the preservation of architecture in its current state) from restoration (the return of architecture to a predetermined historical moment by accurately re-creating features), but their arguments usually centered on well-documented historical styles and building types, such as classical temples or Gothic cathedrals. With almost no American precedent and presumably little awareness of the theoretical debates going on about preservation in Europe, the Association announced that it would transform Mount Vernon "*from what it is,* to *what it was,* under the watchful care of the great Chief, who, although he lived for his country, never forgot nor neglected his much-loved home."[56] Even though "restoring" Mount Vernon would not require the same guesswork as returning a ruined English church to its fourteenth-century glory, the MVLA's plan for Mount Vernon was ambitious; the organization sought to return the building to its appearance more than fifty years before. Cunningham and the MVLA planned to show the exact domestic environment that had enacted such a positive influence on Washington so that it would, in turn, shape generations of Americans to come.[57] The public responded enthusiastically to the plan, especially in light of Mount Vernon's supposedly "crumbling" condition.[58]

As supportive as the public might have been in donating toward the purchase of the site, the women's efforts to raise a restoration fund languished.[59] Sarah Tracy, the Association's secretary and co-caretaker of Mount Vernon during the Civil War, wrote Margaretta Morse (vice regent, Louisiana) in December 1860 that the country was so wrapped in the recent "political agitations" that they had all but forgotten about the urgent need to continue supporting Mount Vernon

Fig. 15. Mount Vernon as it appeared while undergoing repairs in 1862.

after the purchase price was met. She worried that if the women failed to raise money for repairs, the Association would "be in the seriously embarrassed position of having acquired property it cannot sustain."[60] Although the MVLA had successfully rallied the nation to raise the two hundred thousand dollars to purchase Mount Vernon, the Association assumed ownership with virtually no funds for its restoration.

Wartime at Mount Vernon, 1860–1865

When the Association finally acquired the deed to Mount Vernon at the end of 1859, just months before shots were fired at Fort Sumter, keeping its and Mount Vernon's public images out of politics became even more of a challenge. Sarah Tracy wrote that with the dissolution of "our Glorious Republic," the members of the Association's board must "by their united action give the solemn assurance to the country that, they, in unity and harmony, could and would, carry out in future all the purposes to which they are pledged as guardians of the Grave of Washington."[61] As the country focused money and energy on the war, the MVLA struggled to keep Mount Vernon physically standing *and* politically neutral with severely limited financial resources.[62]

Tracy led the herculean effort of keeping Mount Vernon and the organization out of the war, both literally and figuratively.[63] She considered publicity "the greatest trial in the place," and with Ann Pamela Cunningham stuck at her family's South Carolina plantation for the duration of the conflict, Tracy worked tirelessly at Mount Vernon to ensure that the public understood the Association's goals and actions.[64] Thanks to her continual lobbying, both the Union and the Confederacy agreed to protect Mount Vernon and to consider it neutral territory; this prevented either side from claiming it as a symbolic act. After the Union's occupation of Alexandria in May 1861, she convinced General Winfield Scott to ensure that visiting soldiers would respect the property and leave their weapons outside its gates when visiting.[65] Popular magazines and newspapers nationwide reported on the arrangement: "The troops of the Government and the Confederates are carefully ordered not to set foot upon its hallowed soil, and it remains . . . one of the few spots of Virginia soil untouched by a soldier's foot."[66] Scott also provided passes so that Tracy and the board's free African American employees could travel to town for supplies without molestation.[67]

The northern press targeted Cunningham—the self-proclaimed "Southern Matron"—directly. The *New York Times,* which had refused to publish the women's appeals for donations before the war, accused Cunningham of being financially careless and of planning to give Mount Vernon to the Confederacy.[68] An even more libelous and widely published account called Cunningham a "Secession Spy" and accused her of living in luxury at Mount Vernon at the expense of northern donors: "She has a delightful summer retreat, where she can look upon broad and fertile acres, can receive her friends like a very princess, and by means of the easy and forgiving temper of our Washington rulers, can forward to [Jefferson] Davis & co. the latest intelligence from the Federal metropolis."[69] Margaret Comegys (vice regent, Delaware) responded to the articles with the facts that Cunningham was in South Carolina, that she would use her own furniture in the house, and that all black labor employed at Mount Vernon was free.[70] Such accusations wounded Cunningham and the Association's board members deeply after all of their efforts to build a politically neutral reputation for themselves and Mount Vernon.

Furnishing Mount Vernon for Tracy; her male custodial counterpart, Upton Herbert; and their chaperone, Mary McMakin, to occupy initially outweighed any thought of returning it to its eighteenth-century appearance. The MVLA had no discussion about whether or not it should continue using Mount Vernon as a residence. With security a constant threat, the board believed resident caretakers an absolute necessity, and the mansion was the only building in which a group of white people had lived on the plantation since Washington's time.[71] Tracy, Herbert, and McMakin occupied bedchambers in the upper stories and used Washington's study as their dining room (as Washington's descendants had).[72] They reserved the downstairs bedchamber and dining room for Cunningham to use upon her return from South Carolina, making the southern side of the first floor a private suite. Washington's bedchamber, the west parlor, and the northwest bedchamber on the second floor (then thought to be the room in which Lafayette had slept) were open to visitors and mostly unfurnished.[73] John Augustine Washington had left the house empty except for a handful of articles he sold or gave to the Association, so Herbert brought his own furniture, and the Association provided additional items.[74] Tracy found the house "shabby" but tried to "make it very comfortable." Her choices were driven more by need than by concern for authenticity: Tracy wrote to Cunningham in December 1860 that they needed window shades because "'the people' all feel privileged to look in at the windows."[75]

Without a steady stream of income, the Association struggled with basic maintenance of the buildings and paying its employees.[76] Before the war, the Association had imagined that visitors' entrance fees would bring in a steady income.[77] During the conflict, however, few visitors came; Mount Vernon was difficult to get to, and not many people were traveling. By road, the plantation was a kind of no-man's-land in between the Confederate forces at Manassas and the Union troops at Alexandria. Getting to the property by river was nearly impossible. The federal government put a stop to boat landings at the Mount Vernon wharf in the summer of 1862 for the duration of the war, severely impacting the MVLA's already dire financial situation.[78] The Association petitioned the secretary of war for reparations for each month that the boat was out of commission and unable to transport tourists, reminding him: "This property belongs to the Citizens of the United States, purchased by the united contributions of more than a million people."[79] The board would not be successful in procuring the money lost by the steamship's halted operation until after the war ended.[80]

Despite their hardships, the Association and Mount Vernon survived the Civil War unscathed. The board had accomplished its immediate goals of buying Washington's house and keeping it neutral territory throughout the conflict. Hordes of visitors streamed to Mount Vernon after the May 1865 surrender at Appomattox and the revival of the steamboat a month later.[81] For the first time, Washington's house was open to the public and accessible, and people were eager to see if the Association had lived up to its promise to preserve the house. Most came with unrealistic expectations and were immediately disappointed by the empty (or closed) rooms and peeling paint. Visitors pointedly remarked that there was "no attempt . . . to reproduce the Home of Washington."[82] Tracy summed up the MVLA's difficult position: "Now that the public has free access they abuse us heartily for not having accomplished impossibilities."[83] The Association tried to combat the criticism by reaching out to the press, and Mary Hamilton (prompted by Edward Everett) even suggested turning the property over to the federal government. The only thing that would quiet the public's frustration was the reassurance that Mount Vernon was taken care of—and that it resembled the house of Washington illustrated by decades of prints and stories, as well as new sources like Lossing's book.[84]

Early Restoration Efforts, 1865–1873

In the three decades after the Civil War, the Association refocused its energy on determining just how to "restore" Mount Vernon to its eighteenth-century appearance and reassuring a skeptical public that it was up to the task. Even though the Association's plan to restore Mount Vernon "to *what it was*" sounded simple enough, it took it almost thirty years to interpret the house in a way that the public found convincing. The MVLA spent the postwar decades scrambling to organize itself and the house, solidifying its identity as custodian of Mount Vernon while transforming the building into a museum. This early era of the Association's restoration may be divided into two distinct periods according to Ann Pamela Cunningham's role in the organization. After her return to Mount Vernon in the late 1860s, Cunningham oversaw the first significant round of preservation efforts. Following her 1873 retirement (and the end of her occupation of the mansion), the organization professionalized and refined its interpretation of Mount Vernon significantly. By the early 1890s, the Association had finally created the nation's first in situ collection of simulated interiors, as well as a well-oiled tourist attraction and preservation organization. As the members of the board gained confidence, financial stability, and historical knowledge, they were able to improve their methods for restoring Mount Vernon and to get ever-closer to the absolute authenticity they thought possible.

Although the Association did not necessarily have a clear plan for how to make Mount Vernon a house museum, board members knew that they did not want it to end up a curiosity cabinet of Washington-related relics. Instead, objects would be presented in their historic contexts: the vice regents planned to arrange objects in the rooms Washington had known and in scenarios in which he might have used and enjoyed them. With an in situ collection of simulated interiors, the restored Mount Vernon would balance being both a relic and a depository for relics. The house and its immediate surroundings could be both an object to be appreciated and an immersive atmosphere to be experienced.

This multilayered strategy revealed a strong belief in the power of historic objects, spaces, and tableaux to shape contemporary people. The Association trusted that such a place would inspire citizens in the present as it had Washington in the past. Decades of pilgrims obviously also believed in the particular power of Mount Vernon's architecture, objects, and landscapes. They had come to connect with the great man by experiencing his material world. By returning Mount Vernon to its appearance as the private home Washington knew, the Association planned to finally transform it into a public shrine. In an 1866 *Godey's Lady's Book* editorial, Sarah Hale summarized the MVLA's confidence in the place's ability to influence contemporary Americans: "Washington's greatest worth was not in his public example. We must set his private life before Young America, and keep in the hearts of the people the love of his private virtues. This is the lamp of goodness which, like the sacred fire on the altar, should be always burning in the homes of our land."[85]

The board had an extremely limited set of tools with which to reconstruct settings that would viscerally connect visitors to Washington's material life. There were very few precedents for the preservation and interpretation of a Colonial-era building in the United States in the late 1860s. The principal interiors of Independence Hall had been "restored" and Washington's headquarters at Newburgh saved, but neither building had been interpreted with furniture or other period objects.[86] The academic fields of American architectural and art history were as nascent as historic preservation; professional scholars and "relic" hunters were equally uneducated when it came to the identification, significance, and history of the country's early material culture. Throughout the MVLA's early work and despite (or because of) its position as pioneering preservationists, it also continued to face challenges organizing itself and combating a sometimes hostile press. It was experimenting with a place widely understood as sacred, all under the microscope of an anxious and expectant public.

The general concept of using objects to evoke the past preexisted the Association's restoration of Mount Vernon. At the era's wildly popular international expositions as well as at public museums, Victorians packed display cases with things that could supposedly tell stories or impart knowledge directly to observers.[87] Most pertinent to the kinds of objects the Association aimed to display at Mount Vernon in the early years of its restoration were "relics," or items that had direct connections (no matter how brief) with a historic person or event. Nineteenth-century Americans used the word "relic" to describe objects made from other cherished articles (e.g., a box made of wood from Washington's original coffin), natural elements from an important landmark (e.g., a sprig of a bush planted by Washington at Mount Vernon), or things associated with a significant individual (e.g., the bed in which Washington died). A product of the period's sentimentality more generally, secular relics provided a direct connection between the past and the nineteenth-century Americans who collected them.[88] With little information available on the history of American decorative arts at midcentury, relics' associations with historic persons outweighed values of aesthetics or craftsmanship.

There was nothing on the scale of an entire public building with historically interpreted interiors to which the Association could look as models for ways to organize relics, however.[89] The Hasbrouck House in Newburgh, New York, predated Mount Vernon as the country's first house museum, but it was more of a repository for relics than a simulated period environment. Like the vice regents at Mount Vernon, the preservationists at Hasbrouck House rooted their building's significance in its connection to George Washington: the general had used the small stone dwelling as a headquarters from April 1782 until August 1783.[90] The goal of the male politicians who saved the building (and ultimately its owner, New York State) was to "preserve and perpetuate" the spot as a monument to Washington and his shrewd leadership during the Revolutionary War.[91] Hasbrouck House was appropriately a very different kind of historic site than what the Association imagined for Mount Vernon; a simulated domestic atmosphere was not the goal at the site of military history preserved by men.

More likely inspirations for the MVLA's restoration of Mount Vernon and its interiors were what the art historian Beverly Gordon termed "saturated worlds":

temporary theatrical spaces that combined relics, antiques (things identified simply as old), costumes, and stage sets in which nineteenth-century people could physically embody idealized pasts and fictional scenarios.[92] Historical *tableaux vivant,* for example, offered opportunities to dress up and to reenact popular paintings and historical events. During the Civil War, northern white women combined their interest in tableaux with the emerging exposition format in a series of charity events benefiting the United States Sanitary Commission.[93] Half of the twenty-two major "sanitary fairs" featured playful Colonial-themed booths in which women dressed up like their early American ancestors; constructed sets featuring Colonial hearths, furniture, and relics; and served food or demonstrated Colonial-era handicrafts.[94] These exhibits inspired the wildly popular "New England Farmer's Home" at the 1876 Centennial Exposition in Philadelphia.[95] Set in a freestanding log cabin built just for the exposition, the exhibit featured a number of relics including John Alden's writing desk, a spinning wheel brought over on the *Mayflower,* and a teapot used by General Lafayette. As at the sanitary fairs, these objects were appreciated exclusively for their historical associations, and they functioned as props in the re-creation of larger tableaux.[96] At least one of the MVLA's early vice regents was directly involved in the sanitary fairs, while others certainly saw such exhibits. This exposure likely provided the MVLA with examples of reconstructed early American interiors.[97]

Similar to the fairs' Colonial exhibits and often used as fund-raisers for Mount Vernon were the "Martha Washington teas" that became especially popular around the centennial.[98] The events encouraged women to dress in Colonial garb and to socialize over activities identified with Colonial America (namely tea and sewing). Some groups reenacted the elaborate scene of Martha Washington receiving visitors in over-the-top European fashion as painted by Daniel Huntington in *The Republican Court.*[99] Although reviled by critics, the painting provided a model for tableaux that involved large numbers of participants pretending to be an early American aristocracy.[100] Much like the participants in Martha Washington teas, the MVLA's board imagined Mount Vernon as a tasteful stage on which the wealthy and successful planter lived a moral and fashionable domestic life. Its early restoration demonstrated more about its members' visions of the past than what the house was actually like in the 1790s.[101]

Fig. 16. New England Kitchen exhibit, Brooklyn Sanitary Fair, New York, 1864.

Beyond the lack of comparable models, the mansion's continued use as a private house hampered the Association's early restoration efforts. Cunningham moved into her suite of rooms after the war was over, keeping half of the downstairs closed to the public.[102] The necessary function of the building as a repository for relics also undermined the Association's desire to avoid turning the house into a cabinet of curiosities. Items such as documents and clothing that did not fit easily into the simulated domestic atmosphere—no matter how historically significant—were crammed into large relic cases scattered throughout the house. Not until after Ann Pamela Cunningham vacated the building in 1873–74 and the Association replaced the bulky cases with smaller and more contextual pieces of case furniture did Mount Vernon better represent an in situ collection of simulated interiors.

A payment of seven thousand dollars from the U.S. government (technically the only federal money the MVLA has ever accepted) funded the first period of restorations at Mount Vernon in 1869–70. Following up on its previously un-successful petition, the Association accepted the funds as compensation for the prohibition of steamboats landing at its wharf during the war. General Nathaniel Michler, then superintendent of public buildings and grounds for Washington, D.C., oversaw the expenditure of the funds and acted as the first in a long line of outside consultants the MVLA engaged over the coming decades.[103] The Associa-tion's acquisition of government funds inspired criticism, but it did allow for vis-ible improvements to the mansion and significant developments in the operation of the property as a tourist attraction.[104] The funds finally allowed the Association to build a greenhouse on the ruins of Washington's in 1869, for example, provid-ing a place to propagate plants and floral bouquets for sale.[105]

The most dramatic changes made possible by the steamboat money were to the mansion itself.[106] With Cunningham often away and hesitant to make deci-sions, Michler directed the MVLA's first major wave of maintenance and repair work in 1869–70, most notably the repair of the iconic piazza and the prepara-tion of wall plaster for paint and paper.[107] These projects offered highly visible improvements to the building. Setting a precedent for decades to come, the As-sociation respected and retained existing building fabric. When Michler and his team replaced plaster, they retained as much of the original lathe as possible. The methods and materials they used were not dissimilar to those used during the eighteenth century, further minimizing any long-term negative impact.[108]

With the plaster walls repaired, the Association began to paint and wallpaper the interior of the mansion, often using donated materials.[109] For the central pas-sage, the Association's new resident secretary, Sarah Tiffey (hired to replace Sarah Tracy), chose a contemporary geometric block pattern she thought would com-plement the rusticated exterior.[110] Cunningham agonized over choosing paint colors for other rooms. She wrote of her anxiety over the color of the New Room in particular: "I am *not* fitted to decide the very important question of what shall be the color of the 'great room' [of] the Home of the Father of this Country."[111] Since the passing of those who had known Mount Vernon best—namely John Augustine Washington III and George Washington Parke Custis—the Associa-tion had to rely on the accounts of others who had visited the house earlier in the nineteenth century.[112] For the choice of paint colors the Association talked to Nelly Custis's niece and "Daddy" Jim Mitchell, a man formerly enslaved at Mount Vernon. Mitchell claimed the New Room had "always been yellow." He was likely referring to the chrome-yellow color added by Bushrod Washington after George Washington's death.[113] While weighing Mitchell's memory and a range of "delicate tints," Cunningham also considered the opinion of Mary Sweat (vice regent, Maine) that they should "try [not] to *modernize* Washington's Home" and instead "try to keep it to the spirit of his age."[114] Cunningham ultimately chose a grayish-pink called "ashes of roses," a tasteful contemporary shade, in the face of inconclusive historical sources. Besides relying on the memories of others, the Association did do some investigation of the physical evidence offered by the house itself. Cunningham peeled back paper to reveal layers of wall treatment in the upstairs bedrooms.[115] Coupled with Washington's descriptions of the various second-floor bedrooms, this rudimentary forensic analysis helped to guide decisions in those spaces.

With restoration work under way thanks to the steamboat reparations, the Association also began to get serious about furnishing the empty house.[116] Much like the bare and peeling walls, the closed and empty rooms led many visitors to question the board's stewardship.[117] Upton Herbert took with him much of the furniture in the building when he left in January 1869, leaving the downstairs public rooms and the upstairs bedrooms mostly empty.[118] Soon after his departure, Nancy Halsted (vice regent, New Jersey) took charge of the refurnishing, acting as the mansion's first curator. She had Cunningham's almost complete confidence and lived close by in Newark, allowing her to make decisions relatively autonomously and to visit Mount Vernon often. Following a suggestion made by another vice regent before the war, Halsted developed a system by which each of the original states outfitted a single room in the house.[119] She arranged for a steamship company to deliver goods without charge from ports in New York and New Jersey.[120] She also acquired large wood-and-glass cases from the Smithsonian to house relics.[121]

With limited funds with which to buy objects in this first wave of furnishing, the Association appealed to the generosity of Washington descendants and relic collectors to donate to Mount Vernon.[122] The board considered objects used by Washington at some point during his life appropriately authentic, though it preferred items with a Mount Vernon provenance.[123] The MVLA acquired objects ad hoc, as it had in the years just before the war. It had accepted the bust of Washington by Jean-Antoine Houdon, the key to the Bastille, and Washington's globe from John Augustine Washington III. In 1859, Nelly Custis's daughter-in-law had given the Association a double-manual harpsichord that Washington had gifted her and that had occupied Mount Vernon's little parlor during Washington's final years.[124] Illustrated and colorfully described by Benson Lossing as the object at which little Nelly spent "many a tearful hour" practicing at her grandmother Martha's insistence, the harpsichord was one of the relics eighteenth-century visitors often remarked upon and associated with the Washingtons' refined hospitality.[125] It was a fine example of the kind of object the MVLA most desired: intimately connected with Washington, it could serve as both a relic and a prominent prop in visitors' imaginings of his daily life at Mount Vernon. Antiques (often donated or brought from vice regents' own homes) supplemented such genuine Washington articles to give a fuller sense of the rooms' eighteenth-century appearances.

The furnished rooms and painted walls helped the Association's board to feel more confident by its June 1870 meeting. The group hoped that the public would recognize its work over the previous year as a good start, proclaiming in a published report of the meeting: "Every effort has been made to put the place into a presentable condition, so that those who make pilgrimage to the spot are no longer shocked by the ghastly traces of neglect and dilapidation."[126] The almost defensive nature of this report revealed more than the Association's desire to relieve the usual pressure from an expectant public. By the early 1870s, it had a new image problem on its hands: Cunningham's health, laudanum addiction, and mental state were deteriorating in dangerous proximity to the thousands of tourists visiting Mount Vernon each year. She was also proving to be an inadequate manager of the site; the board needed a new model for its organization of the day-to-day operation of the increasingly sophisticated site. Having worked so hard to get Mount Vernon and its own public image under control, it now found itself exposed to another round of hateful accusations.[127] Margaret Sweat wrote of the mounting crisis: "The public was becoming interested to ask specific questions; the newspapers were hostile & sensational, & our Regent impervious to entreaties & scornful of threatening catastrophes."[128]

By 1872, issues with Cunningham had reached their zenith. Susan Hudson (vice regent, Connecticut) wrote that summer: "The servants have hard work to keep her in her room. She frequently goes to the windows in states of undress." Besides potentially exposing herself to visitors, Cunningham sometimes refused to differentiate between her income and that of the Association. The new resident superintendent, Colonel J. McHenry Hollingsworth, struggled to keep reporters from witnessing her deterioration, but the press renewed its attack.[129] A series of syndicated articles accused Cunningham of mishandling funds, once again recalling the MVLA's obligation to the public's contributions to the property's purchase.[130] A particularly scurrilous article called the frail South Carolinian "an habitual drunkard . . . incapable of attending to the business of Mount Vernon, and, while intoxicated, of being seen improperly dressed."[131] The Association tried to quiet the accusations with corrections and positive reports of its activities and finances, but to no avail.[132]

Through a series of maneuvers carefully shielded from the press and befitting the respect it had for their founder, the board finally convinced Cunningham to step down as regent.[133] Citing ill health, she officially resigned at the MVLA's November 1873 meeting and moved out of the mansion quickly thereafter. Cunningham's retirement signaled a new era for the organization and for Mount Vernon. Sweat summarized the shift: "The Association was transformed into an institution based on business principles; open to public view; & proud to call upon the world to study the administration of its affairs."[134] Even more importantly, the mansion was no longer a residence; although employees continued to live in outbuildings and board members slept in the house during their annual meetings until the late 1920s, never again would someone live in the mansion full-time. Twenty years after the "Southern Matron" had written her initial appeal, Mount Vernon was finally transforming into a full-fledged house museum.

America's "First" House Museum, 1873–1890s

In Cunningham's farewell address to the Mount Vernon Ladies' Association (written, no doubt, with Washington's own in mind), she reminded the organization of its obligation to the American people—and to Washington's memory: "Ladies, the Home of our Washington is in your charge. *See to it that you keep it the Home of Washington!*"[135] The newly reformed MVLA took Cunningham's words to heart: its goal remained to bring Mount Vernon ever-closer to what it looked like during Washington's lifetime. As Americans became seriously interested in the material culture of the country's earliest decades, this job became considerably easier. Visitation (and the amount collected from entrance fees) rose almost every year, stabilizing the MVLA's financial situation. Information about historic objects and architecture was increasingly accessible: the number of books about the history of American architecture and interiors had grown from zero to more than a dozen by the 1890s, and the first "systematic study" of American furniture was published in 1891.[136] With financial and historical resources constantly improving and Cunningham out of the picture, the Association sought to be ever more authentic in its interpretation of the mansion and efficient in its operation of the site. Seeing these improvements, the press and public finally began trusting the MVLA.

With Cunningham gone, the Association's board had an opportunity to reorganize itself and to improve the site's management and financial situation. Margaret Sweat wrote that after Cunningham's departure, "every council was a step in advance, every Vice Regent grasped her work with a firmer hold; new committees were formed & clearer division of labor arose; new Vice Regents were appointed & brought fresh energy & larger funds with which to carry out the long-desired restorations; all peril was past."[137] With a new business-savvy regent, Lily Berghmans, at the helm, the board developed a series of committees to divide up the work of managing and restoring Mount Vernon, expanding from only a finance committee in 1876 to separate groups in charge of the mansion, relics, library, tomb, furniture, parliamentary rules, records of the organization, guidebook, farm, library, garden and greenhouse, trees and shrubs, press, and by-laws ten years later.[138] The delegation of labor helped to alleviate the perennial problem of the vice regents' geographic dispersal.[139] Many of the vice regents from faraway states still came to Mount Vernon only once a year for the annual meeting. It also allowed the MVLA to begin thinking about restoration beyond the mansion; the board started turning its attention to the outbuildings as places for employees or its own members to stay.[140]

The MVLA's financial situation also improved dramatically. The vice regents followed up on Cunningham's plan to rely exclusively on private funding sources (especially "gentlemen of wealth") rather than the government.[141] The Washington, D.C., art collector and philanthropist William Wilson Corcoran, for example, funded a handful of restoration projects in the 1870s. Corcoran had been a business partner of the MVLA's treasurer, George W. Riggs, leading to a relationship with the organization.[142] Beginning with a five-hundred-dollar donation from Margaret Sweat's father in 1871, the merchant John Mussey, a new endowment also promised to fund future maintenance and restoration.[143] In twelve years, the endowment grew to twenty-eight thousand dollars.[144] The board was so confident in its ability to expand the endowment that it proclaimed it would eventually do away with Mount Vernon's entrance fee.[145] Its ambitious restoration plans prevented this from ever happening.

The board stepped up its efforts for an "influx of visitors" around the 1876 centennial, anticipating that the anniversary would deepen peoples' interest in Mount Vernon. The Association was right: Americans focused their centennial celebrations more often on Washington than on any other Founding Father.[146] At the Centennial International Exposition in Philadelphia, his image graced everything from trade cards to exhibit booths.[147] A massive (and oft-ridiculed) bust of Washington perched atop a giant eagle dominated the main hall of the Fine Arts Building, while the Smithsonian displayed Washington relics in the United States Government Building.[148] Mount Vernon benefited greatly from this centennial flurry: thirteen thousand people visited in October 1876 alone, and entrance fees for the 1876 fiscal year totaled more than twenty-four thousand dollars.[149] America's birthday celebration also inspired hundreds of donors to give money to Mount Vernon, boosting the MVLA's endowment by nine thousand dollars in a single year.[150] Positive published accounts noting the Association's improvements encouraged even more visitors.[151]

As more people became interested in American history and heard about the improvements at Mount Vernon, the Association made it easier to access. Advances in technology and the Association's careful negotiation brought more tourists from Washington and Alexandria by way of steamboats on the Potomac. The steamboat in use by 1889, for example, ran two trips a day to Mount

Vernon carrying up to nine hundred passengers at a time.[152] Arrival by road continued to be more arduous than the river route until the Electric Railroad Company connected Mount Vernon to a larger streetcar network in 1892. Less than two years later, 51,584 people visited Mount Vernon annually, compared to 34,911 in the year before the rail line.[153] Whether paid on a boat or a streetcar, a portion of each visitor's fee went to the MVLA. The site was also open for increasingly longer periods by 1893, stretching visiting hours to five hours every day of the week but Sunday.[154] Visitors now had the time to wander leisurely about the site. Harrison H. Dodge, Colonel Hollingsworth's replacement as resident superintendent in 1885, saw the "propensity for idleness" encouraged by the extended hours as unfortunate; it gave time for curious tourists to distract employees with questions.[155]

The board worked to devise new ways to handle the crowds of visitors. It did not employ formal tour guides, although commentary from uniformed employees (some of whom were stationed in the house during busy times) enhanced visitors' self-guided inspections.[156] This allowed some unsupervised visitors to misbehave, continuing the tradition of relic hunting left over from earlier pilgrims and trespassers. The Association enclosed the New Room mantelpiece in a cage in 1872 to protect it from those who chipped away at its tiny neoclassical figures (it soon replaced the cage with a more open barrier). After visitors broke off a piece of a clock and stole a baluster from the main hall's stairs in 1884, it installed gates in the mansion's interior doorways.[157] Hired guards and gated (and closed) doorways helped to guide traffic through the house. By 1890, Superintendent Dodge instituted a streamlined path that took visitors up the stairs on the south side of the house, past Washington's bedchamber, through the yellow bedchamber, and down the main stairs, where they could peer over and through gates into the parlors and dining room from the passage.[158] Visitors accessed the New Room and study directly from exterior doors.

To inform tourists wandering through the mansion, the Association began to publish an annual guidebook in 1876. One can imagine visitors carrying the forty-page booklet from room to room, using it to identify objects and architectural features. Sold both at Mount Vernon and on the steamboat, the guide also provided an opportunity for the Association to set the record straight on its intentions for Washington's home (much as the *Mount Vernon Record* had more than a decade before). Rich with descriptions of individual objects, the guidebook was quick to remind the reader that what they were seeing was a house museum in its "incipient state." It carefully identified particular relics (such as the Bastille key and harpsichord), signaling that other items were just standing in until "real" Washington objects could replace them. The book explained the basic organization of the MVLA, justifying the entrance fee as "one of the chief sources of revenue to the Association." It operated as a reminder of decorum, giving a warning to any "land pirates" looking to mutilate the New Room mantelpiece.[159] The first edition included only text; Benson Lossing's engravings illustrated revised editions by 1879.[160] By the late 1890s, the guidebook included photographs of the mansion's exterior and each of the principal interior spaces. The guidebooks functioned as mementoes of visitors' trips and provided a glimpse of the place to those who could not visit it in person.

With Cunningham's departure, a stabilized financial situation, and an influx of visitors, the MVLA's interpretation of the house's interiors more closely approximated what its board members thought was authentic to Washington's era. For the first time, the house was no longer used as a residence; the Association reassigned the rooms Cunningham and her attendants had occupied to various vice regents for furnishing, opening spaces that had been inaccessible to the public for the entire history of the building. The simultaneous flowering of the Colonial Revival, a means of remembering America's early history through the imitation or adoption of its material culture, offered an ever-expanding audience and a bank of information about early American material culture to assist these new curators. With new resources, the Association refined its rather haphazard research methodologies and initial interpretation of the mansion and its interiors.

The delegation of the house's interiors to the individual vice regents led to a range of interpretations of spaces within the house. Individual personalities, state pride, and tastes (and likely the influence of the decorators and architects they consulted for their own homes) influenced decisions. Each vice regent even identified her state with a sign above the door to the room she directed, amplifying the contributions of individual board members—and the differences between their approaches.[161]

The use of the inventory made at Washington's death best exemplified the inconsistencies among board members in this period. It was the most readily available primary document to inform the Association's furnishing decisions: incomplete versions of the inventory appeared in both Edward Everett's 1860 biography of Washington and Benson Lossing's second edition of *Mount Vernon and Its Associations* (published in 1871).[162] Vice regents used the inventory more often than any other primary document when arranging furniture in these early years, although they did not use it faithfully until the mid-twentieth century.[163] The scattered nature of the Washington family's documents made it difficult for them to corroborate the document with the correspondence, diaries, and record books that are the staples of today's museum professionals.[164]

Lucy Pickens of South Carolina used the inventory to outfit the dining room, which Cunningham had used as a parlor, in the early 1880s.[165] With one thousand dollars raised from an elaborate tableau of a Revolutionary-era ball held in Charleston, she hired Emmart and Quarterly of Baltimore to faithfully restore the color and "original style of the fine decorations upon the walls."[166] The decorating firm repaired the ceiling rather than replacing it.[167] When it came to furnishing the space, she chose a sideboard donated by George Washington Parke Custis's daughter, Mary Custis Lee, in 1873. She matched this piece to the "mahoganey [*sic*] side board" listed in the inventory.[168] She also took the liberty to insert items that did not match the inventory, including a bust of Washington atop a column made of wood from a palmetto, the state tree, and portraits of the prominent South Carolinians Ann Pamela Cunningham, William Moultrie, and Thomas Sumter.

When Philoclea Eve (vice regent, Georgia) interpreted the riverfront room next door as "Martha Washington's sitting-room" in the same years, she did not use the inventory. Eve transformed the space previously used by Cunningham as a bedchamber and then as a relic room into a domestic simulation for the first time in 1883.[169] Most likely unaware of the document Pickens was using to guide her furnishing of the adjoining dining room, Eve said that she had "no record of what furniture was used by Mrs. Washington" in the space.[170] Appointing it with a host of antiques, her interpretation gave the room a general domestic feel that did not approach its eighteenth-century appointment as a bedchamber.

A reporter for *Harper's Weekly* criticized Eve's work, recognizing its "unmistakable modernness" against the other rooms, which he understood as successful "reproduction[s]" of the interiors Washington had known.[171]

Whether or not they closely followed the inventory, the vice regents used a combination of antique furniture and relics to suggest lived-in domestic spaces. As the Association acquired articles with Washington provenances, it swapped out antique articles—resulting in what board members believed to be an interpretation that became progressively more authentic. With each of the mansion's twenty rooms assigned to a particular state's board member and at least partly

Fig. 17. The dining room at Mount Vernon in the early 1880s with the sideboard donated by Mary Custis Lee, a bust of Washington atop a palmetto column, and portraits of famous South Carolinians—including Ann Pamela Cunningham.

Fig. 18. Postcard of the New Room at Mount Vernon in the 1880s, showing the monumental *Washington before Yorktown* by Rembrandt Peale.

Mt. Vernon Banquet Hall

furnished by the mid-1880s, the Association believed the mansion to be growing closer to its eighteenth-century appearance and began to talk more confidently and knowledgeably about its interpretation.[172] The 1877 minutes described newly acquired furniture vaguely as "old-fashioned" or "one hundred years old." Explanations for individual items ten years later were more specific and concerned with provenance. With more completely furnished rooms, the house also looked more believable and less like the cabinet of curiosities that the Association had long tried to avoid. As the house was restored room by room after the centennial, the MVLA slowly replaced the large cases Nancy Halsted had procured from the Smithsonian with pieces of case furniture. Items too big for cases and that did not have a place in the simulations of the parlors and bedchambers often settled in the New Room, which acted as a kind of museum within the house.[173] The model of the Bastille made from a piece of the prison's wall and Rembrandt Peale's massive painting *Washington before Yorktown* were highlights of the large space in the 1870s–80s.[174] The painting had never been in the house during Washington's lifetime and was too large to fit anywhere else in the mansion. Its placement in front of the west wall's window damaged the picture and caused the MVLA to loan it to the Corcoran Gallery of Art in 1902 (it never returned to Mount Vernon).[175]

The evolution of the little parlor in the decades after Cunningham's resignation operates as a case study of the board's ongoing attempts to simulate what the house looked like in Washington's lifetime. In the early years of the restoration just after the Civil War, the room acted as a catchall for a variety of items, including the Lee sideboard (before Pickens plucked it for the dining room) and a large relic case.[176] Without the elaborate stucco decoration of the west parlor or the family dining room, the room must have appeared relatively small and plain to the board members' late nineteenth-century eyes. Using the harpsichord to inspire visions of the family gathered in the room to listen to Nelly Custis's skilled playing, the MVLA began to transform the little parlor into one of the principal places in the mansion for imagining Washington's domestic life at Mount Vernon after assigning the space to Elizabeth Broadwell (vice regent, Ohio) in 1878.[177] Like all of the vice regents, Broadwell paid for the restoration of her assigned room with donations from her home state (most of which were raised in a tableau given in Cincinnati) and her own money.[178] The initial work cost one thousand dollars (it is not clear how much of that sum went toward the purchase of furniture). She hired Emmart and Quarterly to "retain every part of the old material in spite of its dilapidated condition . . . without changing a hinge, lock, or board, but simply by repairing."[179] The firm replaced the plaster in the room and chose a blue color believed to be historically accurate.

Broadwell redubbed the space the "music room" and began planning its furnishings around the harpsichord.[180] Since its acquisition, the Association had displayed the harpsichord as the "principal piece of furniture" in the New Room, where it functioned more as a relic than as a prop in a tableau.[181] Although the instrument was not listed in the inventory taken after Washington's death (it was technically owned by Nelly Custis), the Association knew that it had historically occupied the little parlor. To outfit the relic with a sense of verisimilitude, Broadwell placed what the Association thought was Washington's rosewood flute on its surface.[182] A guitar, donated by a Washington cousin, also sat atop the instrument. The resulting ensemble allowed the visitor to imagine the refined family entertaining themselves with music.[183]

Broadwell chose a number of items without any particular connection to Washington to fill out the domestic space, including two chairs, vases, a French clock, and three small rugs.[184] Perhaps to stand in for specific items listed in the inventory, she also acquired a set of chairs and a sofa, a large mirror, and a mahogany pier table.[185] Explanatory labels differentiated between the items that were simply old and those that had documented Washington provenances.[186] Deferring to her desire to believe that Washington would have always wanted the very best things available, Broadwell chose more high-style Federal chairs than the simpler Windsors listed in the inventory.

On the room's north wall, a large Colonial Revival cabinet held a number of relics, including a drawing Washington did in preparation for the construction of the piazza, a pair of his spectacles, and a set of his dishes donated by W. W. Corcoran.[187] Ten years after Broadwell's initial restoration of the space, the MVLA installed a mesh railing that allowed visitors to enter the little parlor from the New Room to examine the relics case more carefully (as opposed to peering over and through the gates at the doorways).[188] The Association praised

Broadwell's reimagination of the little parlor, proclaiming that "if the whole mansion could be as thoroughly and successfully restored as the Ohio room has been, the ghosts of Washington and his familiar friends might also be won back to the home of their earthly forms."[189]

Despite the differences in the vice regents' approaches in their individual rooms, they agreed that new information or relics should guide new interpretations. Accordingly, the Ohio vice regent who succeeded Broadwell continued to tweak Broadwell's interpretation of the little parlor.[190] From the late 1880s through the 1890s, a rather ominous mask of Washington believed to be the work of Houdon hung in a heavy gilt frame above the mantel. The board members ultimately deemed it inauthentic and relegated it to Superintendent Dodge's office in one of the site's outbuildings.[191] In the 1890s, a surplus in entrance fees allowed the MVLA to acquire two items connected to Nelly Custis for the room: a piano stool and a tambour frame.[192] Neither had ever been used at Mount Vernon, but both did have genuine Nelly Custis provenances. Around the turn of the century, the Association moved in an ornate Rococo mirror and pair of wall brackets, both owned by Washington and acquired through Mary Custis Lee.[193] The Association emptied the Colonial Revival case of most of its relics in 1911 and by the late 1910s had replaced it with a Federal secretary believed to be owned by Mary Ball Washington.[194] Over the years, items in the little parlor were more likely to have both Washington provenances and to fit the simulation of the eighteenth-century space rather than one or the other.

In terms of the building's architecture, the Association focused on a conservation-based approach. It recognized that while furnishings could be swapped in and out, changes to the building fabric would be more difficult to reverse. It did not differentiate between George Washington–era features and those added by his successors. The MVLA benefited from the stewardship of the Washington descendants who had owned Mount Vernon after 1799: the family consciously chose not to update the building or to change the house, presumably out of respect for Washington and the building's national significance.[195] As it had in its initial work under General Michler's watch, the Association restricted its architectural interventions to maintaining the house as it had appeared upon its purchase. Other than ongoing replastering and repainting, the MVLA made few changes to Mount Vernon's interior architecture after the initial 1869–70 restoration campaign led by General Michler. The Association was also conscious of conserving the landscape immediately adjacent to the house; it refused suggestions to pepper the grounds with monuments or to tear down all of the outbuildings.[196] In both landscape and architecture, it initially did little that could not be reversed when more research and robust funding became available later.

The MVLA's most significant early attempt at restoration of the mansion was the reconstruction of features added by Bushrod Washington in the early nineteenth century: the one-story Colonial Revival porch on the building's south side and the piazza's chinoiserie balustrade. Both were in bad shape when the Association purchased the house, and photographic evidence suggests that the board decided to remove them during or soon after the Civil War. Anticipating future maintenance and eager to have them reconstituted for the centennial, Nancy Halsted first proposed that the board approach the "wealthy iron-dealers of our country" to rebuild the porch in iron, along with the colonnades and the summerhouse down the hill.[197] W. W. Corcoran ultimately paid for the porch's reconstruction in wood in 1876.[198] Halsted hired an architect from her hometown of Newark named Benjamin Van Campen Taylor to design a "fac similie" of the porch and to direct the reconstruction of the balustrade. Unlike the ongoing and often spirited debates over relics and interior decorations, the Association did not seem to have discussed whether or not these were genuine Washington-era architectural features; the board simply directed Taylor to reconstruct them according to sketches made by Benson Lossing and Thomas P. Rossiter in the 1850s.[199]

Furthering this conservation approach, Halsted engaged Taylor to make the first series of measured drawings of the mansion in 1876–77.[200] Taylor's process reveals the seriousness with which the Association took Mount Vernon's architecture. Fewer than twenty years after Lossing sandwiched the building's rough chronology between biographical anecdotes in his first edition of *Mount Vernon and Its Associations,* a professional architect was studying and accurately recording the building's existing conditions. Using documentation as a preservation technique was a very recent phenomenon; architects were just beginning to record historic American buildings with photographs, sketches, and measured drawings around the time of the centennial.[201] Taylor measured and drew floor plans for each of the mansion's three floors, as well as the east facade, in 1876.[202] The board understood the drawings as a kind of insurance policy; if Mount Vernon were to be damaged by fire, Taylor's drawings could help in a reconstruction of lost architectural features.[203] Taylor published a plan of Mount Vernon's first floor along with a number of details and molding profiles in the British publication the *Building News* in 1877.[204]

The Association's work to stabilize the passage over the last few decades of the nineteenth century revealed a slow and gradual shift beyond merely conserving existing fabric to a cautiously conjectural restoration approach. The MVLA began to balance stabilization of the building with its restoration to its eighteenth-century appearance. In response to concern over the strain put on the passage's ceiling by the weight of visitors on the second floor, it first installed an arch to support the beam above.[205] Deeming the arch to be inadequate by 1882, the MVLA hired the Washington, D.C., architect Robert L. Fleming to replace it with an iron girder supported on either side by engaged Doric columns.[206] Although this stabilized the ceiling, it was visually invasive; the public recognized the columns as an addition and complained that they were "too modern in appearance." With the help of Thomas Mellon Rogers, the architect also at work restoring Independence Hall in the 1890s, Dodge directed the restoration of the passage to its "original" condition in 1898–1900.[207] Investigations into the passage's materials and structure helped him to understand changes made through the various eighteenth-century renovations of the building. Dodge installed iron girders across the ceiling and removed the columns. He hid the new supports in a box cornice on the ceiling (approximating what he thought Washington had installed) and behind the wall paneling and constructed additional brick piers in the basement below. In the process, Dodge and Rogers found what they thought to be the original "delicate colonial tints" of the passage's wood-paneled walls and the stair's flowery wallpaper.[208] Calling himself a "'stickler' for reproduction," Dodge painted the passage's paneling white and glossy "French" gray, even though "the effect differ[ed] from modern ideas" of what was fashionable.[209] Dodge had to convince some of the board members that an authentic restoration was more important than decorating the passage according to their contemporary taste.[210]

Fig. 20. The east side of
Mount Vernon in 1890,
with the recently recon-
structed south porch and
chinoiserie balustrade.

By the end of the nineteenth century, Mount Vernon's fully furnished interiors were probably the most photographed interior spaces in America.[211] The MVLA offered photographs, stereographs, and postcards as widely available evidence of its hard work. Such pictures also allowed the MVLA to control the image of the house and the Association's interpretations of it. Since right after the Civil War, the MVLA had engaged exclusive contracts with professional photographers to ensure that they received income from the sale of Mount Vernon photographs.[212] By 1874, the sale of photographs accounted for 16.4 percent of the total receipts at Mount Vernon.[213] In the long term, the MVLA's exclusive contracts with photographers ensured that it controlled the circulation and content of the images themselves. In 1877, the Association even sued a group of photographers who snuck onto the property to take unauthorized pictures.[214] Sold at Mount Vernon, on the steamboat, and at other locations, these images were constantly updated to represent the Association's work inside and out.[215] The MVLA was careful to ensure not only that it maintained the ability to make money off photographs sold at the site but also that the images offered "the best possible representations of the place" and of its efforts in preservation.[216] Whether or not they came to Mount Vernon in person, Americans could easily find out what Mount Vernon looked like, ensuring that the Association's collection and display of historic objects in their original setting had a tremendous effect on the development of popular tastes in coming decades.

The rising numbers of Americans seeing and coming to Mount Vernon by the mid-1890s liked what they found.[217] After decades of concern over the state of Mount Vernon, the American public finally seemed reassured of the future of Washington's house. Grumblings about the entrance fee still popped up intermittently, but three decades of restoration had largely quieted the heavy condemnation and unfair skepticism of the Association's early decades. The MVLA proclaimed in its 1891 annual report: "It has been and is very gratifying to hear from those who visit Mount Vernon, so many approving comments upon the condition of the mansion and gardens and grounds. The care bestowed upon the estate is evidently being more understood every year, and Americans who come here from all parts of the country, now seem to realize what our Association has done in preserving the place."[218] Forty years after Ann Pamela Cunningham's initial appeal, the Mount Vernon Ladies' Association had finally earned the "sympathy and confidence" of the American public.[219]

In the course of making Mount Vernon a house museum, the Mount Vernon Ladies' Association created a model for hundreds of preservation efforts in the century to come and refocused what Washington's house meant. In the difficult years before and during the Civil War, the MVLA purchased the house with support of people across the nation and refused to let it become embroiled in sectionalism. It consciously framed the visitor's experience and popular imagery of Mount Vernon on its architecture and interpreted interiors. While almost all nineteenth-century visitors had begun their pilgrimages by mourning Washington at his tomb, tourists by the end of the century first experienced his life through the mansion. The establishment of the streetcar connection to Mount Vernon and the construction of the "Texas Gate" in 1899 solidified this shift.[220] Designed "in keeping with all the architecture of the Estate," the white-brick Colonial Revival entrance brought visitors to the north side of the site and to the house, rather than via the traditional route that wound from the wharf and past the tombs before climbing the hill to the mansion.[221] As Americans became increasingly interested in their material past, the MVLA's restored Mount Vernon became its prime example. Easily accessed, well-maintained, and with its image tightly controlled by the Association, Washington's house was well on its way to being an icon by the end of the nineteenth century.

3 ★ Replicas, Replicas, Replicas

1890S–1920S

WITH ITS INTERIORS FULLY FURNISHED and its architecture conserved, Mount Vernon was a prime candidate to embody the ideal American house and home at the turn of the century.[1] A 1906 article in *Atlantic Monthly* called Mount Vernon the "ideal country home of the republican gentleman." Twenty years later, *Garden & Home Builder* continued to claim it as the "perfect example of the Colonial country house" and "the very fountainhead of American traditions and ideals."[2] Its supposed simplicity, tales of its legendary hospitality, and its intimate connection to the nation's most revered hero guaranteed its position as a model American home.

By 1900, many Americans began expressing their love for Mount Vernon in a new way: they copied it in three dimensions and at full scale. It was no longer enough to pilgrimage to Mount Vernon or to hang prints of its famed piazza in parlors; Americans wanted to inhabit Washington's eighteenth-century world for themselves. The Mount Vernon Ladies' Association's continued work preserving and publicizing Mount Vernon made the building more accessible for those wishing to emulate it. A far cry from the empty and partially inhabited mansion the MVLA had opened to the public just before the Civil War, Mount Vernon's architecture and interiors more closely approximated the domestic simulations for which the vice regents had long labored by the 1920s. The Association aimed for the authenticity of the site to inspire Americans' patriotism and reverence for Washington but could never have anticipated the enthusiasm its audience would have for copying the building.

Thanks in large part to the MVLA's work creating an attractive, idealized Colonial world at Mount Vernon, Americans felt free to replicate the house in order to evoke a range of meanings. The house's accessibility and long-standing imagery allowed for considerable flexibility, and as the twentieth century progressed, Americans found more uses and meanings for Mount Vernon. In the decades following Reconstruction, replicas of Mount Vernon most often recalled a mythical "Old South." Tossing aside hard-fought claims by the Mount Vernon Ladies' Association of the Union for the house's sectional neutrality, many white Americans reached back to antebellum images of Mount Vernon as the ideal plantation to inform newly romantic visions of the South. Both northerners and southerners replicated Mount Vernon to evoke these ideas, seeing nothing conflicted about identifying the national shrine with a regionally specific past. By the 1920s, replicas of Mount Vernon recalled versions of history that stretched far beyond the Old South myth. Different groups borrowed Mount Vernon to represent America as they understood it in the present, producing an astonishing range of interpretations of Washington's home. These replicas often contrasted dramatically in intention and aesthetics, even as they depended upon the image of the same building at their core.

As the nation's most famous house, its first house museum, the home of its first hero, and the paragon of early American architecture, Mount Vernon provided fertile ground onto which Americans could project their revisionist histories and architecture in the early twentieth century. A group of rural West Virginia farmers could claim it just as easily as a cadre of white supremacists in Atlanta. It could represent America's quest for freedom as gracefully as it could an ideal southern plantation supported by enslaved labor. It could symbolize both privilege and the rewards of humility and hard work. Mount Vernon's recognizability and rich source material facilitated its malleability. Although each "replica" employed Mount Vernon for very specific and sometimes even conflicting reasons, all depended upon the availability of the house's image to invoke an idealized American home. Each replica, in turn, prompted others to consider reproducing the building's architecture and fed the profusion of Mount Vernon replicas in popular culture and architecture well into the twentieth century.

A New Museum and a More "Authentic" Mount Vernon, 1890s–1920s

The Mount Vernon Ladies' Association's curatorial decisions produced a vision of Mount Vernon that it believed was increasingly accurate over the 1890s–1920s, providing a stable model that Americans could more effortlessly imagine, revere, and copy. Even as the Association expanded its interpretation to the landscape and a new museum in this period, its priorities remained firmly fixed on the mansion as the most effective way to communicate how Washington had lived. The gardens and views provided an appropriate setting for the eighteenth-century architecture; a new museum allowed for the mansion's interiors to better approximate the evocative recreations of eighteenth-century life also seen in contemporary museum period rooms and department store displays.[3]

A consistently improving financial situation facilitated the MVLA's ambitious curatorial and preservation programs in the early twentieth century. As it became easier to get to Mount Vernon, entrance fees generated substantial revenue whether visitors arrived by streetcar, boat, or later, private automobile. More and more people visited each year, with attendance rising from just over 50,000 in 1894 to almost 366,000 thirty years later in 1924.[4] Private donations also swelled. The Grand Council of regent and vice regents had always been composed exclusively of socially and economically elite women, but its Gilded Age representatives were especially wealthy and generous to their chosen charity.[5] In sharp contrast to the pointed and often hateful criticism of earlier decades, Americans almost universally praised the MVLA for refusing to let Mount Vernon devolve into the "noisy hilariousness" of gaudy tourist attractions by 1900.[6] Martha Mitchell (vice regent, Wisconsin) remarked upon the transition from the early days of the organization: "It seems like a dream to look at Mount Vernon now and to contrast it with what it was. . . . Oh those were the days when we went through a baptism of fire which our sister regents now cannot realize!"[7]

Without the financial constraints and negative scrutiny of previous decades, the MVLA was finally able to realize and to expand its plans for improving the

interpretation and maintenance of Mount Vernon. While something as funda-
mental as replacing a testy furnace had severely taxed the organization's funds in
the early 1870s, the MVLA had ample resources to ensure the building's safety
and visitors' comfort twenty years later. Its introduction of state-of-the-art technology also guaranteed against unsightly anachronisms. In the 1890s, the MVLA
installed an underground furnace system fueled by a central plant four hundred
feet from the mansion.[8] New underground reservoirs could use steam power to
pump water for extinguishing fires, and a chemical engine could smother any
fire in less than two minutes.[9] This multipronged system of fire prevention and
suppression was continually updated and became even more important when the
Association installed electricity in the mansion in 1916.[10]

Stable finances expedited the MVLA's relic collecting and allowed it to be
pickier about what items it wished to purchase or accept for donation. The Association could readily purchase items it believed would further the authenticity
of its presentation of the house.[11] Following developments in the academic study
of American decorative arts and architecture, the vice regents began to rely more
consistently on historical documents and scholarly research when making decisions about what to purchase and how to arrange items in the house. The 1911
discovery and subsequent publication of Washington's complete probate inventory was a significant moment in their refinement of the building's interiors.[12]
It prompted the Furniture Committee to pronounce that some of the building's
rooms were "overcrowded" and to promote the retiring of "anything not connected with Washington or Mount Vernon."[13]

The Association furthered the architectural preservation techniques it had established in the 1870s. In 1894, the Philadelphia architect Theophilus P. Chandler
generated fifty-six pages of measured drawings of the building. Coupled with a
number of photographs, the drawings updated those completed by Benjamin
Van Campen Taylor eighteen years before.[14] Although not a trained historian,
Superintendent Harrison H. Dodge experimented with and employed the latest
techniques in historic preservation. He took routine maintenance at Mount Vernon as an opportunity to look closely at the building and supplemented his forensic analysis with research into Washington's papers.[15] He published articles (and
later a monograph) on Mount Vernon's history and outside historians regarded

him as the foremost expert on the subject.[16] Dodge's 1936 obituary in the *Federal Architect* credited his "painstaking archaeological research" and "investigations of an almost Sherlock Holmes character" with inspiring the scholarly approach to preservation at Colonial Williamsburg.[17]

With the house well furnished, in a good state of repair, and safe from fire in the early twentieth century, the Association could also afford to consider the surrounding landscape more carefully as a period-appropriate setting for the mansion. In 1911, it began its long relationship with the prominent botanist Charles Sprague Sargent focused on the history and health of the site's trees. He encouraged the Association to devote the same degree of accuracy in its documentation and interpretation of the landscape as it did to Mount Vernon's architecture and interiors.[18] Landscape history was still in its infancy, however, and neither the vice regents nor their audience were as concerned with the authenticity of the garden spaces as that of the mansion.[19] Instead, the MVLA largely relied on Colonial Revival trends to invent charming "old-fashioned" outdoor spaces that befitted its idealized vision of Washington's gracious life at Mount Vernon.[20] With some rudimentary archaeological investigation, the MVLA focused its attention on more easily researched architectural interventions designed by Washington like walls and drives.[21]

Other than such features that could be directly credited to Washington, the "restored" landscape at Mount Vernon merely acted as context for the site's main attraction: the mansion. The Association continued to regard the house and its re-created interiors as its primary mission. Since Ann Pamela Cunningham's original conception for the restoration of Mount Vernon, the role of relics in the house had been a particular concern; the Association considered display cabinets full of objects like Washington's clothing as distracting from its attempts to create period rooms—regardless of these relics' historical significance.[22] In the fifty years after Cunningham's resignation, the construction of a new, fireproof building to display and safeguard such objects was a constant topic of discussion. As highly regarded institutions such as the Metropolitan Museum of Art installed early American period rooms in the 1920s, pressure mounted on the Association to finally rid Mount Vernon's famous interiors of items that did not "fit." Committed to meeting the latest standards of authenticity, the Association finally built a "relic house" in 1928. The decades-long process of making this decision and constructing the new building revealed the MVLA's struggle to balance best practices for interpreting the house's interiors with a minimal impact on the mansion's larger context.

The idea of a relic house first surfaced with the MVLA's first unofficial curator, Nancy Halsted, who pronounced in 1889 that the MVLA could never "have the home of Washington as it should be until we have a museum."[23] While some of the vice regents agreed with Halsted, others argued that the disadvantages of "placing any building at Mount Vernon which was not there in the time of Washington" outweighed the goal of presenting the interiors as domestic simulations.[24] Those who objected to imposing a modern building on the historic landscape won out; the majority of the late nineteenth-century board deemed a few curiosities or exhibit cases in the mansion to have less of a negative impact on the illusion of authenticity than a completely new building.[25]

The need for a structure for the safekeeping and display of relics gained urgency as Mount Vernon's collections grew over the following decades.[26] At the Association's request in 1921, the architect Milton Bennett Medary Jr. proposed a site for a fireproof relic house along the north lane just behind the spinning house.[27] Medary chose this location for multiple reasons. It was close enough to the mansion that visitors could easily walk to it but was not within direct sight of the house. Planned with exhibition spaces and accommodations for the vice regents during their frequent visits, it could also provide badly needed residential facilities that would put an end to the board members' practice of sleeping in the mansion.[28]

The most attractive reason for choosing this site was Medary's suggestion that it had hosted a structure during Washington's lifetime. Dodge had recently uncovered foundations on the proposed north lane site, which he had identified as the building labeled "Quarters for Families" on the plan drawn by Samuel Vaughan.[29] The fact that Washington had deemed the site appropriate for a building smoothed over decades-old concerns of introducing a new structure to the historic ensemble, and the Association hired Medary to build the new relic house.[30] The Association had already constructed new buildings on the sites of long-demolished eighteenth-century structures: following the general layout of

Fig. 21. A period room in the Metropolitan Museum of Art's American Wing, opened in 1924. The MVLA built a separate relic house in the 1920s at Mount Vernon so that the mansion's interiors would better demonstrate the most recent developments in museum exhibits as well as more accurately present Washington's material world.

Washington's greenhouse and slave-quarter wings along the north side of the upper garden, it built a new greenhouse soon after the Civil War and added wings of sleeping quarters for vice regents in 1889–90.[31]

In the process of discussing the new relic house with Superintendent Dodge, Medary discovered that Washington had demolished the Quarters for Families before his death.[32] Ever mindful of following Washington's wishes, the Association withdrew its plans for the relic house in light of this new information.[33] If Washington had ultimately decided not to have a building at the end of the north lane, his decision would stand.

Still in need of a relic house, the board decided to retrofit an existing outbuilding and chose a small structure on the north lane then known as the carpenter's shop (today recognized as the salt house).[34] It clearly understood interior alterations of a historic outbuilding to be less problematic than the introduction of a new building to the landscape. Following a new set of plans by Medary, Dodge gutted the eighteenth-century building, poured a concrete floor, lined the interior with fireproof tile, and installed a ventilation system and electricity.[35] The Association displayed documents, clothing, and objects in large cases lining the building's walls. By February 1923, the small building held all of the relics deemed not to fit within the house's domestic simulations, and the MVLA finally expelled all remaining exhibition cases from the mansion.[36]

Almost immediately, the improvised relic house proved to be too small, and its poor ventilation seriously compromised the very objects it was intended to

Fig. 22. The interior of the first relic house (housed in the carpenter's shop, now known as the salt house), Mount Vernon, ca. 1925.

safeguard.[37] By 1928, the Association began to examine other options. Rejecting Medary's proposal to reconfigure the existing barn because of the failures of
the retrofitted carpenter's shop, the Association ultimately decided to revisit his
original plan to construct a new building on the site of Washington's Quarters
for Families.[38] The imminent threat posed to the relics in their current location
squelched any discussion about the appropriateness of constructing a building
where Washington had decided to tear one down.

The need to preserve the mansion's interiors as simulations of Washington's
domestic spaces ultimately overcame misgivings about the visual impact of a new
building, even as the MVLA recognized the integrity of Washington's composition of the plantation's buildings and landscape. Accordingly, Medary ensured
that the new relic house would fit in (or at least not stand out) as much as possible
while serving multiple functions. In accordance with the Association's wishes to
keep the new fireproof concrete block building "in harmony with the spirit of the
place," Medary matched its scale and details to the adjacent spinning house.[39] The
new building boasted exhibition space on the first floor, a cement basement for
the storage of the Association's records, and sleeping quarters for the vice regents
on the second floor.

By removing all relics from the house to the new museum, the Association finally succeeded in establishing in situ domestic simulations at Mount Vernon that were comparable to the period rooms becoming more popular in American museums: each room served as an example of a type of eighteenth-century space, as well as a representation of Washington's particular domain. The construction of a new building within the historic ensemble indicated the relative significance the organization placed on the house and its interiors: their authenticity superseded that of the landscape as a whole. The process of planning and constructing the relic house demonstrates how, in many ways, the figure of Washington began to recede as his mansion moved to the forefront: it stood not only as a monument to his taste and character but also as a means to visualize the material life of Colonial Americans more generally.

Mount Vernon (and Its Replicas) and the Search for an American Architecture

In the same decades that the MVLA refined its preservation efforts and refocused its attention on the house's interiors, attitudes toward Mount Vernon's architecture—and American architecture more generally—shifted considerably. Early histories of Mount Vernon and other Colonial buildings focused on their creators' biographies and associated historical events. Spurred by a search for an indigenous national architecture and the increasingly popular Colonial Revival, the scene changed dramatically over the final three decades of the nineteenth century.[40] Architects came to appreciate the aesthetics and development of the country's early architecture and voraciously sought and consumed information about it. Prominent Beaux-Arts–trained or –inspired architects started to incorporate Colonial features into their modern houses by the end of the 1870s, precipitating inquiry into surviving examples of "ancient" architecture. A review of Arthur Little's *Early New England Interiors* of 1878, the first publication of measured drawings of Colonial buildings geared toward architects, made clear the shift to a more studied approach: "the lessons to be drawn from them are much needed, and the demand for them will increase with our civilization."[41] More popular sources provided an eager lay audience for these architects' new "modernized colonial" styles and histories of early buildings.[42] The author of an 1896 article in *Lippincott's Monthly Magazine,* for example, proclaimed: "The people of this country never took so much intelligent interest in architecture as they do to-day."[43]

Mount Vernon was well positioned in this craze for early American architecture. Whereas earlier generations of Americans had chiefly appreciated Mount Vernon's architecture because of its connection to Washington, those at the turn of the century were more likely to revere the building for its architectural significance. As American architects began to document and research historic structures (and to expand their study beyond New England, where most started), they consistently heralded Mount Vernon as a supreme example of Colonial domestic architecture and aimed to cover the building's history and stylistic attributes thoroughly. The sixth volume of *The Georgian Period,* produced by *American Architect and Building News,* published the first measured drawings of the house in America in 1900.[44] Prepared to meet "a steady demand for material illustrating Colonial architecture," the series was one of the first concerted efforts to compile histories and accurate documentation of important early buildings.[45] Fifteen years later, Mount Vernon was so widely considered a paragon of Colonial architecture that one art historian declared: "Mount Vernon has so often been proclaimed 'the finest example of Colonial architecture in the country' that one almost risks the accusation of treason by denying it."[46]

The prominent place of Mount Vernon in this newly forming canon of early American architecture was both curious and predictable. Architecturally, Mount Vernon was not a perfect specimen of eighteenth-century Georgian architecture. The awkwardness of its proportions and uniqueness of its features should have disqualified it from consideration as an archetypal building of its period. Compared to a more perfectly symmetrical composition like Westover on the James, Mount Vernon was a highly idiosyncratic building. Its very unacademic qualities, however, helped to ensure its recognizability and further connected it to the personality of its revered designer. The house's irregularities made it more approachable and appealingly charming. Mount Vernon's accessibility as a well-preserved and well-documented building open to the public also made it a strong contender for the nascent pantheon.

In response to the rising professional and popular interest in Mount Vernon and Colonial architecture, the historian Paul Wilstach published a monograph on Mount Vernon in 1916.[47] Predating the first academic surveys of American architecture by almost a decade, Wilstach's book drew upon Washington's writings, Superintendent Dodge's forensic analysis, and direct observation of the building.[48] Instead of using the house as a setting for stories from Washington's life as Benson Lossing had decades previously, Wilstach approached his work as a biography of the house itself. He published measured floor plans of the house and, most importantly, put to paper Dodge's observations on the evolution of the building: Wilstach related that after inheriting the plantation and house from his half brother Lawrence Washington, the young George renovated the building and later directed the additions to either end during the Revolution.[49] At the time, neither Dodge nor Wilstach realized that Washington also raised the house from one-and-a-half stories to two-and-a-half stories in his first round of renovations or that it could have been built by his father.[50]

Despite Wilstach's attempts to forgo the usual "doubtful tradition" for a more scholarly approach, his book revealed his inability to avoid the idealization most Colonial Revivalists of the period had for the country's early history and for Mount Vernon in particular.[51] Describing Mount Vernon as "the scene of an easy, graceful social life, based on an opulent hospitality," Wilstach's book perpetuated the house's role in Washington's comparison to Cincinnatus and images of happy and well-cared-for slaves.[52] He similarly described the architecture as beyond reproach: "The whole aspect of the house is simple without severity and elegant without ostentation."[53] Wilstach's incapacity to shake such sentimentalization is not surprising; these ideas about Mount Vernon had been firmly entrenched for more than a century. Like most Americans, Wilstach wanted to view the Colonial past in a positive light.

The mixture of "architectural archaeology" and romanticization in Wilstach's book and similar early architectural histories informed a novel way to appreciate historic American buildings: by replicating them in part or in their entirety.[54] Mount Vernon was not the only historic American building replicated in the early twentieth century, but it was undoubtedly copied far more often and more faithfully than any other.[55] Relying upon tableaux such as the Colonial kitchens and the MVLA's simulation of Washington's world at Mount Vernon, turn-of-the-century "replicas" took to new heights these early attempts to re-create historical spaces. Full-scale reproductions of historic buildings provided three-dimensional stages on which Americans could reenact and reimagine the past. They varied in function and degree of authenticity: a world's fair pavilion copied Mount Vernon inside and out as a kind of historical exhibit, while a private house only emulated the house's dimensions and most recognizable features. Both, however, used replication of Mount Vernon's architecture to connect contemporary people to Washington and his beloved home. This manifestation of ideas about the Colonial past was a loose blend of study and fantasy: turn-of-the-century Americans had enough information and interest to imagine the country's material history with some veracity but also felt comfortable adapting it freely with the latest of modern conveniences.

Mount Vernon and the Old South: The Virginia Buildings of 1893 and 1915

The initial wave of replicas of Mount Vernon relied on its double reputation as the most representative American house and the most exemplary southern plantation. Between the 1890s and 1910s, world's fair pavilions and a host of private houses imagined Mount Vernon as the premier "example of an hospitable old Virginia home."[56] With varying degrees of fidelity, these replicas were key participants in the construction of the "Old South" myth by both northern and southern whites at the turn of the twentieth century. This version of the region's history offered an escape to a hierarchical agricultural past as the country transitioned into an urban nation with an expanding middle class and immigrant population.[57] It was loose enough to encompass both the Colonial and antebellum periods, merging a regional narrative with the nationally nostalgic Colonial Revival.[58] Romanticized visions of the grace and beauty of the early South also promoted the idea that slavery had been both benevolent and necessary.[59] For many whites nationwide, this excused their complicity or participation in slavery, justified contemporary Jim Crow legislation's relegation of African Americans to second-class citizens, and facilitated the reconciliation of a nation so recently and violently fractured.

Architecture, and especially the image of the plantation house, was essential to the mythical Old South. To elite white southerners looking to regain political and economic control following Reconstruction, the plantation house symbolized the power and wealth they hoped to reestablish with their ambitious plans for the "New South."[60] For Gilded Age northerners, the plantation house offered a glimpse of an American aristocracy supposedly separated from crass commercialism and industrialism. To white audiences nationwide, historic southern architecture symbolized an idealized world of leisurely hospitality, aesthetic beauty, and a rigidly defined power structure. A *Chautauquan* article describing a plantation published in 1889 positioned the "planter in his manor-house" at the center of an enviable world: "surrounded by his family and retainers, [he] was a feudal patriarch mildly ruling everybody; drank wholesome wine, sherry, or canary, of his own importation; entertained every one; held great festivities at Christmas, with huge fires in the great fire-places, around which the family clan gathered; and everybody, high and low, seemed to be happy."[61]

With its dominant piazza, neoclassical features, and long tradition in national public memory, Mount Vernon was unsurprisingly a paragon for this idealized plantation type. Mount Vernon spanned national and regional memories more easily and effectively than any other historic plantation house. Decades of descriptions of George and Martha Washington's legendary hospitality and the building's dignified architecture lent the building immediately to the tropes of the Old South myth. In the decades after the Civil War, many Americans began to emphasize its specifically southern qualities, diverging from the regionally neutral image so painstakingly argued by the MVLA. An 1887 article in *Century Illustrated Magazine,* for example, elaborated upon the house's three-part composition: "The uses of such covered walks require no explanation to a Southerner, who recalls the many hospitable mansions where from the kitchens situated at a distance from the dwelling a procession of little darkies like an antique frieze was seen to pass and repass, supporting plates of hot batter-cakes."[62] In this article and others, slavery played a newly central role in descriptions of the house and Washington's daily life there. A topic left largely untouched in recent decades, discussions of slavery at Mount Vernon emerged to reinforce the larger Old South myth at the end of the nineteenth century. *Peterson's Magazine* bolstered the supposed pleasantries of slavery in a description of what a visitor might have witnessed at Washington's farm: "He would have heard such melody of mirthful song mingled with merry laughter coming from the lips of a hundred dark-skinned toilers, as never welled up from human souls burdened with a sense of oppression."[63]

In three dimensions and with live actors, two full-scale replicas of Mount Vernon at world's fairs vividly reinforced the house's role in the moonlight- and magnolia-filled vision of the Old South: the Virginia Buildings at the 1893 Chicago World's Columbian Exposition and at the 1915 Panama-Pacific International Exposition in San Francisco. Funded with both public and private money and exhibiting the state's identity and history for tens of millions of people, these buildings were tremendously influential in spreading Mount Vernon's image, in fueling the impulse to replicate it, and in confirming its starring role in popular ideas of the South. Their creators specifically nurtured the Lost Cause, a memory white southerners designed to justify their pride in the ruined Confederacy.[64] Spanning more than twenty years over the turn of the century, the Virginia Buildings testified to the lasting power of Mount Vernon's image to express white Americans' affection for a mythical southern past.

In some ways, Mount Vernon was the obvious model for Virginia's state building at the 1893 World's Columbian Exposition. The exposition's master architect, Daniel Burnham, suggested that states copy significant historic buildings whenever possible.[65] Following his advice, Pennsylvania relied on Independence Hall, and Massachusetts offered a version of John Hancock's house (demolished in the 1860s). Other states constructed more generalized Colonial Revival architecture.[66] The Virginia Building was unique among the other state buildings in the extent to which it relied on its historical model for inspiration. Massachusetts changed the scale and architectural features of the Hancock House to make it appear more "civic," and Pennsylvania copied only Independence Hall's iconic tower. In contrast, the Virginia Building was an accurate replica of Mount Vernon in scale, detail, and floor plan.[67] According to all reports, the only concessions that the Virginia Building made to the practical needs of its guests were a reading room in which visitors could peruse books by Virginia-born authors (perhaps in the room that approximated Washington's study) and a counter for sending postcards and telegrams. The singular significant architectural divergence made in the translation from the original was orientation: with the state's site at the rear of the fairgrounds giving visitors little reason to walk around the back of the pavilion, planners chose Mount Vernon's east side as the building's front. The piazza was undoubtedly the most recognizable feature of Mount Vernon and the natural choice for the "face" of the state at the exposition.

By replicating Mount Vernon so carefully even as other states only approximated or casually referenced historic buildings, the Virginia Building's exclusively white planners revealed the seriousness with which they took the opportunity to show themselves to the world in 1893. In subtly infusing their re-creation of Mount Vernon with connections to their Confederate past, they simultaneously excused their state's participation in secession and offered a history around which all white Americans could unite.[68] The strategy worked: Virginia's exhibit was among the most popular of the state buildings.[69] A lecturer at the Exposition's Historical Congress, for example, praised the sunny picture offered by the Virginia Building and confirmed its reliance on the Old South myth: "From the pretty and vivid picture [drawn] of the home-life of Washington, we may learn how unpretentious the truly great can dare to be, and the simple manner of living chosen by the family of that honored son of old Virginia. . . . It is really an enjoyment to be here to witness the tranquil happiness that reigns throughout the house."[70]

The idea of replicating Mount Vernon for the Virginia state pavilion probably originated with the newly formed Daughters of the American Revolution (DAR) and the Ladies' Auxiliary Board of the Board of World's Fair Managers of Virginia, who commandeered much of the fund-raising and planning for the building as soon as the state legislature agreed to participate in the exposition.[71] The DAR had considered replicating Mount Vernon during the fair's initial planning stages but ultimately limited its participation to an exhibit in the Women's Building.[72] Lucy Preston Beale, a member of one of southwest Virginia's "oldest and wealthiest families" and a leader in both groups, probably promoted the idea of replicating Mount Vernon to her fellow Virginians once the DAR had dropped it.[73] As a central figure in both organizations, Beale was uniquely positioned to suggest the idea of reproducing Mount Vernon for her state's pavilion once the national organization abandoned the plan.[74]

As soon as the Board of World's Fair Managers agreed upon Mount Vernon as the model for the Virginia Building, Beale actively sought the approval and assistance of the Mount Vernon Ladies' Association in order to ensure the building's fidelity to its model. The Association refused to loan her genuine Washington relics, granting her generous access to the house instead; she visited multiple times to study "details of the Mansion and the arrangement of its furniture."[75] The MVLA also helped the building's architect, Edgerton Stewart Rogers, obtain exact measurements of Mount Vernon's plan and features.[76] Rogers presumably made measured drawings of the building over multiple trips.[77] He published two

Fig. 24. Virginia Building, Edgerton Stewart Rogers (architect), at the World's Columbian Exposition, Chicago, Illinois, 1893, in *The Columbian Exposition Album* . . . (Chicago: Rand, McNally, 1893).

interior views of the replica in the *Inland Architect and News Record* shortly before the exposition opened, using the titles "Mount Vernon" and "Virginia Building" interchangeably.[78] A historian of the fair described the extent of the replica's fidelity: "The carved mantels and wood trimmings were exact facsimiles, as well as the windows, with small panes and sashes fastened with wooden buttons."[79]

The Virginians furnished simulations of Mount Vernon's interiors, including the central passage, the New Room (used as the reception room), Washington's study and bedchamber, and the garret bedchamber to which Martha Washington retired after her husband's passing.[80] The Board of World's Fair Managers' curatorial strategy for the Virginia Building was much the same as that which the Association had until recently employed at Mount Vernon: it chose objects associated with the state's heroes as well as articles that simply looked old in order to convincingly re-create a historic environment.[81] Objects relating to Washington ranged from articles of clothing to a reproduction of the bed in which he died.[82] The board also wanted to ensure that visitors acknowledged other founding Virginians: the exhibit displayed Thomas Jefferson's watch and eyeglasses, along with Dolley Madison's piano.[83]

But the Virginia Building did not merely tell a story of the state's role in Colonial history. Relics of Founding heroes sat alongside the whiskey flasks and mahogany table of the Confederate States of America president Jefferson Davis, Confederate money, and a photograph of the Confederate general Stonewall Jackson.[84] By weaving these relics into the interiors of the highly recognizable national shrine, the Virginia Building's proponents normalized their Lost Cause narrative and suggested that the Confederate statesmen had merely been following the constitutional principles laid out by Washington, Jefferson, and the rest of the (notably Virginia-born) Founding Fathers.[85] The Virginia Building established Washington and Mount Vernon as steadfast symbols in an uninterrupted progression that began with union making, inevitably led to union breaking, and ended with union reconciling.

The Virginians could have pursued other options for displaying historic objects, but a replica of Mount Vernon positioned them as productive members of a national culture without sacrificing their pride in the Confederate cause. Some of the same Virginians at work on the Chicago building were simultaneously preserving the "White House of the Confederacy," the former Richmond residence of the Confederate president Jefferson Davis, with a very different approach.[86] Rather than interpret the building as a house museum, they conceived it as a depository for relics that exemplified the bravery and beauty of a fallen civilization.[87] Opened on George Washington's birthday three years after the World's Columbian Exposition, their museum of the Confederacy featured large relic cases crammed with bloodstained military memorabilia and tattered homespun demonstrating the valor of both those on the battlefield and those on the home front.[88] The same Virginians determined emotional, war-torn relics fit for a presentation of the recent past in Richmond and chose a more inviting, domestic presentation for an international audience in Chicago.

Mount Vernon in Chicago re-created more than just the material aspects of the "home-life of Washington" infused with reminders of more recent events. It also imitated a working plantation house in which both mistress and slaves charmed audiences with their legendary southern hospitality. Lucy Preston Beale greeted guests at the Virginia Building and oversaw its daily operation.[89] In Virginia's official report, her "thoughtful and genial hospitality" was credited with "whatever social advantages, attentions and comforts Virginians have received at the Mt. Vernon."[90] Described as "a charming representative of the Virginia matron," Beale stood in the role of the magnanimous and dignified plantation mistress praised in contemporary Lost Cause histories of the antebellum South.[91]

Accounts of the fair also consistently commented on the "old Virginia negroes" who worked alongside Beale.[92] The historian Hubert Bancroft wrote of the complete faithfulness of the replica in his account of the fair: "The result was a perfect mirror of the times, even to the aged negroes appointed for domestic service."[93] An African American janitress mentioned by Bancroft and others was most likely Sarah Robinson, a woman then employed by the MVLA.[94] Ignoring her contemporary status as a paid employee at Mount Vernon, newspapers reported that she was a descendant of the Washington family's former slaves.[95] Assuming that Sarah's last name must be "Washington" after her former owners, one reporter made clear his interpretation of her as a stand-in for an enslaved person: "Sarah Washington . . . a direct descendant of the old Washington house servants, proud of her name and of the worthy ancestors who adopted it. She is grave, dignified, and courteous as becomes her place and name, and in her one may behold a typical survival of the servant of the old school."[96] The Virginia Building's re-created world was convincing enough that the public easily made the leap and compared its black employees to their enslaved ancestors. This simulated plantation united white audiences around the idea that slavery had been a benign institution. As if re-illustrating the images of happy, faithful slaves such as those in Junius Brutus Stearns's 1851 painting of Mount Vernon, the Virginia Building provided a stage for the enactment of mythical relationships between kind mistresses and faithful slaves.[97] By suggesting that Sarah was a "Washington" who had chosen to stay at Mount Vernon long after emancipation, the Virginia Building reinforced stereotypes of blacks who were more interested in serving their former masters than asserting their newfound freedom. Across the exposition grounds in the fair's Agriculture Building, Nancy Green played a similar role selling pancake mix as "Aunt Jemima" for the R. T. Davis Milling Company. Representing an ever-smiling mammy or a dutiful "servant of the old school," Aunt Jemima and Sarah "Washington" offered white audiences unthreatening visions of African American citizenship that patently ignored emancipation and denied advancements made during Reconstruction.[98] Against the backdrop of exhibits of African "natives" on the fair's Midway, both Nancy Green and Sarah Robinson also undoubtedly confirmed the supposed civilizing benefits of slavery for many white visitors.[99]

Following the success of Mount Vernon in Chicago, the Old Dominion and many other states continued to evoke their Colonial architectural heritage with reproductions at subsequent world's fairs. Virginians opted to construct a replica of Thomas Jefferson's Monticello at the 1904 Louisiana Purchase Exposition in St. Louis, commemorating the defining moment of the Virginian's presidency. In 1915, Virginia once again decided to replicate Mount Vernon for its state building at the 1915 Panama-Pacific International Exposition in San Francisco. Across the country from the original, the replica had the potential to expose a whole new coast to Washington's home. The state's commission for the exposition decided at its very first meeting to reproduce Mount Vernon.[100] Positioned alongside replicas of the Trenton barracks where George Washington and his troops quartered during the Revolutionary War, the Old Massachusetts State House, the Alamo, and Independence Hall, Mount Vernon was the darling of the Avenue of States.[101] It hosted more than 3 million visitors during the fair and was pronounced "a perfect picture of Mount Vernon as it was 115 years ago."[102] The marina beyond the building's trademark piazza suggested the Potomac, providing a suitable waterfront setting for the house.[103]

The Virginia Building's architect, Charles Kirkpatrick Bryant, made the state's decision to reproduce Mount Vernon at San Francisco an even easier one. He drew up plans for the job and supervised its construction without taking a salary.[104] Bryant likely volunteered because he had access to Edgerton Stewart Rogers's measured drawings of the mansion produced for the Chicago fair. Bryant's business partner, Benjamin West Poindexter, had inherited all of Rogers's "professional books" after the architect's death, presumably including the drawings for the 1893 Virginia Building.[105] With such resources at his disposal, Bryant surely saw the commission for the 1915 Virginia Building as an opportunity to drum up new business back in Richmond. In fact, he would come to dominate the business of reproducing Mount Vernon at world's fairs for the next two decades.

Bryant also made a new set of measured drawings of Mount Vernon to ensure an "exact replica" in San Francisco.[106] Unlike its generosity toward Rogers and Lucy Preston Beale less than twenty years earlier, the MVLA was concerned that Bryant's Virginia Building would be too precise. A complete replica threatened its increasing desire to control the house's image by the 1910s: Mount Vernon's interiors were closer to their eighteenth-century appearance than ever, and the MVLA's board members clearly did not want their hard work or reputation compromised by a shoddy copy. After a discussion over whether or not to grant Virginia the "privilege of using the Mansion at Mount Vernon as a model," the MVLA unanimously decided to sanction the exposition building on the grounds that it would be temporary and that "only the outside of the building was to be reproduced."[107]

Virginia and Bryant obliged the Association's request and reproduced only Mount Vernon's exterior architectural features, desiring the organization's support for publicity and general goodwill. Thanks to the state's pioneering Chicago pavilion and the spread of the historic preservation movement, the replica and period room were also no longer novelties.[108] A complete replica would not have been as intriguing as it had in 1893.[109] Instead, Bryant replicated Mount Vernon's floor plan and finished the interiors with Colonial Revival details; the Virginians outfitted the interiors as a combination of exhibit spaces and period rooms.[110] Relics and antiques in the dining room, west parlor, and New Room simulated those spaces at Mount Vernon; exhibits on the state's educational system, agricultural and manufacturing achievements, and a proposed monument to George Washington occupied the rest of the first floor.[111] The only room open to the public on the second story was "Washington's bedchamber," featuring a copy of his bed. The rest of the upstairs bedchambers were reserved for the state's commissioners and the building's hostess, Nannie Randolph Heth.[112] One dependency reproduced Mount Vernon's kitchen; the other held additional exhibits.[113] No contemporary reports mentioned (or objected to) the interiors' lack of fidelity to the original, testifying to the success of Bryant's generically historic atmosphere and to the public's satisfaction with an approximation of Mount Vernon.

Without accurate simulations of Mount Vernon's interiors or a host of Colonial or Confederate relics, the 1915 Virginia Building focused on what museum professionals today would identify as a living-history interpretation in order to provide an even subtler connection between Colonial, antebellum, and contemporary Virginias than offered by the 1893 version. The building's hostess, Nannie Randolph Heth, consciously played the role of the plantation mistress Martha Washington. Living in the exhibition building, she spent most of her days at the fair greeting visitors dressed in Martha Washington's own jewelry and copies of the first lady's dresses.[114] Heth embodied the living legacy that connected Washington with the Confederacy: she was the goddaughter of Robert E. Lee, who had married the daughter of George Washington Parke Custis, George Washington's adopted grandson.[115] Visitors did not comment upon any African American employees "performing" with Heth.[116]

The choice of a historical actor over material objects or architectural fidelity to connect various periods in the state's history indicated the success of the Lost Cause narrative in the twenty years since the World's Columbian Exposition: a generalized Mount Vernon with a woman playing Martha Washington was enough to retell the Old South myth. By 1915, white Americans had largely reunited around such an idyllic image of the plantation. The Confederate memorial organizations that had been in their infancy in 1893 were well-established and

Fig. 25. Nannie Randolph Heth dressed as Martha Washington in the Virginia Building at the 1915 Panama-Pacific International Exposition, in Frances A. Groff, "Lovely Woman at the Exposition," *Sunset Magazine*, May 1915.

gaining increasing control over the narrative of southern history by 1915. Through forums ranging from textbooks to public monuments, the Lost Cause had successfully convinced many Americans of a romantic and patriarchal southern past in which slavery was conflict-free.[117] As the South's most famous building, Mount Vernon could easily and quickly conjure images of such an imagined past—even in approximation.

Mount Vernon and Domestic Architecture in America, 1890s–1910s

Within a decade of these earliest full-scale replicas of Mount Vernon and the first American publication of drawings of the house in *The Georgian Period*, its iconic piazza began to appear on private houses. The most notable, and perhaps the first, example of the explicit replication of Mount Vernon's architectural features on a contemporary house was McKim, Mead and White's Hill-Stead of 1899–1902. In the following decades, Mount Vernon's famed piazza became a favorite motif of the American country house. Mount Vernon appealed to Gilded Age patrons and their socially connected architects for the same reasons it had inspired the creators of the 1893 and 1915 Virginia Buildings: it was identified with an American elite. Country houses like Hill-Stead were idealized agricultural getaways bought with fortunes made in busy urban centers; they were a large, semi-public, and somewhat permanent means of conspicuous consumption for the outrageously wealthy.[118] Mount Vernon's role as the perfect plantation was particularly well suited to this new class of Americans clamoring to prove their gentility and taste. Its connection to Washington suggested that owners of a version of the building would similarly lead the United States to greatness.

The demand for tasteful and historically inspired domestic architecture emerged with the rise of American architectural history, a more academically informed architectural profession, and increasing consumer choices more generally.[119] Architects like Charles McKim, Richard Morris Hunt, and Stanford White distinguished themselves among their late nineteenth-century peers with their literacy and proficiency in historical styles. These architects practiced eclecticism alongside the principles of clear and unified composition taught at the exclusive École des Beaux-Arts in Paris; they used the study of historic architecture to inform their designs, to connect themselves to larger social and cultural themes, and to please their wealthy and educated clients.

Demonstrating one's fluency in historic architecture was imperative for a successful architect of the period; replicating entire designs verbatim was discouraged.[120] Although many architects were as comfortable designing in the Colonial as the Tudor, Mediterranean, or various eras of classicism, most sought to apply a style's principles to the particular requirements of a building's site, client, and function. They consciously avoided losing artistic integrity to the "snare of the predetermined style."[121] Most architects adapted historic styles to meet their clients' expectations for the most modern conveniences: residential "replicas" of Mount Vernon usually integrated the house's architectural features into a modern floor plan that included the latest plumbing and lighting technologies. The architect Frank E. Wallis described this approach: "I believe a new and better era in architecture is with us . . . a Colonial revival—not a faddish copying, but a sincere and studied acceptance of our most precious architectural heritage—is a thing to be hopefully and prayerfully looked forward to."[122]

For the client, style was one of the most important decisions to make in the process of designing a house; most saw the choice of historic style as a means of identifying themselves with the values of past cultures, people, and events.[123] Discussions and examples of different architectural styles were abundant in popular magazines and literature, providing a host of material from which clients could educate themselves. The introduction to *Architectural Styles for Country Houses,* a book published in 1919 featuring essays on historic styles ranging from the Colonial to the "Swiss Chalet Type," warned the reader to choose the right style from the beginning of the design process: "While the failure to include back stairs may cause a temporary inconvenience, and may in time be remedied, the style of our house will abide with us for the rest of our days, and if we have chosen unwisely in our haste there is nothing about the whole structure that may become so insistently repellent."[124] With its long identification as a simple yet dignified design, associations with the Old South, and a direct connection to George Washington, Mount Vernon had tremendous appeal for Americans building a house in the Colonial style.

There was no question as to which style Theodate Pope Riddle would choose for her parents' country house, Hill-Stead, in Farmington, Connecticut, at the turn of the twentieth century: only the Colonial would do. She had already remodeled an eighteenth-century building as her own residence, and her library included the latest American architectural histories, including *The Georgian Period* with its drawings of Mount Vernon. Riddle and her parents hired McKim, Mead and White to help with the drafting and planning of the project, with Riddle remaining in full control of the house's design.[125] She imagined a large white mansion with the vernacular character of the rambling farmhouses both she and her male architects admired. Not until after the family was occupying Hill-Stead in the fall of 1901, however, did the house begin to reference Mount Vernon directly with a version of Washington's trademark piazza. Who made the decision to add the truncated piazza (it has six square columns instead of Mount Vernon's eight) with chinoiserie railing is unclear. Riddle had visited Mount Vernon in

1900, and McKim, Mead and White was designing a Mount Vernon piazza for the Orchard, a residential commission in Long Island, at the same time.[126]

Regardless of how the decision was made, the piazza was included in the first published images of the building in the November 1902 issue of *Architectural Review*. When the architectural critic Barr Ferree covered Hill-Stead for *American Homes and Gardens* more extensively later in the decade, he praised the "appropriateness of the design" for rural Connecticut. Without even needing to name the source for the piazza directly, he noted the building's ability to balance historic character with modern convenience: "To all intents and purposes, therefore, we have here a fine old time farm house; not a reproduction, not a duplication of another building . . . but a quiet harmonious design, worked out in the style of its period, with detailing of the most modern kind, a house that is at once scholarly and refined, modern and old."[127] In both the general style of the Colonial and the specific reference to Mount Vernon, Hill-Stead's character struck the balance so desired in the American country house: relaxed yet urbane, impressive yet simple.

In 1898–1907, McKim, Mead and White added a Mount Vernon piazza to the Orchard, the revamped and much-enlarged suburban home of Stanford White and Charles McKim's friend and wealthy stockbroker James L. Breese in Southampton, Long Island. Breese wanted to reference Mount Vernon in particular from the start: "There was one dominating idea in Mr. Breese's mind when he called in his friend, Charles Follen McKim, to help him remodel his old farmhouse, and that was to retain the quaint straightforwardness of the early American builder's work and to bring to the new home something of the dignity and simplicity of Mount Vernon."[128] Like at Hill-Stead, the piazza formalized the rambling white house. At the Orchard, McKim chose to use rounded Doric columns on all but the piazza's ends and designed delicate stucco medallions for the hall and dining room ceilings similar to that on the ceiling of Mount Vernon's west parlor. The H-shaped plan suggested the Palladian organization of Mount Vernon; McKim used matching conservatory spaces on either side of the main block of the building to connect it to flanking wings.[129] Shortly after the house was finished, Barre Ferree evaluated the "frank adaptation of the old Southern Colonial house": "The word 'Hospitality' is writ large over this fine mansion; for

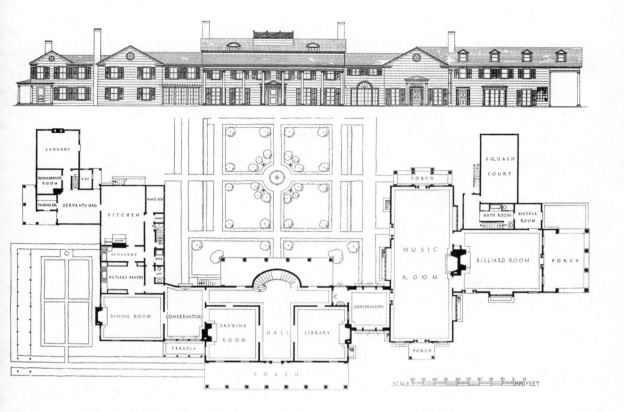

the house is a mansion, though the design is simple, the architecture restrained, the decorative elements refined and subdued."[130]

Hill-Stead might have been the first time professional architects had used Mount Vernon's piazza in a contemporary context, but the Orchard was more widely published. It ended up being more influential on the following generations of architects looking to emulate the illustrious New York firm and Washington's beloved home. The editor of *Architecture* used the Orchard as the best example of the American country house in 1912 because of its ability to offset its size with a character that was "unpretentious, unaffected and homelike."[131] The bible for Americans aspiring to or living the life of the wealthy, *Country Life in America,* named the Orchard one of the "best twelve country houses in

Fig. 26. The Orchard (residence of James L. Breese), McKim, Mead and White (architects), Southampton, New York, 1906 in McKim, Mead and White, *A Monograph of the Work of McKim, Mead & White,* vol. 3 (New York: Architectural Book Publishing, 1915), plate 270.

America."[132] Photographs and to-scale drawings of the house were featured in McKim, Mead and White's seminal multivolume monograph, published between 1915 and 1920.[133] Again and again, critics and architects praised the Orchard for its quality of being both simple and magnificent, conflicting attributes reconciled by the familiar piazza of Mount Vernon. Built during the firm's impressive rise to fame, the Orchard only became more notable as the firm did.[134]

Following McKim, Mead and White's success and the ever-growing popularity of the Colonial Revival, young American architects followed with a second wave of Mount Vernon–inspired American country houses in the 1910s.[135] In *Country Life in America,* numerous articles on Mount Vernon's history by Paul Wilstach and others were published alongside photographs and drawings of the modern interpretations.[136] The magazine's editors prompted readers to draw direct connections between the glamorous lives of contemporary millionaires and Washington. Through this and other similar venues, Mount Vernon maintained its status as the premier example of American domestic architecture, and its piazza appeared on even more houses as replicas were published in a variety of venues.

Before he became known for his monumental Classical Revival public buildings, John Russell Pope designed at least two well-published Mount Vernon–inspired country houses. Beginning his career under McKim's mentorship, Pope quickly mastered academic eclecticism.[137] In 1911, his enormous white residence for the publishing magnate Robert J. Collier in Wickatunk, New Jersey, featured not one, but two facades inspired by Mount Vernon. Five tall, thin, square columns marked the recessed entrance on the front of "Rest Hill," while the garden-facing facade boasted a full, eight-columned piazza.[138] Pope was most likely appealing to Collier's deep patriotism with his choice of Mount Vernon as a historical reference.[139] Pope had recently designed a neoclassical temple to enclose Abraham Lincoln's Kentucky birthplace for Collier.[140] Pope also used the Mount Vernon piazza in a more modest Long Island residence for the New York businessman J. Randolph Robinson in 1917. Picking up on Charles McKim's variation at the Orchard, Pope used rounded, rather than squared, columns.[141] The house was lauded for its simultaneous simplicity and monumentality, echoing the ambiguity of Mount Vernon's appeal to eighteenth-century audiences.[142]

The École des Beaux-Arts alumnus William Adams Delano used the house's

Fig. 27. Muttontown
Meadows (Egerton L.
Winthrop House), Delano
and Aldrich (architects),
Syosset, New York, 1903,
in *Architecture* 41, no. 4
(April 1920): plate 55.

west facade for his well-published and highly praised Long Island country house, Muttontown Meadows, in 1903.[143] Built for the prominent New York attorney Egerton L. Winthrop Jr. at the same time McKim, Mead and White were building the Orchard close by, the house typified the characteristic understatement of country houses by Delano's New York–based firm, Delano and Aldrich.[144] Demonstrating his knowledge of Mount Vernon beyond its most famous feature, the architect designed a symmetrical facade with a pedimented door surround, rusticated wood siding, a heavy Doric cornice, dormer windows, and a cupola.[145] Attuned to the colors and landscape of Mount Vernon, the architect contrasted the white exterior walls with "apple green" shutters and introduced the facade with a circular drive.[146] The caption for the building in *American Country Houses of To-day* signaled Delano's triumph in the interpretation of his model: "This is a view of a Long Island home, not a picture of old Virginia. It has the qualities of repose, of excellent properties, of attention to detail."[147]

By the late 1910s, houses with Mount Vernon's trademark features were known as the "southern type," categorizing a geographically determined category of domestic architecture the same way in which the "Swiss chalet" or "French castle" might. The white-painted porch, even with rounded columns or when attached to a brick building, differentiated Mount Vernon–inspired houses from other Colonial Revival buildings and added a regional flair. Authors of a 1918 article in *House Beautiful* clustered a photograph of the Orchard with that of a brick house featuring a Mount Vernon piazza as examples of the "old Southern type," despite the fact that both were built far north of the Mason-Dixon Line.[148] The Southern Pine Association used an image of a Colonial Revival house with a Mount Vernon–style piazza in an advertisement that ran in popular design magazines in the late 1910s.[149] The Colonial and southern associations of Mount Vernon could overlap or be separated in architectural evocations, but both were equally essential to the house's popular image. The ease with which it could represent either made it ever more attractive to architects and clients looking to reference the American past.

The images and descriptions of such large mansions and the glamorous lives they hosted inspired others to use Mount Vernon's trademark architectural features more widely in American domestic architecture by the end of World War I. Architecture magazines and books expanded from the Mount Vernon–inspired country houses in posh New York and Philadelphia suburbs to more affordable versions.[150] Publications offered a range of ways in which Americans without the vast fortunes of the Popes or the Colliers could attain more modest versions of Mount Vernon. In 1917, the editors of the *White Pine Series of Architectural Monographs,* a magazine "suggesting the architectural uses" of the inexpensive building material, held a design competition for a frame house costing under $12,500.[151] The program of the competition did not specify style, but almost all of the winning entries were Colonial Revival. More specifically, four of the twelve designs recognized by the jury borrowed elements of Mount Vernon in their compositions. Three used the piazza outright; another imaginatively adapted the details of the mansion's colonnades and dependencies with a small, attached porch. The 1915 publication *Inexpensive Homes of Individuality* similarly offered a brick Colonial Revival house with a Mount Vernon piazza and chinoiserie balustrade as an example of the "the stately high-columned Colonial porch that was common in early Southern work."[152] Although Washington's piazza was anything but typical in the eighteenth century, it was an increasingly common feature in domestic architecture by the end of the 1910s. With its easily referenced architecture and popular associations with a mythical South, Mount Vernon became a favorite source of inspiration for domestic architecture among contemporary architects and an increasingly wide variety of clients.

Mount Vernon Replicas of the 1920s

Following World War I, Americans began to see possibilities for the adaptation of Mount Vernon's iconic architectural features in building types other than the private house. Just as the white piazza, cupola, and trademark asymmetry traveled from elite suburban mansions to more affordable residences in the 1910s, so too did they migrate from residential architecture to a variety of commercial and civic structures nationwide in the 1920s. The MVLA's increasingly refined interpretation of the building and the availability of its image stimulated its popularity, ensuring it as prime inspiration for a new surge of replicas. As more Americans became familiar with Mount Vernon, they could more easily recognize an intentional reference to it. In designs for college campuses, hotels, a children's summer camp, an exposition pavilion, and even a women's prison, architects and clients across the country hoped Mount Vernon's image would conjure idealized visions of the simplicity of Colonial America, the patriotism of George Washington, and the glamour and grace of the Old South.[153]

Mount Vernon enjoyed this groundswell in popularity just as the national past became more approachable and fashionable across all strata of society and visual culture.[154] Facilitated by rapidly developing technology and a healthy economy, more Americans began to collect antiques and to travel to history-related destinations in the 1920s.[155] A growing number of house museums and public collections of American decorative arts fed voracious appetites for Colonial history.[156] The opening of the Metropolitan Museum of Art's American Wing in 1924 heralded an especially high point in the appreciation of early American design and the accessibility of its history. With the first permanent exhibition of historic American interiors in a major art museum, the Metropolitan confirmed that American objects were worthy of reverence for their aesthetic value as well

Fig. 28. Design for an "attractive" women's prison, Alfred Hopkins (architect), in Alfred Hopkins, *Prisons and Prison Building* (New York: Architectural Book Publishing, 1930), plate 10.

as their associative provenance: a chair's craftsmanship and style was becoming just as important as whether or not an important historical figure had sat in it.[157] For many, the quest for finding and defining a traditional American aesthetic was also a reaction against unfamiliar (and arguably foreign) Modernism.[158]

The boosted interest in Colonial objects and architecture manifested in two major trends, both of which shaped the new wave of Mount Vernon replicas of the 1920s: the increasing availability of Colonial Revival goods and the use of history to assert American nationalism. As historic American furniture became increasingly revered and the general population became more attentive to the nation's early material culture, manufacturers and retailers started to create and aggressively market reproduction furniture, decorative arts, and architectural elements. While only the wealthiest Americans might have afforded (or collected) genuine Colonial objects at the end of the nineteenth century, copies of museum-quality pieces were widely available by the mid-1920s.[159] The Mount Vernon piazza began to appear on more affordable homes just as Colonial Revival goods allowed more Americans than ever to revel in their material heritage.

As a backlash against this democratization and commodification of national history, many native-born, white Americans used historic architecture and material culture to assert their supposedly rightful claims to the nation's past.[160] They were also responding to the increasing heterogeneity of the population: the foreign-born population of the United States nearly tripled between 1900 and 1920. The influx of immigrants (especially those from southern and eastern Europe) threatened many native-born Americans, who shunned the waves of people from cultures they perceived as inferior. This culminated in the passage of the National Origins Act of 1924, which limited the number of new immigrants to the United States according to country of origin. As part of this xenophobia, many native-born Americans used national history and Colonial Revival goods to define what was American and, by exclusion, what was not. The curator for the Metropolitan Museum's American Wing, R. T. Halsey, revealed the prejudice driving that exhibit in particular: "The tremendous changes in the character of our nation and the influx of foreign ideas utterly at variance with those held by the men who gave us the Republic threaten, and unless checked, may shake, the foundations of our Republic."[161] By enshrining American decorative arts in a museum, exhibits like Halsey's carefully designated "American" objects as English in origin and at least eighteenth-century in vintage.

Groups selling Colonial Revival goods and using history to lay xenophobic claims of ownership on history had opposing objectives. The first worked toward including more Americans in the appreciation of history (or at least to take monetary advantage of it). The other used history to exclude select groups based on their race or ethnicity. Despite their differences, both depended on a wide population to be significantly engaged with the nation's past: in order for an individual to decide to purchase a Colonial Revival object or to feel ostracized for not having American ancestry, she or he had to believe that the past was important in the present.

This rich range of uses for the material past primed a fertile ground for a rush of Mount Vernon replicas. Because so many Americans knew what Mount Vernon looked like and had already seen an alternative version of it (either as a private house or world's fair pavilion), it offered more opportunities for connecting past and present than any other American building. In turn, the reproductions of the 1920s took advantage of Mount Vernon's recognizability and used its iconic piazza to conjure a range of meanings reaching far beyond recollections of the Old South.

Four select examples of nonresidential replicas designed in the decade reveal the various methods and reasons behind Americans' choices to reproduce Mount Vernon. Each building publicly represented the identity and mission of an organization; each organization carefully chose the readily identifiable piazza to make specific arguments about its position in the rapidly changing nation. The Metropolitan Philadelphia branch of the Young Women's Christian Association (YWCA) and West Virginia's 4-H program co-opted Washington's home for dining halls in order to convey the importance of civic responsibility in a democracy. Both rooted in the Progressive Era, the YWCA and 4-H saw the appropriation of Mount Vernon as an opportunity to attract and serve a wide audience with free or affordable social services. In the same years, two different college campuses in Georgia, Wesleyan College and the short-lived Lanier University, used architecture to legitimize their respective programs, to root their missions in a southern identity, and to guide their students' moral and historical educations. Their reasons for harnessing Mount Vernon were as different as they were similar. Lanier used the graceful white piazza to promote white supremacy, while Wesleyan College encouraged conservatism without such blatant politicization. Comparison of these four examples demonstrates that Mount Vernon was popular and familiar enough by the 1920s to accommodate such widely divergent interpretations. It could conjure feelings of inclusiveness and generosity at the same time that it could project hate and racism.

Depending on more than a century of tales of the Washingtons' boundless hospitality, the Metropolitan Philadelphia branch of the Young Women's Christian Association built a Mount Vernon–inspired "hostess house" to serve visitors and female employees of the Philadelphia Sesquicentennial Exposition in 1926. Designed by the local architecture firm Magaziner, Eberhard and Harris, the "Mount Vernon House" embodied "every phase" of the organization's services.[162] The only part of Mount Vernon that the YWCA chose to replicate faithfully was the east facade, which functioned as the front of the building and most easily conjured ideas of a gracious Old South. Even though the interiors served a range of practical functions and did not attempt to suggest period rooms, the YWCA did outfit them with domestic Colonial Revival touches (much like the 1915 Virginia Building).[163] The building hosted more than eighty thousand "tired tourists" over the course of the fair.

Beyond its "slim white pillars and broad piazza," the YWCA building and its evocation of the Old South offered a progressive range of services to working women much like those that the organization promoted in urban areas nationwide.[164] Beginning amid the country's urban expansion of the 1870s and 1880s (the Philadelphia branch was formed in 1870), the YWCA constructed boardinghouses that offered safe and respectable places for "women adrift": young and immigrant women living independently of their families.[165] The organization gradually expanded to provide job training and placement, to advocate for workers' rights, and to ensure that women were paid fairly so that dire financial circumstances did not drive them into prostitution.[166] By providing safe homes and promoting the protection of working women, the YWCA furthered the Victorian-era idea that the feminine domestic sphere was the wellspring for society's morality.[167]

By wrapping its services in the envelope of the home that had shaped America's most revered citizen, the YWCA asserted the importance of the domestic realm in protecting the mental and physical health of the nation's citizens. Just as the organization welcomed women adrift in the city, it took on the responsibility to help orient and assist visitors and female employees at the Sesquicentennial. An information booth immediately inside the entrance offered general guidance about the fair, directions to and from sites throughout the city, emergency and social services, and a lost-and-found.[168] The booth gave suggestions for suitable lodging and services to women and foreigners new to Philadelphia.[169] Interpreters provided "understanding and sympathetic assistance" to foreign-language speakers, translating maps and other fair literature.[170] Booth employees and volunteers also coordinated with the women on the Sesquicentennial police force (the first female officers at a world's fair) to help find lost children, to report unsanitary conditions, and to watch over young women after nighttime events "to see that they did not leave the grounds in improper company."[171] Although the information booth in the Mount Vernon House was not the only one at the fair, the breadth and depth of its services demonstrated the organization's dedication to the well-being of the fair's more disadvantaged visitors.

Mirroring the YWCA's larger mission to bring cafeterias into the workplace, the main attraction of the Mount Vernon House's largely open-plan first floor was a three-hundred-seat cafeteria (served by a commercial kitchen at the rear of the building). More than 20 percent of visitors to the Sesquicentennial ate at the Mount Vernon House, deemed by some to have the best food on the exposition grounds.[172] Whether at the fair or in a factory, the YWCA's cafeterias offered healthy meal choices in an efficient way; this allowed women to have time to pray during their short lunch hours.[173] To ensure that women working at the fair did not waste time waiting in the cafeteria's long lines, the YWCA also opened a small service counter just for female employees of the Sesquicentennial.[174] In keeping with the organization's advocacy of a vice-free life, the Mount Vernon House cafeteria did not sell cigars or candy.[175]

The Mount Vernon House was also the headquarters for the YWCA's vocal support of workers' rights on the Sesquicentennial grounds.[176] The second floor was intended for the use of female fair employees and largely closed to the general public.[177] It featured substantial restroom facilities, a lounge and recreation room, and a large assembly room. The Metropolitan branch offered a variety of entertainments for female fair employees (providing an alternative to potentially salacious activities elsewhere).

In the same year that the YWCA constructed its temporary Mount Vernon House in Philadelphia, West Virginia's 4-H program built another dining hall based on Washington's home more than four hundred miles away. On the center axis of the "Jackson's Mill" statewide 4-H camp, the dining hall commanded the campus's highest and most dramatic vantage point.[178] The architect R. A. Gillis designed the one-and-a-half-story frame and random-course sandstone building with a cupola, pedimented doorways, heavy Doric cornice, and piazza with eight square columns and a chinoiserie balustrade. Much like the YWCA's hostess house, the majority of the open first floor was left to communal dining tables that accommodated as many as 450 children.[179] The second floor served as a dormitory for camp leaders.

Just as Mount Vernon had fostered Washington's exemplary citizenship, so

MT. VERNON DINING HALL, STATE 4-H CAMP, WESTON, W. VA.

would its distinctive piazza inspire campers at Jackson's Mill. Beginning in the decades after the Civil War and expanding in the early twentieth century, 4-H programs started in many local communities as a means of interesting school-children in new agricultural methods.[180] The programs taught life skills and championed personal responsibility, a commitment to community service, and maintenance of physical and moral health. Camping became a central part of 4-H by the 1920s, and statewide 4-H camps like Jackson's Mill offered solutions for developing "local leadership" and producing "better citizens needed for a safe democracy" in the interwar years.[181] Campers followed strict routines that required them to "live cooperatively, assume leadership roles, and learn skills not taught in the classroom or even at home."[182] These attributes echoed those long admired in George Washington.

Fig. 29. Dining hall, Jackson's Mill 4-H Camp, R. A. Gillis (architect), West Virginia, 1926. Undated postcard published by Teacraft Company, Tenafly, New Jersey.

With its Mount Vernon dining hall, Jackson's Mill was the first permanent statewide 4-H camp in the nation. Its founder, William "Teepi" Kendrick, saw the camp as a standard-bearer for permanent camps in other states.[183] Kendrick, a longtime trailblazer in 4-H philosophy, designed the Jackson's Mill master plan in 1920 with the help of the state 4-H administrator Charles H. Hartley and Tell W. Nicolet of Morris-Knowles Engineers. The Monongahela West Penn Public Service Company donated land at a dramatic bend in the West Fork River in Weston, and West Virginia appropriated fifteen thousand dollars via the state extension service for the camp's initial construction.[184] Camper and volunteer labor built many of the structures with inexpensive materials over the next fifteen years according to Kendrick's master plan.[185] 4-H still operates the camp today.

Choices of architecture and site were central to Kendrick's vision for a camp that would successfully inculcate civic responsibility in its campers. In an instruction book he published for 4-H guides in the same year that he directed the construction of the dining hall, Kendrick wrote: "The fundamentals of our civilization are to be brought out in the type of building so that when the camp is complete it will have an atmosphere conducive to bringing out the best there is in our boys and girls."[186] At Jackson's Mill, Kendrick developed a campus steeped in American history; using buildings and places associated with famous individuals, he shaped a landscape for his "leadership laboratory" that provided tangible links to the past.[187]

Kendrick was initially attracted to the Jackson's Mill site because it was the childhood home of the Confederate general Stonewall Jackson.[188] Although the house in which Jackson had lived in the 1830s had long since burned, a gristmill built by Jackson's uncle remained. To enhance the camp's historic character, Kendrick moved a 1790s log cabin adjacent to the mill and reconstructed it on the footprint of a cabin supposedly built by Jackson's grandfather.[189] To complement the aesthetic of the log cabin and to remind campers of the pioneering beginnings of their West Virginia ancestors, he designed many of the new buildings at Jackson's Mill with roughly hewn logs and heavy stone chimneys.[190] Kendrick even specified that cypress, stone, and spruce were particularly appropriate materials for 4-H camps as they recalled "the Pioneer Spirit."[191]

The idea for using Mount Vernon as the model for the dining hall supposedly came from campers, but it also fit perfectly with Kendrick's use of architecture to remind young people of historical figures' courage and civic commitment.[192] Kendrick wrote of the building: "George Washington said to his soldiers at Valley Forge 'Take Courage, for we can yet go over into the mountains of West Augusta and recruit an army that will win this war.' For that reason, we built this, keeping faith in him."[193] The most highly finished and expensive building on the Jackson's Mill campus, the dining hall was an integral part of the symbolic landscape Kendrick crafted to "discover and train leadership" in West Virginia's youth.[194] It also proclaimed the politically peripheral state's sense of belonging to the nation; West Virginia had as much of a right to Mount Vernon as any other state.[195] Built in coarse stone, this Mount Vernon had a West Virginia flair that differentiated it from the refined Georgian rustication of the original and gestured to the pioneer emphasis of the rest of the camp's carefully crafted history.

Kendrick planned the camp's Mount Vernon dining hall on axis with the Jackson homesite, the reconstructed cabin, and the mill, connecting the various layers of history at the core of the camp and focusing the young campers' activities around them.[196] The rest of the campus radiated from these buildings much like a town around a central green. Kendrick compounded Mount Vernon with the myth of the pioneering log cabin, seamlessly mashing layers of Founding myths into a landscape meant to inspire a new generation of leaders.[197]

Both the Metropolitan Philadelphia branch of the YWCA and the West Virginia 4-H aimed for their Mount Vernons to be uplifting places that could actively shape socially disadvantaged populations. Jackson's Mill provided a place that could help West Virginia's largely rural and poor youth rise from their humble childhoods; the YWCA offered services that its organizers believed would make the lives of women working at the Sesquicentennial easier, healthier, and more moral. Both organizations deemed Mount Vernon the ideal architectural model for these civic-minded goals. As altruistic as these buildings and the organizations they represented might have appeared at first glance, however, things were not so simple. These buildings participated in the xenophobic exclusivity that infected many attempts to harness early American history in the period. Just as they were statements of Mount Vernon's potential to belong to everyone, the YWCA's hostess house and 4-H dining hall also suggested that the privileges begotten under the broad white piazza—and by extension, American history and patriotism—were only for the "right" people.

Jackson's Mill, like all statewide 4-H camps, was built exclusively for white children. Although 4-H programs for African American youth developed alongside those for whites, they never received full financial or administrative support. As a result, camping opportunities and facilities for black children lagged far behind.[198] Camp Washington-Carver, West Virginia's segregated statewide 4-H camp for African American children, was not built until 1937. Constructed in Fayette County by the Works Progress Administration, the camp was smaller than Jackson's Mill and lacked the strong ties to national and local history championed by William Kendrick either in architectural style or associational significance.[199] As much as Kendrick and his colleagues were devoted to teaching children civic values at Jackson's Mill, they provided those opportunities to white children only.

The YWCA's Mount Vernon House was not so blatantly exclusive. There is no evidence that the organization turned anyone away because of the color of their skin or their country of origin. In fact, the YWCA celebrated the cultures of those newly immigrated to the United States through exhibits of Romanian, Latvian, and Armenian handicrafts and performances of traditional ethnic dances hosted in the cafeteria space.[200] The choice of Mount Vernon—undoubtedly the South's most famous plantation—for the Metropolitan branch's hostess house, however, might have been an affront to Philadelphia's African American YWCA branches. In the early 1920s, they and a number of other black organizations and businesses publicly accused the Metropolitan YWCA of racism. After black women had provided invaluable assistance in the campaigns to build a new central YWCA branch, the Metropolitan branch had refused to participate in efforts to build much-needed new segregated facilities.[201]

In the same years that the YWCA and 4-H built dining halls, two Georgia colleges also copied Washington's legendary piazza: Lanier University in Atlanta designed (but never built) a dormitory, and Wesleyan College, a Methodist women's college in Macon, erected a student activities building. Like Teepi Kendrick in West Virginia and the YWCA in Philadelphia, the colleges' administrators hoped that Mount Vernon's architecture would play an active role in their students' education. Both Lanier and Wesleyan specifically relied on the popular association of Mount Vernon with a graceful and heroic southern past. Where the two colleges differed was in the ways in which they politicized the Old South myth. Wesleyan College promoted a conservative view of women's roles in the contemporary South without an obvious political agenda. Taken over by the Ku Klux Klan soon after its founding, Lanier University used Mount Vernon to endorse a vision of the South that was not only conservative but also deliberately divisive and unquestionably racist.

Differentiating their college from more liberal women's colleges like Smith and Wellesley, Wesleyan College's administrators wished to ensure the persistence of tradition when they built a new campus on the outskirts of Macon, Georgia, in the early 1920s.[202] In close collaboration with the school's administrators, the architects Walker and Weeks of Cleveland opted for the "restrained and chaste colonial architecture" for all of the buildings on the new "Greater Wesleyan."[203] Wesleyan and its architects hoped to evoke the same sense of southern hospitality and Washington's impeccable character that the YWCA and 4-H's dining halls intended to express. They chose Mount Vernon as the specific model for the new student activities building at the symbolic and geographic center of the new campus.[204] Facing a wide green, an enormous piazza with a chinoiserie balustrade dominated the side-gabled brick building. Begun in 1926, the student activities building and most of the other structures on the 132-acre campus were finished in time for the start of the 1928–29 school year.[205]

Wesleyan was the first college chartered to grant degrees to women, and its administrators hoped that the new Wesleyan would "remain true to the fine standards of Christian womanhood established by the old Wesleyan."[206] Central to this traditional understanding of femininity was its connection to a socially conservative, mythical Old South. President William F. Quillian said to the students on the opening day of the fall 1926 semester: "While endorsing all modern movements for the larger freedom of womanhood, Wesleyan has sought to maintain that reserve and refinement which is peculiar to the young womanhood of the South."[207] Students at Wesleyan were not allowed to attend "questionable places of amusement" in downtown Macon, smoke, play cards, or dance. "Talking to young men too long or when not allowed" was grounds for expulsion.[208] An editorial in the student newspaper, the *Watchtower*, confirmed that Quillian's view and its implications were welcomed by much of the student population: "There is no tradition of which Wesleyan is more proud than she is of that atmosphere of culture of the old South, so beautiful now in the midst of the rush and hurry of this day. Wesleyan girls should do what they can to keep this beauty alive."[209] From its students to its president, Wesleyan saw itself as a mainstay of conservative gender roles and as a vision of a patriarchal South—despite its pioneering role in women's education.

The student activities building depended upon Mount Vernon to root its various residential and civic functions in this conservative image of the South. It operated as the face of a large, irregular quadrant of dormitories to its rear; the campus's main dining hall commanded the majority of its interior space; and it hosted the offices of the student government association. The *Watchtower* characterized the building: "The dormitory and dining hall group are more domestic in character, being a prototype of the Virginia architecture, similar to Washington's home at Mount Vernon. The portico of the dining room, which is, perhaps, the main architectural feature of the entire group, creates an air of Southern hospitality."[210] The Student Government Association evoked Washington through its activities in the building promoting a "consciousness of responsibility and pride in the fact that every young woman is on her honor gives to the college an atmosphere of dignity and strength."[211]

In the same years that Wesleyan built a student activities building with Washington's trademark piazza, the coeducational Lanier University planned a campus with a Mount Vernon dormitory in Atlanta. The Baptist preacher Charles Lewis Fowler founded the Baptist-affiliated school in 1917 with hopes to distinguish it as an "all-Southern university of the highest grade."[212] In a design by the architect A. Ten Eyck Brown, most of Lanier's buildings replicated the white-columned plantation houses of prominent southerners.[213] The college's bulletin described the role of the campus's architecture in the daily lives of Lanier students: "to live in the atmosphere of these buildings and to imbibe the wholesome spirit of the illustrious men and women who made these buildings famous during the bellum and ante-bellum days will constitute a liberal education."[214] Fowler clearly hoped that such an architectural strategy could legitimize and distinguish Lanier by

by Lanier University

attaching it to Mount Vernon's prominent roles in national and distinctly southern narratives.

From its beginnings, Lanier University was also intimately tied to the racist
and xenophobic Ku Klux Klan (KKK). In 1921, the Klan purchased the school
and reimagined it as an "All American University."[215] Revived in Atlanta just two
years earlier under the leadership of Imperial Wizard William Joseph Simmons,
the KKK harnessed the fear and racism of native-born, Protestant whites nationwide with a platform of white supremacy, anti-Semitism, and anti-Catholicism.
Threatened by the influx of immigrants and their perceived disruption of patriarchal social and economic structures, the national KKK became a tremendously
powerful political and social force in the late 1910s and early 1920s.[216]

Developed at the same time that the KKK was rising to power in Atlanta and

Fig. 30. Lanier University,
A. Ten Eyck Brown
(architect), Atlanta,
Georgia, 1917 (never
completed). Undated
postcard published by
I. F. Co., Inc., Atlanta.

with many of the same players at the helm, Lanier's mission fit neatly within the renewed KKK's supposedly progressive mind-set. The founder Charles Fowler differentiated the school from other Baptist-affiliated colleges by its coeducational nature; he proclaimed it was "never natural or wise" to separate the sexes, conjuring the rampant anti-Catholicism of the Klan and the Atlanta branch's contemporaneous campaign to rid the public school system of all Catholic teachers.[217] All students were required to take a "special course in Civil War and Reconstruction History" taught by KKK Imperial Wizard Simmons, "supreme leader" of the Klan.[218] Although Simmons had never published a book on southern history, it is easy to imagine his white-supremacist perspective extending far beyond the Lost Cause apologists that preceded him. In a lecture given while teaching at Lanier, he lambasted the National Association for the Advancement of Colored People (NAACP) for encouraging racial equality: "God created certain barriers between the races . . . and declared that the set of men who sought to break them down would sooner or later have to pay the penalty."[219] Fowler himself was an outspoken proponent of the KKK and published a book defending the Klan's often violent actions in 1922, the year after the purchase of the university by the organization.[220]

Architecture was an important strategy for Fowler's developing university. Within months of opening the school with 150 students and rented space, he announced that sponsors had donated property in the Druid Hills suburb and that A. Ten Eyck Brown had developed a compelling plan for the campus.[221] Much like the 1893 and 1915 Virginia Buildings—but with a far less conciliatory bent—Brown planned "reproductions of homes famous in southern history" that reaffirmed a longing for the days when white Protestants held absolute power in the region.[222] In addition to a dormitory modeled after Mount Vernon, the plan included replicas of the plantation houses of the Confederate generals Robert E. Lee (Arlington House) and Stonewall Jackson, as well as Thomas Jefferson's Monticello. Even more indicative of Lanier's political leanings were the proposed replicas of a number of houses identified with prominent white supremacists in Georgia: John B. Gordon, head of the state's KKK in the 1870s and governor following Reconstruction; Henry W. Grady, the editor of the *Atlanta Constitution* who helped to ensure Gordon's election; Robert Toombs, the famously "unreconstructed" southerner who led Georgia's secession and refused to regain his U.S. citizenship after the Civil War; Confederate States of America president Jefferson Davis; and Benjamin Hill, prominent Confederate and champion of the white South.[223] Although only the replica of Arlington House was actually built and published renderings of the campus did not individually identify its various structures, each of these buildings featured porticos with large white columns befitting the mythical view of the region's antebellum architecture. Gordon's house, for example, was described in a contemporary history of Georgia landmarks: "Its colossal and elegant proportions, broad wings, ample grounds and stately forest oaks, all suggest the opulent and splendid days of the Old South."[224] These buildings were a central component of Fowler's campaign to raise money for the college, as he clearly believed that they would appeal to the regional and racial pride of the same Atlanta population that was resurrecting the Ku Klux Klan.[225]

Despite impressive attempts to drum up enthusiasm for the project, Fowler's plan began to languish by 1920. To save the school and to provide the Klan an opportunity to expand into higher education, the organization purchased Lanier and assumed its debts in 1921. Fowler resigned, and the new board, composed almost entirely of KKK leadership, elected Simmons as president of the university.[226] Nathan Bedford Forrest, grandson to the founder of the nineteenth-century KKK, became secretary and business manager.[227] Expanding Fowler's initial vision for the university, the Klan distinguished the school by "laying unusual stress upon . . . the ideals of pure Americanism."[228] The new administration renamed Lanier the "University of America" and developed a curriculum based on fundamentalist teachings of the Bible and the U.S. Constitution in order to better inculcate students with the Klan's white-supremacist brand of patriotism.[229] It planned to construct a "Hall of the Invisibles" for the "teaching of Klankraft and the ideals and principles of Ku Kluxism" on the campus.[230] Due to Simmons's loss of control of the national organization, the expanded university never materialized.[231] Lanier closed its doors amid bankruptcy proceedings in 1922, leaving the replica of Arlington House as its only physical reminder.[232]

Lanier University and Wesleyan College's almost simultaneous uses of Mount Vernon testify to the adaptability of the house's image by the 1920s, especially in its identification with the Old South. Its connection to memories of an elegant and beautiful aristocratic world were inseparable from those of a brutal, patriarchal society built on slavery—whether or not people chose to see beyond an idealization. By the onset of the Great Depression, Mount Vernon was more visible in popular American culture and architecture than ever before, and the proliferation of the building's image on the American landscape had become even more varied.

4 ★ Battles of "Authenticity"

REPLICAS AND RESEARCH
IN THE 1930S

BUILDING ON THE MOMENTUM ESTABLISHED BY the Mount Vernon Ladies' Association's preservation efforts, three imitative world's fair pavilions, and a growing number of replicas, the popularity of Mount Vernon skyrocketed in the 1930s. The decade's celebration of the bicentennial of George Washington's birth and continued commercialization of the Colonial Revival offered opportunities for Mount Vernon to charm even bigger audiences.[1]

Mount Vernon's iconic visage had proven to be both flexible and deeply meaningful by the 1930s. A variety of products banked on its most well-established ideals, emphasizing the building's southern hospitality and refined, patriotic simplicity. A magazine advertisement for Mount Vernon Brand Straight Rye Whiskey in 1939, for example, suggested that the modern "gentleman" could host his guests "in style" just as Washington had more than a century ago.[2] Alongside Mount Vernon's name in an old-timey black-letter typeface, the advertisement's pictorial cues only briefly identified Washington's house: the partially visible mantelpiece and Ionic door surround placed the scene in the house's west parlor. A smiling enslaved African American man in livery exited one corner of the picture with silver tray in hand. George Washington sat in an armchair with his back to the viewer; the bushy white ponytail of his profile clearly recalled Gilbert Stuart's archetypal portraits.[3] Mount Vernon was so familiar by the end of the

1930s that the liquor company found only idealized snippets necessary to visually pinpoint it in the advertisement.

As companies and individuals used Mount Vernon to sell everything from whiskey to roof shingles, the Mount Vernon Ladies' Association became increasingly concerned with its perceived loss of control over the shrine's public image.[4] The Association asked the producer of Mount Vernon Straight Rye Whiskey to consider the historical inaccuracies in the advertisement.[5] Under no legal obligation to heed the MVLA, the company declined to reply and continued with the ad campaign. The incident was just one example of the growing tension between Mount Vernon's public image and that maintained by the Association. Increasingly over the 1930s, the MVLA took substantial measures to prevent what it saw as the tasteless and frivolous commercialization of George Washington and his home. Using a variety of strategies, the Association intervened directly in some of the decade's most significant attempts to co-opt Mount Vernon's likeness. Its attempts to interpret Washington's home based on well-founded facts in the same years were a further affront to the increasingly casual adaptation of the building's image.

"Trying to Stem These Reproductions": The MVLA and the Mount Vernon Replicas of the 1930s

More Americans than ever were visiting Mount Vernon in the 1930s. The construction of the George Washington Parkway in 1932 made it easier to get there by car and provided an attractive and efficient alternative to the steamboat and trolley routes.[6] The Association opened the site on Sundays for the first time in 1934, ending a long debate between the merits of observing the Sabbath and providing an opportunity for working Americans to see the house on weekends.[7] The site's attendance record shattered in 1936 with 530,000 paying tourists.[8]

As the Mount Vernon Ladies' Association worked to offer an experience rooted in historical accuracy to this upsurge of tourists, it became increasingly concerned with the interpretation of the house's memory beyond its gates. In 1929, the board had consented to the mansion's use in advertising for the Gutta Percha Company's "Barreled Sunlight" white paint in exchange for the company's agreement to repaint all of the plantation's buildings.[9] Just a few years later, the board began to take a strong stance against the commercialization of Mount Vernon's image. Working both defensively and offensively, the Association refused to endorse the widespread commercialization of the house and embarked upon an aggressive preservation and research campaign in an effort to maintain its hold on an "authentic" vision of Washington's home. The vice regents worried that the exploitation of the building was unseemly and damaging to Washington's legacy but also that the public might accuse *them* of profiting from Mount Vernon. With increasing skill over the early twentieth century, the board's members avoided any situation that might cause the public to distrust them.[10] By refusing to willingly allow Mount Vernon's image to be used in advertising by the 1930s, the Association hoped to protect both its and the house's integrity.

The kind of commercial exploitation that worried the Association most was full-scale replication. Architectural reproductions were more permanent than any singular product; the very nature of a replica threatened its quest for authenticity far more gravely than advertisement copy. Whereas the MVLA facilitated the 1893 and 1915 world's fair pavilions and refrained from comment on the buildings inspired by Mount Vernon in the 1920s, it began to take a much stronger stand against replicas by Washington's bicentennial in 1932. But as more information on Mount Vernon became available and as interest in the Colonial period expanded, the MVLA also had more to worry about.

No replicas had more success in promoting Mount Vernon as a model for contemporary architecture or in motivating the Mount Vernon Ladies' Association to develop a stringent policy against reproductions than those planned by the leading producer and retailer of prefabricated buildings in America in the early 1930s: Sears, Roebuck and Company. In 1931–32, Sears created two full-scale exhibition replicas and began to market a mail-order house with a version of the iconic piazza. While millions worldwide saw the two replicas, the publication of a Mount Vernon look-alike in Sears's catalogue ushered in a new age of Mount Vernon interpretations. In addition to the houses of the well-to-do published in glossy design magazines, architectural catalogues aimed at the middle class began to feature buildings of all sizes inspired by Washington's home following Sears's debut. Much as the Association feared, Mount Vernon was "commonize[d]" over the 1930s—and Sears led the way.[11]

Sears and Roebuck first got into the Mount Vernon business in 1931, when they built a full-scale replica as the United States pavilion at the Colonial and Overseas Exposition in Paris. As the country's first-ever government pavilion at a European colonial exposition, the building had tremendous publicity potential at home and abroad. A year into the Great Depression and following a decade of isolationism, the exhibit offered the country a chance to reassert its past and potential successes. Sears manufactured and constructed the exhibition pavilion in record time, providing evidence of the country's resilient industrial prowess despite the economic crisis. The image of Mount Vernon and its recollection of George Washington's friendship with the French hero Lafayette also reminded an international audience of America's political origins and positive historic relationship with Europe.[12]

After briefly considering designing an exhibition pavilion that would draw from the various cultures of the United States' overseas territories in its architecture, the U.S. commission in charge of the government's involvement in the fair decided that the American building would be a "home of the colonial type" that was most representative of the "national style."[13] The idea to replicate Mount Vernon came soon thereafter, and the choice fulfilled all of the U.S. government's many logistical and ideological requirements. The building would be easily identified by an international audience and Americans back home, and its Palladian composition would lend itself to the assorted administrative and exhibition needs of the U.S. commission.[14] Besides the precedent set by previous world's fair replicas, other countries used architectural reproduction as a strategy in their buildings at the 1931 Paris exposition: France constructed a copy of Angkor Wat from its Indochinese colonies, while the Dutch synthesized features indigenous to their East Asian territories in their pavilion.[15] William Adams Delano, an architect well versed in replicating Mount Vernon, was at the head of the U.S. committee and surely encouraged Washington's home as the ideal model for America's national pavilion.[16]

The commission also hoped that a replica of Mount Vernon would inspire interest in the upcoming bicentennial celebration of George Washington's birth, an event that the federal government depended upon to galvanize the American people amid the difficulties of the Depression. Although the federal commission for the 1932 George Washington Bicentennial was established in 1924—long before the onset of the Depression—it took on new meaning after the crash of the stock market in 1929. Initial plans focused on a world's fair to be held in New York City akin to the celebrations of the nation's birthday held in 1876 and 1926.[17] The federal George Washington Bicentennial Commission ultimately decided that a unique program designed to elicit "spiritual and patriotic appeal" from every corner of the country was more in keeping with the nation's deep reverence for its Founding Father.[18] The government distributed a series of pageants, plays, musical scores, films, essay contests, commemorative postage stamps, medals, genealogies, classroom lesson plans, and suggestions for celebrations of holidays and anniversaries spanning from Washington's inauguration to Columbus Day. Considering the hardships faced by city and state governments throughout the United States, this wide range of government-provided programs allowed localities to pick and choose how to celebrate the anniversary of Washington's birth according to their budgets and interests. In the end, 894,224 local committees presented more than 4.7 million programs using images, scripts, and essays provided by the federal Bicentennial Commission.[19] Bicentennial material unsurprisingly touted Mount Vernon as a root of Washington's character, reinforcing its importance to American history and present-day patriotism.[20] The author of one publication insisted: "We must visit Mount Vernon to know the real Washington; and, to know him as we ought, we should visit it many times . . . for the more we know of Washington the more we appreciate his home."[21] During the country's greatest economic depression in both the United States and in its representation in Paris, the U.S. government deemed George Washington and his supposedly simple life at Mount Vernon outstanding examples for how to weather seemingly impossible odds.

The early involvement of Charles Kirkpatrick Bryant, the architect of the Virginia Building at the 1915 Panama-Pacific Exposition, also facilitated the decision to replicate Mount Vernon as the U.S. pavilion. Bryant offered his services as soon as he heard about the United States' involvement in the Paris fair. Writing to President Herbert Hoover, he claimed (erroneously) to have the only complete and detailed measured drawings of Mount Vernon and suggested that the building be manufactured in the United States and sent to Paris to save money and to ensure quality.[22] Less than a month later, Sears, Roebuck and Company had signed on to manufacture the replica and its accompanying exhibition buildings for only 10 percent overhead. Sears saw the building in Paris as an opportunity to revive its mail-order home business, which had begun to decline even before the crash.[23]

Set in a grove of trees on 2.5-acres in the Parisian park Bois de Vincennes, the completed ten-building U.S. complex centered on a full-scale replica of Mount

Fig. 32. Newspaper clipping about the production of Sears, Roebuck and Company's United States Building at the Paris Colonial and Overseas Exposition, 1931.

Taking Mt. Vernon to France

(Top) Replica of the Mt. Vernon mansion group now under construction, which will house American government exhibits at the French International Colonial Exposition in Paris next summer. (Below) Fleet of trucks leaving Port of Newark plant of Sears, Roebuck and Co. with 300,000 feet of specially prepared millwork enroute to France for the buildings and (right) loading the lumber for Paris.

Vernon. The project's landscape architect, Jacques Gréber, was careful to reproduce the circular carriage drive with its bollards and chains; he also added a sundial to match that in Virginia.[24] After some discussion, the commission decided to arrange the replica just as contemporary visitors approached the house in Virginia, with the building's west facade serving as the front.[25] A wide, sloped lawn approximated the site along the Potomac.[26] Outfitted with period rooms matching those in Virginia, the main block of the replica served as a house museum; the dependencies housed modern exhibits, including displays on Alaska and Native Americans, as well as a version of Mount Vernon's kitchen. Bryant tucked additional structures for exhibits of the United States' overseas territories on either side of the house and coordinated them with architectural elements borrowed from Washington's house. The entire composition approximated the organization of Mount Vernon's outbuildings along the plantation's service lanes and allowed for an unobstructed view of the replica from either direction.

The planning, manufacturing, and construction of a replica of America's most famous house in Paris promised good publicity for Sears. The Chicago-based corporation had begun selling building materials in its catalogues in 1895, expanded to offer millwork by 1902, and released its first *Modern Homes* catalogue in 1908.[27] The company ensured its dominance of the prefabricated housing market by extending lines of credit, offering mortgages earlier and more generously than federal organizations.[28] In 1930 (while the construction of the United States Building was under way), Sears reorganized its Modern Homes department to maximize profits and to make up for the decrease in new construction affecting similar mail-order businesses across the country.[29] In style, most of the buildings in the Sears catalogues by the 1930s were Colonial Revival or Arts and Crafts–inspired bungalows. The simplicity, modesty, and relatively small scale of Colonial Revival buildings were especially appealing to a wide range of Americans and easily adaptable to the company's fabrication and assemblage techniques.[30]

The construction of the United States Building confirmed the efficiency of modern American technology and provided physical evidence of the health of the country's industry. French and American newspapers enthusiastically followed each step of its manufacture and construction, giving Sears plenty of free advertising. The process was similar to that of any other Sears house: the company milled and cut the lumber at its plant in Newark, New Jersey, and then sent it along with plans and details to France, where a company representative, Gustav Meissner, was on hand to manage a work crew as it assembled the building and installed utilities.[31] Bryant and Sears adhered to and even surpassed the promised construction timetable: Bryant delivered the drawings to Sears on October 15, and just seven days later, the materials for the two initial exhibit halls were bound for Paris.[32] He described the process in a press release: "More than 30,000 feet of lumber and special millwork, cut and numbered in the United States like steel 'fabricated' for a modern skyscraper structure, have arrived in Paris or is on the highseas enroute [*sic*] to France."[33] French and American newspapers published photographs of the milled lumber along with Bryant's rendering of the complex. By mid-November and ahead of schedule, the two exhibit halls neared completion. In order to prove to the public (and government officials back in Washington) that construction was really that far along, Bryant and Meissner staged photographs standing on the roof of one of the buildings.[34] The quick turnaround of the U.S. pavilion had special significance in the context of a world's fair: when the American commission declared its buildings complete by the April deadline (the fair was set to open on May 1), the government's efficiency flew in the face of a long tradition of exposition buildings taking far longer than expected (meant to commemorate Columbus's 1892 voyage, the famed World's Columbian Exposition of 1893 opened a year late).[35]

The fast construction timetable of Mount Vernon's Parisian twin was even more notable considering that Sears also reproduced the famous interiors' mantels, moldings, and elaborate stuccowork.[36] Working with a consortium of Grand Rapids furniture manufacturers and historians from the Smithsonian, the U.S. commission outfitted the interiors as period rooms with a mixture of reproduction Colonial Revival goods and genuine antiques; the result approximated Mount Vernon's interiors more closely than any previous world's fair replica.[37] Like Sears and Roebuck, the Grand Rapids furniture companies saw the building as a "first-class stimulant" to their businesses and provided the furniture at a low cost.[38] By 1931, Michigan was losing its hold on the market for Colonial Revival reproduction furniture to southern manufacturers, the Depression, and shifts in the ways in which Americans consumed furniture; the industry saw the

Fig. 33. Dining room in the United States Building at the Paris Colonial and Overseas Exposition, with the highly finished ceiling and mantel and furniture by Grand Rapids furniture companies.

exhibition pavilion as "one of the greatest opportunities ever offered to Grand Rapids."[39] The vast majority of articles were "near approximation[s] in both size and design" to pieces in Mount Vernon rather than line-by-line copies.[40] The dining table in the banquet hall, for example, was a reproduction of a table in the style of Duncan Phyfe. Although not a copy of a table at Mount Vernon or even one from the eighteenth century, it was based on a museum-quality object. A few key pieces were inspired by actual items in Mount Vernon: using photographs, Kindel Furniture Company created an "accurate replica" of the bed in which Washington died.[41]

With its reproduction architecture and furnishings, the United States Building was more of a Colonial *Revival* exhibit than a historical one; it was a testament to American style of the past as well as the present. The press claimed that because the majority of the goods were pieces already in production, the replica gave "credit to the taste of an American public."[42] Publications also widely praised the appropriateness of the building's modest elegance in the face of economic ruin.[43] At a fair held during an international economic crisis, this Mount Vernon was restrained rather than showy. In the press and the building's guest books, the "charm," "simplicity," and "good taste" of the exhibit especially wowed European visitors.[44] A French exposition organizer gushed over the "quiet, stately building of Mount Vernon": "In this moment of world depression, when all suffer, it stands symbolic of simple, austere living which cannot be compared with the overflowing life of too-prosperous times. We must all, in all countries, struggle to rise above the material life if we are to see our civilization survive."[45] *Good Housekeeping* reported that many Europeans had a similar "revelation" about American style once they visited the Mount Vernon exhibition building: "There has been a false conception of our standards of taste and living which has caused many foreigners to visualize us as indulging universally in the undistinguished, the pretentious, and the gaudy. Mount Vernon, Vincennes, has given an object lesson, the importance of which can hardly be overestimated, of the inaccuracy of this conception."[46] That almost everything in the Mount Vernon replica was for sale in some form—whether a Sears "Colonial" house or a Mount Vernon–inspired sideboard—also made the exhibit economically democratic. Unlike many previous replicas of Mount Vernon, these items were not priceless heirlooms available only to the economically or genealogically advantaged. The building emphasized the modesty and attainability of American style.

While the press praised the Mount Vernon replica and the values it represented, the Mount Vernon Ladies' Association worried over it. The board realized that the Paris version was different from the replicas it had previously approved and initially refused to endorse it: with its closely copied interior details, period rooms, and immediate landscape, the United States Building was far closer to the real thing than either the 1893 or 1915 Virginia Buildings.[47] The Association's board was also insulted by the fact that no one had asked its permission to reproduce Mount Vernon in Paris. By the time the MVLA considered the matter in late 1930, Bryant had already supplied the drawings to Sears and the U.S. commission was moving forward with its plan to copy Mount Vernon.[48] Responding to the MVLA's alarm upon hearing about the project, the commission's officers quickly tried to reassure the organization that they would "do nothing that would in any way mar the position that Mount Vernon has before the world" and "sacredly [avoid] any misuse of the building."[49] Faced with little choice, the Association agreed to sanction the exhibit, and Superintendent Harrison H. Dodge traveled to France to see it under construction.[50] He ultimately pronounced the building a success and a credit to the Association, although he found the details and setting lacking "that thrilling charm that pervades the *real* Mount Vernon."[51]

As a result of the United States Building's successes, the Association became more vigilant about full-scale replicas of Mount Vernon, while Sears and other commercial enterprises fully exploited the possibilities for such buildings. Within months of the Paris exposition's closing and the start of the George Washington bicentennial year, the MVLA, Sears, and Charles K. Bryant were each deluged with requests for measured drawings of the mansion by individuals and businesses wishing to copy it for all manner of purposes.[52] The battle of the reproduction was on, although it was one that the MVLA could and would not win. As then regent Alice Richards said in 1932: "I am very busy now trying to stem these reproductions, we have no legal rights . . . and can only try persuasion."[53] Whether for private houses or models made in elementary school classrooms, the MVLA and its staff flattened all requests for information on Mount Vernon if the inquirer so much as hinted that he or she planned to replicate the house.[54] Without referencing specific adaptations, the Association cited the "many unsatisfactory reproductions in the past" to justify its unwillingness to provide measurements and details.[55] The board could only control what people did with the information they obtained directly from the MVLA; the Association could do nothing about information already available. The MVLA's lawyer reminded the board that the building in its charge was "like the Parthenon, or old St. Peter's or Westminster Abbey or the Liberty Bell: the design, the method of construction, the dimensions, all are in the public domain" and although they could "deplore" the "indiscriminate erection of copies," they could not prevent it from happening entirely.[56]

With measured drawings in hand and the MVLA's blessing on the Paris building behind it, Sears and Roebuck went forward with a second replica in 1932— again without first asking the MVLA's permission.[57] The company, along with many of the same Grand Rapids furniture manufacturers that had been involved with the building in Paris, worked with the New York City municipal government to create another full-scale copy of the house in Prospect Park, Brooklyn, as part of the city's celebration of Washington's bicentennial. The building's proponents predicted that 15 million people could see the building and that such an experience would have both "spiritual and material benefits": such a patriotic display could rally despondent spirits, while the visitors it drew could boost the city and region's economy.[58] Alice Richards wrote to the Park Association of New York City, urging the organization to halt the replica of Mount Vernon until fully weighing "the question, whether such reproductions may not detract from the sacredness and dignity of the Home of Washington, the man whose memory is being specially honoured this year." Neither organization could stop the replica, and plans were already under way.[59] In the end, Sears built the Mount Vernon along with a full-scale reconstruction of the city's long-since-demolished Federal Hall in Manhattan's Bryant Park.[60] Together, the buildings opened to great fanfare in the spring of 1932 to "show two sides of Washington's life."[61]

The New York Bicentennial Commission initially hoped to dismantle the United States Building in Paris and move it to New York, but a private entity had already purchased and moved the building by the time the commission began planning the exhibit (it still survives as a private house outside of Paris today).[62]

Bryant and Sears ultimately agreed to build Mount Vernon in Brooklyn, and the city projected that a twenty-five-cent admission charge would cover the design and construction fees.[63] Located near Washington's position during the Battle of Brooklyn, the Mount Vernon replica looked out over Prospect Park Lake in a setting deemed to be appropriate for the riverfront building.[64] Bryant included the two attached dependencies in his New York version, along with matching parterre gardens on either side of the house; the gardens hinted at the symmetry and detail of those at Mount Vernon and included boxwood that supposedly derived from a specimen planted by Washington himself.[65]

While millions had visited and lauded Mount Vernon in Paris, the Brooklyn version was a flop. Despite the praise of Brooklyn "housewives" that the building provided "an example of good taste," the admission fee, the political wrangling of the New York Bicentennial Commission, and insufficient publicity prevented its success.[66] New York City never made a profit on either Federal Hall or Mount Vernon and ended up owing Sears and Roebuck for both buildings.[67] The Brooklyn Mount Vernon fell into disrepair and failed to open for a second year.

Sears and Roebuck, however, used the publicity around the Paris and Brooklyn replicas to usher in a new product: the company's first Mount Vernon–inspired house plan appeared in the 1932 *Modern Homes* catalogue. Sears called the house "The Jefferson," probably because Mount Vernon's moniker was already ascribed to an existing plan and Thomas Jefferson was another Virginia-born Founding Father enjoying a resurgence of popularity.[68] Perhaps Sears consciously avoided a direct comparison to Mount Vernon because of the MVLA's wariness over the two exhibition replicas. Regardless of its name, the two-story, white-brick house with a central hall, trademark piazza, and chinoiserie balustrade was undoubtedly modeled after Mount Vernon.[69] A small sunroom attached to the side of the building approximated the massing of the porch on the south side, off of Washington's study. The catalogue testified to the staying power of Mount Vernon's characteristic features and echoed the southern identification of the country houses of the previous decades: "Designed along the same lines as historic Mt. Vernon, this southern colonial home spells success. Many types of colonial architecture have 'stood up' for years with American home builders. Among these types the southern colonial has held its share of popularity and today is classed

The JEFFERSON
No. 3349—Eight Rooms and Two Baths

DESIGNED along the same lines as historic Mt. Vernon, this southern colonial home spells success. Many types of colonial architecture have "stood up" for years with American home builders. Among these types the southern colonial has held its share of popularity and today is classed as one of the truest types. Exterior walls of whitewashed brick form a pleasing background for the dark green shutters and roof.

LIVING ROOM AND SUN ROOM, dining room and kitchen open off the center hall on the first floor. Note many convenient closets for outer wraps. Second floor plan contains hall, four large bedrooms and two baths. This roomy home boasts a total of ten closets.

Fill out Information Blank and we will send you complete delivered price, photographic architectural elevations and floor plans, also outline of specifications.

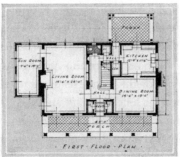

FIRST FLOOR PLAN

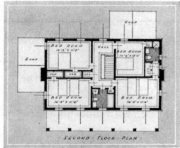

SECOND FLOOR PLAN

SEARS, ROEBUCK and CO.

Fig. 34. The "Jefferson" house design in the 1932 Sears, Roebuck and Company's *Homes of Today* catalogue.

as one of the truest types."[70] More elaborate than Sears's other Colonial Revival designs, the Jefferson offered a dramatic alternative to the company's cozy bungalows and modest two-story Colonials.

The appearance of a Mount Vernon adaptation in the Sears and Roebuck catalogue signified the form's final transition from one employed by Beaux-Arts–trained architects for wealthy clients to a version that was mass-produced and economically accessible to the middle class. Magazines like the *White Pine Series of Architectural Monographs* might have provided examples of ways to interpret Mount Vernon by the late 1910s, but architectural catalogues had a far greater reach a decade later. The importance of the building's appearance in the 1932, 1933, and 1937 Sears and Roebuck catalogues is incalculable. In a form meant to be easily digested and disseminated, the Jefferson was far more adaptable for the average American homebuilder or real estate developer than the palatial country houses by big-city architects artistically photographed in design magazines.

Following the publication of the 1932 Sears catalogue, versions of Mount Vernon began to appear in the repertoire of seemingly every builder that constructed houses for the middle class; they continue to be a staple in home designs today. The Aladdin Company, named after the Arabian Nights story in which a genie builds a palace overnight, first published a Mount Vernon–inspired model in 1941.[71] Founded as a mail-order retailer of precut houses in the early twentieth century, Aladdin was closing in on Sears in the number of houses sold by the early 1940s.[72] "The Kingston," a one-story, two-bedroom white cottage designed "for those who love a porch," featured a piazza with four square columns and a simplified chinoiserie balustrade across the front. Frame in construction and half the size of Sears's brick Jefferson, it was also simpler and more affordable. The catalogue's description did not mention Mount Vernon as the specific inspiration, but it described the porch as the building's distinguished feature and echoed the language and sentiment Sears evoked for the Jefferson: "Its square columns, embellished with short pillars and railing above are in architectural harmony and also give the whole picture individuality and distinction."[73] That same year, Aladdin also featured a small cottage with Colonial details on its cover called "The Mt. Vernon." Without any specific architectural references to Washington's house, it still evoked the "simplicity of form," and "cleanness of lines" that the public so

Figure 35. The "Colonial Cottage" house design in the Garlinghouse Company's 1940 *All-American Homes Catalog.*

admired in Mount Vernon.[74] Like Sears, Aladdin used Mount Vernon both in name and in image to entice home buyers.

Other mail-order companies sold only the plans of buildings that looked like Mount Vernon, offering yet another way Americans could have their very own version of Washington's home.[75] The Kansas-based Garlinghouse Company's 1940 *All-American Homes Catalog* featured a two-bedroom cottage much like Aladdin's "Kingston," with a balustraded piazza across the front. Pairs of small square columns supported the "spacious porch," and quoins suggested Mount Vernon's rusticated facade. Costing only $12.50, the plans for the house presented an affordable alternative to Sears and Aladdin's precut homes.[76] The Special Home Planning Department of the Gordon–Van Tine Company offered to turn a client's "photograph, picture, rough pencil sketch, or just a written description" into a full set of blueprints for free. The 1932 catalogue illustrated its description of this service with a photograph of a stately two-story frame home with a Mount Vernon–inspired piazza.[77]

In addition to such catalogues, design magazines continued to provide ways for average Americans to build their own version of Washington's mansion in the decade before World War II. Tremendously popular among middle-class Americans of both sexes, the *Ladies' Home Journal* promoted an entire Mount Vernon–inspired lifestyle with a special booklet and multiple articles in 1937.[78] The magazine had been a pioneer among those publishing reform-minded model-house designs since the late 1890s. Similar to companies like Garlinghouse in its publication of complete plans and renderings of ideal houses, the *Ladies' Home Journal* also accompanied its designs with contextual descriptions and decorating ideas.[79] The special-issue booklet *Mount Vernon Rooms* echoed decades of praise for Washington's house and wishes to connect its perceived values to the present day: "Because of its beauty, Mount Vernon has become much more than a shrine. For just as the man who made it still appears in our minds and hearts as something far more personal than a great historical figure, this first house of the land, in its architecture and decoration, has become in a very real sense an inspiration. We can follow its lead with full knowledge that there is nothing finer. . . . However, [the Mount Vernon house] is not a copy. It is an interpretation from the primitive perfection of the eighteenth century into the practical perfection of today. It is the Mount Vernon that we would like to live in now."[80]

Sure enough, the three-bedroom, two-bathroom house was not a true replica: like the Jefferson, it adapted and simplified the features of Mount Vernon for a contemporary audience. With a three-part Palladian plan, the central-hall house featured two wings attached to the building's main block: one served as a garage, while the other housed a kitchen and maid's room. The exterior gestured at the two "fronts" of Mount Vernon: one side had regularly distributed windows and a central pedimented door; the other predictably featured a piazza with six square columns. A small cupola topped the hipped roof of the main block of the house. The interiors and suggested furnishings borrowed freely from Mount Vernon and other Colonial Revival sources. An illustration of a banjo clock featuring Mount Vernon's image sat alongside that of a lantern adapted directly from the one hanging in the mansion's central passage. The wallpaper in the "Washington Bedroom" approximated that installed in the mansion in the early 1930s, and the booklet's text assured readers that the well-appointed kitchen would have had Martha Washington's approval. The magazine used words like "charm," "elegant,"

Fig. 36. Detail of the cover
of *Ladies' Home Journal*'s
Mount Vernon Rooms
booklet (Curtis, 1937).

"dignified," and "simple" to describe the various rooms and fixtures, all in the supposedly "perfect taste" of the eighteenth century.[81]

Although *Ladies' Home Journal* did not claim the house to be an exact replica of Mount Vernon, it did use the word "authentic" to describe various features and articles of furniture. Concerned that the description of the replica's features as "authentic" was misleading, Charles Cecil Wall, Dodge's replacement as Mount Vernon's superintendent, asked the magazine's architecture editor for clarification on the point. The editor responded with an apology indicating that he did not fully understand the MVLA's objection: "We wanted to imply that [the features] were 'authentic' in the sense that they were in the spirit of the time."[82] Such weakening of the term "authentic" greatly worried the MVLA, which used increasingly professional methods to interpret Mount Vernon. Yet to *Ladies' Home Journal,* the word provided its audience with the reassurance that the design ideas were based in the style of the eighteenth century.

A New Strategy: The MVLA and the Colonial Village at the 1934 Chicago Century of Progress International Exposition

Whether employed in full scale in Paris, in whiskey advertisements, or on the pages of the *Ladies' Home Journal,* Mount Vernon's architecture offered a highly marketable image over which the Mount Vernon Ladies' Association had little say. But the Association did not respond merely by protesting. It also reacted with more proactive strategies to what it saw as the gross commercialization of a precious shrine: the Association took advantage of some commercial ventures for its own publicity and simultaneously reinvigorated its efforts to preserve and research Mount Vernon. These approaches gave the MVLA an opportunity to control the building's interpretation more efficiently and to improve its own image in the process.

Still reeling from Sears and Roebuck's initially unsanctioned replicas in Paris and Brooklyn, the board was shocked to hear that another version of Washington's house was planned for the second year of the Century of Progress International Exposition in Chicago, Illinois, in 1934. An ⅝th-scale replica of Mount Vernon, the centerpiece of the 2.5-acre "Colonial Village" concession, was already under construction by the time the Association became aware of the project in April 1934. The architect-historian Thomas Eddy Tallmadge designed the structure to anchor an ensemble of reproduced Colonial buildings ranging from Ben Franklin's long-lost Philadelphia print shop to the newly reconstructed Governor's Mansion in Colonial Williamsburg. Descriptions of the attraction read like a movie set: "Builders of the American Colonial Village have captured the atmosphere of Revolutionary days—and make characters who lived then seem to return to walk in the shaded old streets. And, walking with them, the modern visitor quickly becomes part of the scene."[83] A local antiques dealer and members of the Daughters of the American Revolution (DAR) planned to operate the Mount Vernon replica in period costume, using the interior spaces for historical exhibits, salesrooms, and meeting spaces.[84] Unlike the Sears replicas that were legitimized by their official sanction of the U.S. and New York City governments, the Colonial Village's Mount Vernon was unabashedly part of a commercial concession. One of fourteen "foreign" villages, it deployed a clever mix of historical

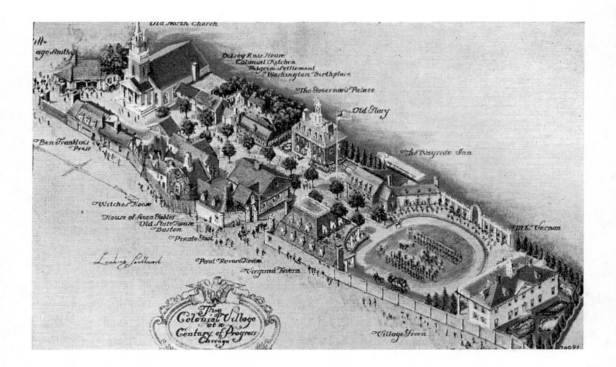

Fig. 37. Mount Vernon replica at the near end of the Colonial Village, Thomas Eddy Tallmadge (architect), Century of Progress International Exposition, Chicago, 1934. Postcard published by Gerson Brothers, Chicago, 1934.

references and playful fantasy to entice audiences to spend time and money in idealized realizations of other times and places.[85]

Calling the Colonial Village Mount Vernon "a more flagrant infringement of our rights than has hitherto occurred," the board's vice regents strongly objected among themselves to the for-profit nature of the replica.[86] The project lacked the legitimacy and prestige the U.S. government had bestowed upon the first Sears replica. With the project already under way, however, they chose to respond to it as an opportunity rather than to fruitlessly and publicly denounce it. The Illinois vice regent, Harriet Carpenter, wrote to Alice Richards: "I feel that this is the most valuable kind of publicity that we could obtain under any circumstances at any time and that their mistake will rebound to our good."[87] The board directly conferred with Tallmadge, the local chapter of the DAR, and the concession's operators to positively influence visitors' impressions of the replica and the MVLA, choosing to take a stand for the representation of Mount Vernon and the Association in what was otherwise a situation entirely out of its control.

The idea for a Mount Vernon replica in 1934 probably originated with Thomas Eddy Tallmadge, although Sears—most likely wary from the Brooklyn fiasco—was first offered and then declined the opportunity to reproduce Washington's house in the fair's 1933 season.[88] The Chicago-based architect was on the Advisory Committee of Architects for Colonial Williamsburg and the author of one of the earliest survey histories of American architecture.[89] Because of his demonstrated commitment to academic architectural history and restoration, the MVLA's board was frustrated that Tallmadge had chosen to replicate Mount Vernon so loosely and without its permission.[90] More interested in an approximation than an exact copy, he had made do with readily available books and magazine articles rather than asking the MVLA to undertake a new set of measured drawings.[91]

The Colonial Village's Mount Vernon was very different in purpose and treatment than the previous five replicas built at world's fairs: it was not intended to represent a specific group's civic identity or version of patriotism, nor did it attempt to replicate faithfully Washington's house inside or out. For Tallmadge, the Colonial Village was a playful means of educating a wide public on the country's early history and material culture. His Mount Vernon followed the more generalized approach of Sears and Roebuck's design for the Jefferson rather than the company's fair pavilions: it did not reproduce the mansion's outbuildings, connected dependencies, or detailed interiors, and the piazza facade functioned as the front of the building. He also added a series of steps leading up to the piazza and a small boxwood parterre garden behind the building, providing pleasant places to sit or stroll. Like the adaptations in contemporary architecture catalogues, the building was symmetrical; Tallmadge regularized the window arrangement and placed a cupola on the centerline of the building directly above the front door. Whereas earlier world's fair replicas had recognized the asymmetrical window pattern as one of the distinctive features of the house, Tallmadge's strove to be a more perfect example of Georgian architecture.[92] In the end, Tallmadge and the vice regents warmed up to one another by the time construction wrapped.[93]

With little possibility of influencing Tallmadge's take on Mount Vernon already under construction, the Association moved to ensure that the exhibit

Fig. 38. The "minute girls" performing in front of the Mount Vernon replica at the Century of Progress International Exposition, Chicago, 1934 (Kaufman & Fabry, photographers).

presented accurate information about the house's history and its stewardship. After a newspaper article claimed the DAR as the caretakers of Washington's home, the Association was especially keen to stake its claim to Mount Vernon's preservation at the version in Chicago.[94] The board insisted that Tallmadge erect a sign that identified the organization and that specified the building as a reproduction, just in case someone mistook it for the real thing. The final sign read: "A reproduction of Mount Vernon, Virginia / The home of / General Washington / Which is Owned and Maintained by the / Mount Vernon Ladies' Association of the Union / Founded 1853 / The Object of this association is to preserve unchanged, as far as possible, the home and tomb of Washington."[95] The Association also took advantage of the commercial nature of the exhibit to generate income and to ensure that accurate information was available for sale in the replica's gift shop. The items it offered included those already for sale at Mount

Vernon (postcards, guidebooks, and a history of the organization by Thomas Nelson Page) as well as a set of watercolors of the mansion commissioned especially for the fair. The amount generated in sales was ultimately "negligible," but the MVLA's involvement in the concession allowed it to keep a close eye day to day on the exhibit's depiction of Mount Vernon.[96] More importantly, it generated significant publicity for the organization. More than 1.4 million visitors came to the Colonial Village, with two hundred thousand paying the admission fee to see the DAR's exhibits inside the Mount Vernon replica. 158 newspaper articles about the Colonial Village mentioned the exhibit over the course of the fair.[97] Perhaps after learning from the replicas in Paris and Brooklyn that it could not stop outsiders from replicating Mount Vernon, the MVLA went on the offensive with the pavilion at the Century of Progress. By becoming involved with the exhibit, the organization benefited from its publicity and clarified its mission to a wide audience it might not otherwise have reached.

Research and Preservation at Mount Vernon in the 1930s

Just as Tallmadge's liberal adaptation of Mount Vernon in Chicago drove the vice regents' active involvement in a form they had so recently shunned, so did the "indiscriminate erection of copies" help to move the board to launch its most aggressive preservation and publicity campaigns since the organization's early decades.[98] Regarding such replicas as caricatures, the MVLA sought to improve the historical accuracy of its own interpretation of Mount Vernon as well as the information circulated beyond the site. Just as it had for decades, the Association's board sought the latest techniques and outside expertise to inform its decision making. Its choices were often closely aligned with those at the recently opened and much-celebrated Colonial Williamsburg, and the two organizations developed a collegial relationship over the 1930s. What inspired the board's changes at Mount Vernon was not a sense of competition with Williamsburg or any other historic destination, however. The vice regents were instead concerned that the organization was losing control of Mount Vernon's image and that the public was becoming more familiar with willy-nilly copies than with the original in Virginia.[99]

Following the trend at other historic sites and the expansion of the fields of American art and architectural history, the MVLA began to hire preservation "professionals" and to focus its attention more closely on the aesthetics of Mount Vernon's architecture and decorative arts. Since the late 1890s, historic preservation had become an increasingly specialized and male-dominated field.[100] Although women organized along the lines of the MVLA had tried to purchase and restore Thomas Jefferson's Monticello, for example, a group of male lawyers and businessmen ultimately formed the Thomas Jefferson Memorial Foundation and transformed the building into a house museum in the mid-1920s. The academic architect and historian Fiske Kimball restored the house, and the foundation's board granted him tremendous authority over the restoration, furnishing, and interpretation of the building.[101] The architecture firm Perry, Shaw and Hepburn, along with an advisory committee of professional architects that included Kimball and Thomas Eddy Tallmadge, directed the restoration and reconstruction of Colonial Williamsburg in the same period. Colonial Williamsburg's staff of design professionals and historians was almost exclusively male. The Great Depression and resulting government-funded programs like the Historic American Buildings Survey (HABS) quickened the professionalization of preservation; with new construction slowing, many architects sought employment documenting or restoring buildings rather than designing new ones.

In its campaign to make its presentation of Mount Vernon more accurate, the MVLA professionalized in much the same way as Colonial Williamsburg and Monticello: for the first time in 1936, the board hired a full-time employee in charge of preservation. Its choice was Morley Jeffers Williams, a landscape architect on the faculty at Harvard.[102] Besides a graduate degree in landscape architecture from Harvard's Graduate School of Design, Williams's pedigree included training in archaeology by Arthur Shurcliff, the head landscape architect at Colonial Williamsburg.[103] Along with Tallmadge, Kimball, and others, Williams was a key player in the transition of preservation from a field driven by patriotic females to one dominated by academically trained male architects and historians. At Mount Vernon, Williams remained beholden to the Association's board; its members regarded his opinion with the utmost respect and often deferred to his expertise but never fully relinquished their vision for Washington's home to him or any other employee. Unlike Monticello or Colonial Williamsburg, the all-female board remained the primary decision maker at Mount Vernon.

The death of Superintendent Harrison H. Dodge in 1937 eased the transition to a more professional Mount Vernon.[104] Having worked for the Association since 1885, Dodge was in many ways typical of the early preservation movement: he was an amateur historian who learned by doing rather than academic training. His departure offered an opportunity for new staff to execute emerging research and preservation techniques with authority, led by Morley Jeffers Williams. Williams first came to Mount Vernon in 1931 to study the landscape as part of a Harvard grant program. The project also took him to Monticello and Stratford Hall, where his excavations led to a commission to design a garden based on his findings.[105] Williams published his conclusions on Mount Vernon in *Landscape Architecture* a year after his first visit. He began the article with a statement of the plantation's significance that managed to balance the MVLA's priority of presenting a vision of Washington's impeccable taste with those of academic historians: "Mount Vernon is the most important of American estates, both because it was the home of the greatest American and also because it is a highly developed example of landscape design."[106] His relationship with Mount Vernon continued informally until the MVLA hired him full-time as the director of research in 1936, just months before Dodge's death.[107] Bringing along fellow landscape architect Alden Hopkins, Williams established a new Office of Research and Restoration for Mount Vernon.[108]

Not everyone on Mount Vernon's staff respected and deferred to Williams's expertise. The new superintendent, Charles Cecil Wall, was threatened by Williams's degrees and previous experience and challenged his authority in making major decisions.[109] First hired as assistant superintendent in the early 1930s before replacing Dodge, Wall did not have formal training in design or history. He was a businessman who, like Dodge, developed expertise through experience working at Mount Vernon.[110] The scramble for power between Wall and Williams in the second half of the 1930s revealed the persistence of the amateur perspective in daily decision making at Mount Vernon.

Applying the methodologies of archaeology, documentation, and documentary analysis far more methodically than Dodge ever had, Williams made a number of significant changes and discoveries at Mount Vernon between his initial survey in 1931 and his eventual ousting by Wall in 1939.[111] Williams and his staff set out to make (but never finished) a series of measured drawings of the house based on the new standards of the Historic American Buildings Survey.[112] They compared Mount Vernon with its contemporaries to determine where Washington might have gleaned his design ideas.[113] Williams identified Batty Langley's popular English pattern book as the source for the New Room's Venetian window and aspects of the landscape, for example.[114] Their archaeological investigations revealed the different periods of Washington's landscape, evidence of long-demolished outbuildings, and the location of ha-ha walls and other significant features. Williams's work also confirmed the accuracy and importance of the drawing Samuel Vaughan made of the property in 1787.[115]

In the first two months of 1938, Williams's small staff produced the MVLA's first publicity campaign based on scholarly content. The board wanted to reassert Mount Vernon's dignity and historical significance against what it saw as the building's brash commercialization, as well as to satisfy the public's voracious desire for information on the house's architecture and history. In a "triple burst" of articles published in venues that bridged the academic with the "popular and general," Williams laid out the conclusions made from his staff's recent research.[116] By revealing the processes of Washington's design decisions, Williams refined discussions of the general's relationship with the place and provided direct evidence of his talent as a landscape designer and architect.[117] The articles also provided a cache of vetted information on Mount Vernon for other venues to republish for years to come.

Benson Lossing, Paul Wilstach, and others had previously attempted to lay out the evolution of the mansion, but a 1938 article in the *New York Times* orchestrated by Williams illustrated and more accurately described the progression of the building and its immediate landscape.[118] A series of Williams's drawings demonstrated the additions of features and rooms, while the article emphasized that "new evidence" was "backed by [Washington's] diaries, letters and accounts." He corrected Dodge's earlier assumption (perpetuated by Wilstach) that Washington merely rehabilitated the interior of the building in the late 1750s with a drawing that clearly indicated that he had added another story shortly before marrying

Martha Custis.[119] The article made special mention of the building's most iconic feature, connecting its initial creation to present adaptations: "Not precisely dated is the piazza or portico—so much copied that it has created an enduring fashion and thus, by some, is counted an original contribution of Washington to American architecture."[120] Published in such a widely read newspaper, the article attempted to guarantee the authority of the MVLA and its staff.

Williams laid out his findings on the development of Mount Vernon's landscape in the more academic publication *Landscape Architecture* within two weeks of the *New York Times* article.[121] Using photographs, an illustration of the drawing by Samuel Vaughan, and Williams's own renderings, the article presented the most thorough account of the development of the mansion's immediate setting that had ever been published. Williams contextualized Washington's alterations to the mansion's architecture with his reorganization of views and design of landscape elements such as the picturesque bowling green, service lanes, and outbuildings. He identified Washington's design sources and deftly described the motivations for Washington's deviations from them. He ended the article with a statement on the relationship between the MVLA's new research agenda and ongoing preservation at Mount Vernon: "With the passing of time has come new responsibility and with it a desire for knowledge. What were conditions as Washington left them? Contemporary diaries, sketches, and letters, to-day's obvious commonplace facts—all now need interpretation. That they are receiving careful study and attention by the Association's new Department of Research and Restoration is a tribute to the way in which the Ladies are meeting their responsibility."[122] Whether or not this closing comment was meant as an affront to Superintendent Wall, it was certainly a defense of Williams's own research agenda and a reassertion of the MVLA's primacy in historic preservation.

While the articles in the *New York Times* and *Landscape Architecture* reached a wide general audience and professional landscape architects, respectively, a third article published in *American Architect and Architecture* reached yet another audience: architects and architectural enthusiasts.[123] With only brief text to describe the basic development of the mansion and the "meticulously accurate" process by which Williams and his staff had surveyed the building, the majority of the

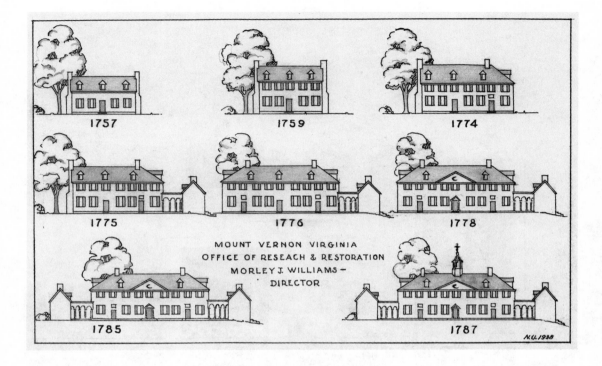

1757

1759

1774

1775

1776

1778

MOUNT VERNON VIRGINIA
OFFICE OF RESEACH & RESTORATION
MORLEY J. WILLIAMS —
DIRECTOR

1785

1787

N.U. 1938

fourteen-page article consisted of measured drawings and photographs. The Association used photographs by Frances Benjamin Johnston commissioned the year before as part of its efforts to document the mansion more accurately.[124] The leading architectural photographer of the period, Johnston used the medium to record Colonial buildings with an almost scientific precision; her work helped to ensure that "straight" photography would be considered alongside measured drawings as a means of preservation by documentation.[125] Like in her other projects, Johnston removed furniture and decorative arts in order to focus her images on the architectural details and proportions of Mount Vernon's interiors. The very fact that the Association allowed its carefully curated objects to be relocated and left out of published photographs indicates its eagerness to adhere to the new standards for preservation.

Fig. 39. Illustration of the evolution of Mount Vernon, 1938.

Although Williams understood why the Association wanted to publish his findings immediately, he worried that the organization was "becoming sadly publicity conscious."[126] He wished to focus on applying his findings to new interpretations of the site rather than writing or overseeing publications. He reminded the vice regents that their greatest publicity and educational tool was the restored mansion and landscape.

Prompted by Williams and Superintendent Wall, the MVLA did make its most aggressive physical alterations to the mansion to date in the 1930s. Williams, the board, and Wall continued to carefully orchestrate articles in major newspapers and magazines, creating opportunities for the public to see the "new" Mount Vernon and to learn about how the board made preservation and interpretation decisions.[127] The MVLA's research and publicity fought the replicas of Mount Vernon hand in hand.

The Association made a significant departure from its 1870s decision to reconstruct the small porch on the south side when it removed the feature in 1931.[128] Following its demolition, Dodge directed his staff to match the porch's former door opening to the windows on the second floor and the newly constructed cellar entrance to that on the north side.[129] Even more dramatic (and even traumatic) was the removal of the chinoiserie balustrade atop the iconic piazza in 1936. With the railing missing from all of the early depictions of the mansion, it had long been evident that the railing was not on the house during Washington's time.[130] Morley Jeffers Williams further argued that Washington would never have designed "a piece of applied decoration" with so little logical connection to the building.[131] The decision to remove the balustrade was a difficult one: the Mansion Committee reported on the momentous event: "Many of us have great feeling for this railing, but we must not let sentiment alone govern us in so serious a matter."[132] While the vice regents ultimately were unanimous in their recognition that the feature was added after Washington's death, Dodge protested the removal of the balustrade and regarded the decision as a mistake.[133] The board might have been willing to put its "sentiment" aside for authenticity, but Dodge would not accept the conclusions of Williams or other professionals. He believed the feature too essential to Mount Vernon's architectural history to throw away.

Thanks to new discoveries and the departure of many items to the new museum, the MVLA also made significant changes to the interior of the mansion to attempt greater accuracy in this period. The board returned to the inventory, using it to purge the house of anachronistic items.[134] As with the decisions to change the railing and to remove the south porch, the vice regents did not hesitate to make measurable changes when clear evidence was available. They sought out expertise in areas not represented by their staff in the newly established American departments at the Metropolitan Museum of Art and Philadelphia Art Museum, Colonial Williamsburg, and from the Harvard architecture professor Charles W. Killam.[135] Heeding the inventory, the Association finally began to interpret the first-floor space long known as the "Martha Washington Sitting Room" as a bedchamber. Closer reading of Washington's documents also revealed that the second-floor room in which Lafayette slept was not that on the west side of the house (as first decorated by Nancy Halsted) but that on the east, and the interpretation changed to bespeak the discovery.[136]

Before his death, Dodge had directed the reproduction and installation of a pattern in Washington's bedchamber after discovering a fragment of wallpaper there in 1929.[137] The new paper featured prominently in bicentennial coverage of Mount Vernon and in Sears's replicas in Paris and Brooklyn, prompting many requests to replicate it (which the MVLA flatly refused).[138] The public's desire to copy the famous bedroom's wallpaper became especially problematic after Wall and Williams figured out that what Dodge had discovered did not, in fact, date to Washington's time. Williams claimed that "knowledge was lacking and proper research not done," suggesting his disdain not only for Dodge's conclusions but also for his methods.[139] The wallpaper was finally removed in 1949–50 and the room whitewashed following additional research.[140]

The quest for authenticity and the availability of Williams's expertise also led the Association to think more carefully about its interpretation of outbuildings. The board had long realized the importance of the structures along the north and south lanes to Washington's farming enterprise, but Williams's research helped it to consider the buildings as a more conscious part of the general's design for the plantation. Archaeology identified the foundations of early outbuildings and of the blacksmith shop, dung repository, and carpenter shop appearing on the 1787 drawing by Samuel Vaughan; Williams's work also confirmed that the north lane's icehouse (built partly on the foundation of the blacksmith shop) dated to a period after Washington's lifetime.[141] The summerhouse, an 1880s reconstruction based on Benson Lossing's drawings, was finally removed.[142] Williams also drew plans for a reconstruction of the eighteenth-century buildings no longer extant in the upper garden, including the general's large greenhouse and attached slave-quarter wings, based on existing documentary evidence.[143] He never completed the project and left Mount Vernon shortly thereafter in 1939.

Armed with new information and confidence in the importance of the outbuildings, the vice regents persisted in their interest in the structures after Williams's abrupt departure. In 1941, the board hired Walter Mayo Macomber, the "highly experienced" architect representing Colonial Williamsburg's principal design firm, Perry, Shaw and Hepburn in Virginia, to pick up on Williams's plans for an accurate reconstruction of the buildings in the upper garden.[144] All major restorations were put on hold during the war, however, and the board and Macomber returned to Williams's research and suggestions after its conclusion.[145]

Alongside the MVLA's new emphasis on research and its active application in preservation, the house continued to display the vice regents' personal tastes. Both when definitive information was known and when research had not yet revealed conclusive results, the Association approximated or decorated the mansion and landscape in keeping with the aesthetic preferences of the Colonial Revival. The New Room, long the depository of relics that did not fit elsewhere in the house, received a dramatic makeover. The replacement of the anachronistic brass railing around the precious mantel with a moveable and less visually intrusive barrier and the refurnishing of the space with pieces newly acquired from Martha Washington's descendants gave it a more domestic feel and aesthetic focus.[146] The Association did not closely adhere to the inventory in its choices of furniture or pictures as it did in other rooms; it did not even consider including the twenty-seven chairs listed in the inventory, for example.[147] The board's choice of "light green" for the wall color followed evidence of a scrap of wallpaper found earlier in the twentieth century as much as it did the vice regents' aesthetic preferences.[148] Although the decision was surely made in part based on family lore, the shade was also chosen because it matched the impressive, recently acquired carpet supposedly presented to President Washington by Louis XVI.[149] Just as it had been since the nineteenth century, the Association's adherence to authenticity remained somewhat selective in the 1930s.

Beyond the mansion, even Morley Williams fell victim to the Colonial Revival's influence. Following brief excavations in the lower garden and an examination of Washington's farm journal and landscape design influences, he designed a new plan for the walled space. The "kitchen garden" opened to the public in 1937, much in the vein of the gardens designed by Williams's mentor at Williamsburg and the one he had recently completed for the Garden Club of Virginia at Stratford Hall.[150]

At the same time that the Association was "bewildered by the mass of research material that should be studied" in its interpretation of Mount Vernon, others outside the organization were more comfortable than ever to exploit the house's image for commercial gain.[151] As the MVLA committed anew to close accuracy at Mount Vernon, those replicating the building borrowed the house's iconic features even more freely. No matter what the motivation, the vast majority chose Mount Vernon for the same reasons that the MVLA so vehemently fought to protect it: it represented something aesthetic, revered, and intimately related to America's greatest hero. What drove the MVLA's careful restoration and advertisers' replication was not as different as its board's members believed.

5 ★ "In This Changing and Troubled World"

SOCIAL HISTORY AND THE AMERICAN ROADSIDE, 1950S–1980S

I
N 1952, ONE YEAR BEFORE the Mount Vernon Ladies' Association celebrated its centennial, Mount Vernon passed a tremendous milestone: more than 1 million tourists visited the mansion in a single year.[1] The *Saturday Evening Post* featured Mount Vernon in its "Face of America" campaign, calling it a "noble shrine to one of the noblest Americans."[2] Thirty years later, numbers of paying tourists at Mount Vernon were plunging and the MVLA was under intense fire for its interpretation of the site. In a scathing article in the *Washington Post,* the reporter Dorothy Gilliam lambasted the MVLA's presentation of slavery at the historic plantation: "This absence of proper recognition is an atrocity that adds insult to the already deep moral injury of slavery."[3] Some were no longer interested solely in narratives of George Washington and Mount Vernon's greatness.

Between the years following World War II and the early 1980s, America—and Mount Vernon—underwent tremendous change. Decades of social upheaval, war, and racial strife diverted the traditional narratives of American history away from the singular achievements of rich, white men like Washington. Whereas the great hero's home was a popular destination and symbol in a postwar period emphasizing America's supposed greatness, its image became much more contested in just a few short decades. The MVLA tried to perpetuate its positive narrative of George Washington's achievements and life at Mount Vernon while anticipating the public's changing expectations. But by the 1980s, community leaders and the press accused the all-white board of coming up short in its efforts to present the history of Mount Vernon's enslaved community.

As the presentation of the past became increasingly controversial at Mount Vernon, replicas of Washington's iconic piazza were more popular than ever. America's commercial roadsides expanded at midcentury, giving forth to two new building types that boosted the visage of Washington's house: the motel and the purpose-built funeral home. Generally evoking Mount Vernon's legendary hospitality and peaceful domesticity, these versions of Mount Vernon were far more superficial than previous replicas. At least on the surface, they were free from the complicated realities of contemporary race relations and the culture wars to come. Whereas elite Virginians, the YWCA, Gilded Age millionaires, and even Sears and Roebuck had replicated Mount Vernon for very specific political or ideological reasons, Americans increasingly copied Mount Vernon to make a nostalgic gesture to a vaguely imagined and idealized past. In order to sell products and services, history was watered down, hollowed out, and ultimately divorced from the same issues that made telling Mount Vernon's story increasingly difficult for the MVLA. As preservation grew more professional and history more inclusive, the gulf between historic site interpretation and popular architecture was wider than ever.

The Interpretation of Slavery at Mount Vernon, 1950s–1960s

Through experimental technology and ambitious new interpretation programs, the Mount Vernon Ladies' Association and its staff endeavored to enhance the experiences of visitors to Mount Vernon after the war. An ever-improving highway system, more leisure time, higher levels of education, and economic stability meant that not only were more Americans traveling by the 1950s but also that their expectations for amenities and entertainment were growing steeper.[4] The Association had to compete with other heritage destinations as well as with commercial attractions like Disneyland (opened in 1955) for visitors' attention.

The Association's primary strategy for attracting audiences and differentiating the site from other destinations remained what had drawn visitors for almost a century: the in situ re-creation of the settings in which Washington and his family had lived. The Association hoped Washington would continue to come alive through the ever-improving accuracy of the site's buildings, landscapes, and interiors. In a 1954 interview, Charles Cecil Wall stated that his goal as superintendent was to help visitors imagine Washington "in a personal and intimate sense" that went beyond the "remote, cold, formidable general and President, someone whose picture was hung on a schoolroom wall."[5]

The Association's most ambitious project of the 1950s was the reconstruction of the greenhouse and its attached slave-quarter wings in the plantation's upper garden. Initiated with a vision in line with the organization's preservation efforts over the previous sixty years, the reconstruction ended up humanizing Washington in ways completely unanticipated by the MVLA's board members. Unlike all of the spaces that the Association had previously interpreted, the primary purpose of the complex's wings was housing enslaved laborers. Not until they worked out the particulars of the project did the vice regents realize the difficulty of reconciling their heroic vision of Washington with the flawed slaveholder of reality.

As at most contemporary historic sites, slavery was barely mentioned in the interpretation at Mount Vernon over the first half of the twentieth century.[6] The

Fig. 41. Greenhouse and adjacent slave-quarter wings in the upper garden at Mount Vernon, Walter Mayo Macomber (architect), 1950s.

only formal acknowledgment of the lives of the enslaved was a memorial stone placed at the plantation's slave cemetery in 1929. The stone's inscription echoed the image of the faithful slave enduring from the Lost Cause: "In memory of the many faithful colored servants of the Washington family, buried at Mount Vernon from 1760 to 1860. Their unidentified graves surround this spot."[7] In contrast to this romanticized remembrance, the introduction of the slave-quarter wings explicitly and irrevocably introduced slavery's physical and material hardships to the MVLA's narrative at Mount Vernon. After a decade of heated discussion and concern within the Association, Mount Vernon became one of the earliest historic house museums to interpret the material realities of the lives of the enslaved in 1962. For the first time, the national shrine was revealed as a conflicted place of elegant entertaining and human bondage.

The greenhouse and slave-quarter wings were some of the last documented Washington-era structures no longer standing in the historic area that the Association had not already reconstructed. Built by Washington over 1784–92 and clearly visible in the period depictions by Samuel Vaughan and Edward Savage, it burned in 1835. The Association later erected a commercial greenhouse for propagating plants on the site; it subsequently added sleeping quarters for vice regents to either side. Although these modern buildings were built roughly on the footprint of the original structure, there was no attempt to reconstruct the building as it looked during the Washington era.[8]

The necessity of repairs on the nineteenth-century greenhouse prompted the Association to decide finally to reconstruct the eighteenth-century building in 1941.[9] After conducting rudimentary archaeological investigations and examining Washington's letters and drawings, the architect Walter Mayo Macomber determined the dimensions and details of the building. In his initial plans, he imagined that the interiors of the slave-quarter wings on either side of the greenhouse would remain "serviceable" as rooms for the vice regents to occupy while visiting for the board's annual meetings.[10] Later that year, however, he revised his plans: "The Green House and Quarters should be restored as closely to its original appearance as possible, inside and out."[11] It is unclear what shifted Macomber's perspective, but it was most likely his professional interest in fully interpreting a historical reconstruction—a point of view surely honed while working at Colonial

Williamsburg. The board agreed, set forth to furnish the "slave quarters," and began to make accommodations for its displaced sleeping quarters elsewhere on the estate.[12] The war intervened, however, and the MVLA put Macomber's plans on hold.

Talk of the reconstruction picked up after the war, along with a greater attention to the estate's outbuildings as a whole. A new Committee on Furnishings for Outbuildings and curatorial assistant focused almost exclusively on these structures. The vice regents put a premium on the long-uninterpreted buildings as "important elements of the Mount Vernon picture" and viewed them as a means to better serve their audience with a more accurate picture of Washington's surroundings.[13] Using the inventory, account books, and other comparable examples as guides, the curatorial assistant Frank Morse set about finding everything from period clothing to casually drape on pegs to fake hams to hang in the smokehouse.[14] Morse had previously worked as a history teacher and came to Mount Vernon as a guard and handyman after the war.[15] Collaborating with members of the Committee on Furnishings for Outbuildings, Morse and the Association's staff "restored and re-equipped" the plantation's ten original outbuildings "as stage settings, as if persons had either walked off or were about to walk on." The final building in the roster was the salt house (the former carpenter's shop/relic house), restored and furnished in 1966.[16] The construction of a motel-like dormitory in 1950 to accommodate the majority of the vice regents during their annual visits facilitated the effort and opened almost the entire historic core of the plantation to interpretation for the first time.[17]

The board officially put Macomber on retainer as Mount Vernon's consultant "Architect for Restoration" in 1946 and set him to work resurrecting his prewar scheme for the greenhouse and its wings.[18] With the help of a newly discovered insurance drawing made in 1803, Macomber's revised plans included furnished simulations of the eighteenth-century greenhouse, living quarters for enslaved laborers (two rooms in either wing, divided by gender), and a shoemaker's shop. The rest of the reconstruction accommodated a sitting room for sick tourists and a garden salesroom.[19] Construction began in the summer of 1950 using thirty thousand bricks from the recently gutted White House.[20] After researching Washington's work orders and letters, Macomber determined that the slaves'

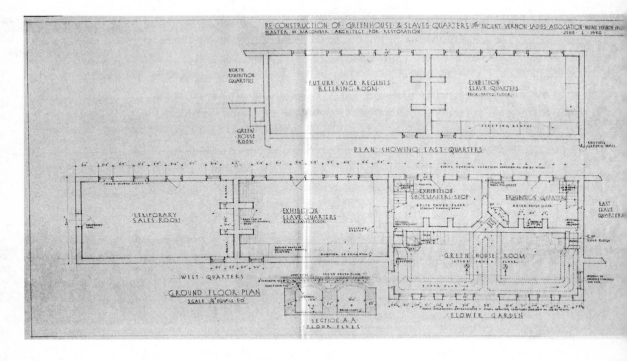

Fig. 42. Walter Mayo Macomber, *Re-construction of Greenhouse & Slave Quarters for Mount Vernon Ladies [sic] Association, Mount Vernon, Virginia,* June 1, 1950.

dwelling spaces' original interior configuration consisted of a series of two-tiered bunks laid on wooden sills along the interior walls. After installing the bunks, the board's Committee on Furnishings for Outbuildings began to bring the spaces to life with furnishings and textiles.[21]

When the entire board finally viewed the nearly finished slave-quarter interiors during its annual meeting in 1952, some vice regents were "very much upset" by what they saw. Sara Butler (vice regent, Louisiana) wrote Macomber that the "prison arrangement" of the bunks gave the undesired appearance that "the General was not careful of the morals of his slaves." Without any formal training in history or historical archaeology, Butler argued that she had "never seen nor heard of any arrangements for slaves."[22] Always wishing to see Washington in a heroic light, Butler and her fellow board members recoiled at the arrangement of the bunks; the slave-quarter wings' crowded interiors confounded their desire to see Washington as a benevolent patriarch who treated his human chattel as extended family.[23] When the MVLA opened and widely publicized the green-house in 1952—the year of Mount Vernon's highest attendance to date—the doors to the slave quarters remained closed.[24] The board wanted to be sure that its first interpretation of a slave space was as accurate as possible, but it was unable to reconcile Macomber's findings with its rose-colored view of Washington.

With African American history and vernacular architecture far outside the agendas of most preservation professionals of the period, the vice regents and their staff were ill-equipped to balance their idealistic expectations for what Washington might have built for his slaves with the realities of eighteenth-century plantation life. Likely the only other interpreted slave quarters that board members had seen was a cabin reconstructed and furnished at Stratford Hall in 1939.[25] That interpretation easily conformed to the idea that enslaved families lived relatively independently and comfortably in single-family dwellings; it was quite unlike the communal arrangement of the slave-quarter wings Macomber projected at Mount Vernon. The vice regents were hesitant to suggest that Washington would have planned something so far from the typical (and supposedly benevolent) means of housing slaves.[26]

The board also understood that, as the country's first and most visited house museum, Mount Vernon had a special responsibility to present the slave-quarter wings as accurately as possible. Frank Morse wrote to the board: "From the standpoint of historical responsibility, Mount Vernon will be considered gospel to most tourists. This would appear to make absolute accuracy important as to the Quarters."[27] The MVLA directed Morse to work up a bibliography of slave life and to prepare a report that could verify or refute Macomber's arrangement.[28] Morse's initial reports confirmed the board members' concern that there was "insufficient evidence" for Macomber's reconstruction of the wings' interiors, agreeing that the bunks seemed "to indicate a rather callous disregard for the blacks." He noted that the combination of the bunks and the vice regents' tasteful choice in textiles and other details resulted in "a forced marriage between a chain gang barracks and the phoney Uncle Tom's cabin propaganda of the mid-nineteenth century."[29] In order that space within the historic area not go to waste during this period of indecision, Superintendent Wall outfitted one of the wings as an auxiliary exhibition space for the adjacent museum and used the other for storage.[30]

As the slave-quarter wings' interiors remained uninterpreted, discussions continued between the board and its staff on Washington's usage of the word "berths" to describe the structures on which slaves slept. Although he could have meant it to indicate bunks, as Macomber had assumed, Morse and others presented the possibility that Washington might have meant it to refer to "small compartments," such as those on ships.[31] Hesitant to abandon positive visions of the Old South, Morse deemed the latter more likely as it seemed more compatible "with both Washington's regard for the family life of the negroes and the general southern way of caring for negroes."[32] Morse, Wall, and the vice regents continued to consult historians across the country about the conditions of slave quarters at southern plantations. They dismissed opinions that concurred with Macomber's initial design, justifying their continued line of questioning by the fact that no one could offer another example of a bunk-like arrangement in the eighteenth century.[33]

In 1961, Morse discovered a nineteenth-century history of the American Revolution that supported "the hypothesis that George Washington would have been familiar with two-tiered bunk construction" during the war. Further research confirmed that Washington used the words "bunk" and "berth" interchangeably in his descriptions of sleeping arrangements in military camps, providing what the board finally determined to be conclusive evidence that he used "berth" to mean bunk.[34] This discovery pushed the Association to complete furnishing the west quarter wing and to open it to the public. The regent Francis Beirne told her board: "For two years I have urged Council to take some action in opening the West Negro Quarters, and while I understand the complexity of the situation, I do feel that the time has come when something must be done."[35] The bunks were slightly widened to suggest double occupancy before the opening of the exhibit in 1962, but otherwise looked just as Macomber had designed them almost fifteen years previously.[36]

Spinning the unusual space to reflect positively on Washington, the Association explained the bunks as evidence of his ingenuity and commitment to efficiency: "The setting here restored may well have been unique in General Washington's time, his own original conception; he was not averse to progressive innovation in any of his various fields of activity."[37] The MVLA featured the finished space in its illustrated annual report in 1962 and opened it amid the

Fig. 43. The interior of the slave-quarter wing at Mount Vernon, 1962.

"pomp and circumstance" of its annual celebration of Washington's birthday; board members were relieved that it "produced no adverse comments."[38] The press failed to cover Mount Vernon's newest interpreted interiors so long after the opening of the rest of the greenhouse. After a decade of consternation, the greenhouse's quarters slid quietly into the MVLA's increasingly comprehensive restoration of Washington's eighteenth-century world at Mount Vernon. As the nation transitioned into the Cold War and the civil rights movement escalated, the MVLA's Washington largely remained a symbol of ingenuity, morality, and strength at Mount Vernon.

Whether in the mansion or in the reconstructed slave-quarter wings, the MVLA depended on the same limited means of interpretation they had for decades; midcentury visitors learned about the restored landscape and buildings using the continually revamped guidebook and by asking questions of guards stationed around the estate. Like most house museums of the period, the MVLA mostly counted on the visual and physical experience of the restored architecture

and simulated interiors to speak for themselves. In the early 1950s, Superintendent Wall began to raise the alarm to the board that although unprecedented
numbers of tourists were coming to Mount Vernon, few were leaving with ade-
quate knowledge of Washington or early American history.[39] To better engage its
audience, the MVLA began to experiment with a handful of new techniques and
to consider visitors' experiences more directly. These new methods were more
actively didactic than the restorations under way in the outbuildings: unlike the
mute bunks in the reconstructed slave-quarter wings, they delivered explicit messages in both words and images. Slavery gained a steady foothold in these new interpretation strategies, although its inclusion never disrupted a positive memory
of Washington.

Over the summer of 1965, the MVLA experimented with a method that di-
verged dramatically from its typically preservation-driven approach to interpretation: a forty-eight-minute, pretaped tour via a Solocast personal record player.
While the interpretation of the slave-quarter wings had begun as a by-product of
a larger architectural reconstruction project, the Solocast tour was a conscious
attempt to better control the message visitors took away from their Mount Vernon experience.[40] Colonial Williamsburg, the Metropolitan Museum of Art, and
Independence Hall were already using Solocast's portable record players to inform visitors of their vast collections and landscapes.[41] For one dollar, visitors
could rent small personal players and headphones with records (available for sale
at the end of the tour) that directed them through these sites, providing a narrative carefully controlled by the museums' staffs. Unsurprisingly, the narrative
offered to renters of Mount Vernon's Solocast machines perpetuated the MVLA's
unwaveringly positive view of Washington. Mount Vernon's tour began at the
Texas Gate and ended at the greenhouse (and its small gift shop).[42] It "developed
a portrait of George Washington through his relationship to Mount Vernon and
provided visitors with a scholarly but enjoyable commentary on country life in
eighteenth century America."[43] The Solocast tour was the first "guided" tour ever
offered by the MVLA; specially trained guides would not entirely replace the
employees who stood guard in the mansion until 1986.[44] In keeping with the Association's desire to make Washington relatable and appealing to the masses, the
narrative told the visitor: "The public man is indeed so well known that it is hard

to see the real man beneath his dignities. Mt. Vernon expresses the real man—his intelligence, his interests, his taste and industry."[45]

Although the Solocast Company wrote the tour's script, Wall and the board had considerable control over its content. Released within months of the Voting Rights Act, slavery was something the Association clearly felt it had to address directly. Such gains in the fight for civil rights prompted a more careful consideration of African Americans' historic achievements. Committed to an unambiguously inspiring view of Washington, however, the MVLA acknowledged slavery without abandoning its view of an unambiguously admirable Washington. While standing on the North Lane gazing at the plantation's outbuildings, the Solocast audience heard the narrator introduce Washington the slaveholder: "George Washington owned well over a hundred slaves, though he seldom referred to them as such. He called them 'the people' or 'my people.' . . . [H]e seemed embarrassed by the system." Like the MVLA's explanation of the bunks in the Annual Report a few years earlier, the Solocast tour transformed Washington's complicity in slavery into a positive aspect of his character; in this case, the narrative focused the audience on Washington's kindness and humility. An actor voicing George Washington followed this with: "I never mean (unless some particular circumstance should compel me to it) to possess another slave by purchase; it being among my first wishes to see some plan adopted by which slavery in this country may be abolished by slow, sure, imperceptible degrees."[46] By pitching Washington as an almost accidental slave owner in his own words, the MVLA attempted to distance the general and his home from slavery's violent history. As depicted in the Solocast tour, the general hoped to see slavery diminish without disrupting society—an impossibly naïve perspective that contrasted mightily with current events. Not surprisingly, the MVLA was unable to abandon its idealized Washington; the tour offered slavery as an institution Washington was reluctant about rather than as a system on which his comfort and wealth depended.

At the end of the study period, the MVLA choose not to commit to the Solocast technology beyond the trial period. The visitors who used the machines found it enjoyable and informative, but the MVLA deemed it too expensive (the organization had to buy the machines and to hire employees to rent them to visitors) and admitted that "most people have little or no awareness of such a device or the usefulness of it."[47] Regardless of the conservatism of its narrative, the Association's willingness to experiment with the technology—and to address slavery directly through it at all—indicated its concern over the message Mount Vernon was sending and its rightful anticipation of the impact of social change on that narrative.

Mount Vernon on the Roadside: Funeral Homes and Motels, 1950s–1960s

As the MVLA tread carefully in interpreting slavery at Mount Vernon and agonized over the details of historical reconstruction, Americans replicated the building's trademark architectural features along roadsides across the country at an unprecedented rate. The Mount Vernon replica became so ubiquitous by the 1950s that it represented the values long associated with Washington's home— hospitality, good taste, and patriotism—more often than it directly referenced the historic structure itself. The MVLA might have been worried about how its audience understood Mount Vernon amid the period's social and cultural upheaval, but commercial replicas were unconcerned with the building's direct connection to a potentially controversial past.

The copying of Mount Vernon was so widespread and varied at midcentury that the MVLA could not hope to curb it; the days of politely asking Sears and Roebuck to refrain from duplicating Washington's house were long over. Because there was so much information widely available on Mount Vernon's architecture, architects and business owners who wanted to copy the house had no need to approach the MVLA for drawings or other material; few would follow the dimensions and details of the original closely anyway. Popular magazines promoted this loose adaptation of the architecture of the past, rejecting the strict academic nature of many earlier replicas. In a 1952 article titled "How to Merge What You've Got (the Past) with What You Want (the Future)," *House Beautiful*'s architectural editor preached: "Many people say . . . that they want their house 'to look just like Mount Vernon.' . . . You cannot copy the past. All you can do is learn from it. And the first thing you can learn from American history is this: Contemporary problems always demand contemporary solutions. . . . Good design is ageless."[48] With mass consumption expanding and Mount Vernon reaching its peak of popularity and visitorship, Americans found a whole new range of contemporary purposes for the iconic building. The recognizable features of Mount Vernon's architecture made it ideal for adaptation along the expanding commercial strip.

With many professional architects committed to the stylistic abstractions of Modernism by the 1950s, designing historically derivative contemporary buildings was usually left to builders or commercial architects without the pretensions of the academy. Business owners with an eye on the newly expanding field of advertising often decided what they wanted their structures to look like and directed their building professionals accordingly. As Denise Scott Brown and Robert Venturi would famously explain to fellow architectural theorists in their 1972 book *Learning from Las Vegas*, commercial developers and entrepreneurs exploited the compositions and details of what were otherwise rather standardized structures to communicate ideas; prominent "signs" could easily transform the identity of a simple "shed."[49] In this way, retrospective styles—and especially copies of well-known historic buildings—migrated from world's fairs to the roadside in the years before and after the war. They offered easily digestible symbolic meanings that a broad audience could read passing quickly in moving cars.[50]

By the time Disneyland opened with its fantastic stage sets referencing different dreamlike destinations, Americans were also growing more adept at simulating environments to grab customers' attentions. Like the fake Victorian shop fronts along Disneyland's Main Street, the commercial Mount Vernon replicas idealized their model, resulting in adaptations that were bolder and simpler than the original.[51] Following its already long history of reproduction in a range of building types, the Mount Vernon replica became more standardized by the 1950s: commercial buildings referencing Washington's house were usually symmetrical, rectangular buildings with side-gabled roofs and long facades. Exteriors were either painted white or faced with red brick, indicating a generalization of Virginia architecture made famous by Colonial Williamsburg. Details were domestic and Colonial in character, although they rarely referenced Mount Vernon in particular: false dormers, door surrounds with broken pediments or fanlights, and inoperable chimneys, sash windows, and shutters were most common. Rustication, cupolas, and a green/white/red color scheme were options for those who wished to reference Mount Vernon more specifically. Mount Vernon's Palladian composition also lent it to a variety of programmatic functions: it could just as easily be a single rectangular block or stretched on either side into a larger complex.

Since the first replicas of the 1890s, the iconic piazza remained Americans' favorite way to reference Mount Vernon. Whether with rounded columns or square pillars, a long, often two-story, flat- or shed-roofed porch evoked Mount Vernon's revered values easily and efficiently. Replicated piazzas often included the chinoiserie railing that the MVLA had removed from the original in 1936 as well. Photographs, prints, and descriptions had included the characteristic feature for so long that it continued to be identified with the house even after it was gone from the original. The fact that the MVLA had long deemed it an anachronism revealed the divide between the original and the replicas.

This shorthand language for referencing Mount Vernon proved especially appealing to the proprietors of two new building types: the motel and the purpose-built funeral home. Both began developing before World War II but came to fruition just as Mount Vernon was reaching its peak popularity and number of visitors in the 1950s. Both also had functions closely related to that of traditional domestic architecture. Before the twentieth century, most travelers stayed in taverns or private homes, while funerals were held at home or in houses converted into commercial parlors. As relatively new concepts, motels and funeral homes shared the need to convey trustworthiness, familiarity, sincerity, tradition, and security; many people had never stayed in a motel or opted to mourn their loved ones in a purpose-built funeral home before the 1950s. As a piece of highly recognizable domestic architecture that had communicated values along these lines for more than a century, Mount Vernon was the perfect model for these new building types.

Motels and funeral homes' adaptations of the prevailing southern plantation house also suggested racial coding in many parts of the country. While it is impossible to know for sure how many Mount Vernon–inspired structures hosted segregated businesses, many surely did. Cloaked in the image of white gentility, these buildings' services were usually intended only for white customers. Until the Civil Rights Act of 1964 prohibited discrimination in public places, most motels in and out of the South were racially segregated.[52] The American funeral industry had long been divided by race, regardless of Jim Crow. White cemeteries across the country had refused to bury African Americans since the end of the Civil War, leading to the creation of burial societies and later funeral homes that catered only to black communities.[53] Minorities often undertook cleaning, serving, and maintenance positions at such establishments, however.[54] The proprietors and architects of these buildings most likely never considered the potential meaning of their use of a former plantation house as the model for their segregated businesses. In light of the MVLA's careful consideration of the history of slavery at Mount Vernon at the same time, however, it is important to contrast the Association's concerns with the overwhelming assumption of the apolitical nature of the replicas.

The motel emerged in the years after the war to accommodate an increasingly mobile American public. Architecture magazines tracked its progress, anticipating the role that the profession would play in the development of the new building type. In 1933, *Architectural Record* described the clusters of small, detached cabins of the motor camp as "a new and rapidly enlarging field of building construction."[55] After the war, better roads, greater rates of car ownership, a booming economy, and shortened work weeks prompted the evolution of the "motel," a combination of the words "motor" and "hotel," from these modestly appointed establishments.[56] The motel was a series of individual rooms-for-rent, each appointed with an en suite bathroom, arranged contiguously and most often in a single story. The long row of rooms opened onto a parking lot and usually featured a lobby at the center or one end of the row. The entire ensemble most often directly faced a major thoroughfare.[57] Perceived as more convenient and inexpensive than the downtown hotel and more comfortable and modern than the prewar motor camp, the motel's popularity was almost instantaneous.[58] Whereas in 1928 only around 3,000 motels served tourists traveling by private automobile, 29,426 motels greeted "a new breed of Americans-on-the-go" by 1954. Less than a decade later, the number of motels had more than doubled.[59]

The use of Mount Vernon's name and architectural features for buildings in which people ate and slept was hardly new. Besides the cafeterias built by the YWCA, Wesleyan College, and the West Virginia 4-H program in the 1920s, hotels had also borrowed Mount Vernon's architecture. Adjacent to the campus of the University of North Carolina in Chapel Hill, Arthur C. Nash designed the Carolina Inn in 1923–24 with a Mount Vernon–inspired piazza, balustrade, and cupola to convey an "old fashioned, home-like appearance."[60] The red-brick building complemented the neoclassical buildings of the campus recently finished by McKim, Mead and White; its well-appointed guest rooms, ballroom, reception areas, and dining room provided domestic luxury for hire.[61] The Lowell Inn offered a similar vision of Mount Vernon–inspired hospitality to visitors to Stillwater, Minnesota. Designed in 1927 by the architect William Ingeman, the four-story, red-brick hotel boasted an impressive thirteen-columned piazza complete with chinoiserie balustrade.[62] Known as the "Mount Vernon of the West," the hotel gained considerable notoriety after Duncan Hines recognized it in his 1938 *Adventures in Good Eating* restaurant guidebook.[63] The bright-orange hipped roof, pediment, and cupola of the Howard Johnson restaurant chain also bore a striking resemblance to Mount Vernon's distinctive red top. Developed in the 1930s by the roofer Norman W. Pemberton, the form became a central part of the franchise's branding strategy and even the basis for its logo. The largest and most highly publicized Howard Johnson's restaurant located in Rego Park, Queens, looked especially like Mount Vernon. Seen by millions on their way to the 1939 World's Fair, the large, rectangular, white building with dormer windows and a cupola atop its gigantic orange hipped roof approximated the dimensions and composition of the west side of Washington's house.[64] Regardless of whether these earlier Mount Vernon–inspired buildings directly influenced the motels of the 1950s and 1960s, all borrowed Mount Vernon's famous piazza to welcome travelers and to assure them of the proprietors' trustworthiness and commitment to hospitality.

Fig. 44. Logo for Howard Johnson's, ca. 1950s. The orange hipped roof, cupola, and pediment all recall Mount Vernon's iconic roofline.

A survey of midcentury advertising postcards reveals that motels' designs referenced Mount Vernon more often than any historic building besides the Alamo.[65] Both Washington's house and the Texas landmark suggested allegiance to a regional form and were easy to adapt: a piazza quickly said Mount Vernon, while smooth walls and an arched facade suggested the Alamo. Both historic buildings were "traffic-stoppers" that conveyed a sense of familiar patriotism; they offered a traditional alternative to travelers who might be wary of the glass walls, flat roofs, and sharp edges of more Modern motels.[66] When America's largest early motel chain, the Alamo Plaza Hotel Courts, expanded with a new Nashville location in 1941, it swapped out its usual Alamo-inspired facade for a Mount Vernon piazza and dormers.[67]

Formally, Mount Vernon's Palladian arrangement lent itself to the organization of a motel: a lobby space could take on the character of the mansion's main block, while the long rows of rooms stretched out on either side like its colonnades and dependencies. When the first Howard Johnson's motor lodge opened in Savannah, Georgia, in 1954, its lobby featured a Mount Vernon piazza, balustrade, and cupola with guest rooms attached in long rows to either side.[68] Other motels referenced Mount Vernon without a central lobby building, using the piazza's details to accent the typical long rows of guest rooms. The "Colonial setting" of Dale's Mt. Vernon Motel in Canandaigua, New York, for example, was limited to a cupola and white piazza with chinoiserie balustrade shading the row of guest rooms.[69] The Colony Motor Lodge of Strongsville, Ohio, similarly consisted of only a single block of rooms topped with a chinoiserie balustrade.[70] Other motels relied almost entirely on the use of Mount Vernon's name. The Mt. Vernon Motor Lodge in Springfield, Missouri, featured a white-columned piazza fronting the U-shaped line of rooms and a small cupola that gestured at Mount Vernon's trademark features. Prominently displayed on a neon-lit sign, the name of the motel secured the architecture's tenuous connection to Washington's house.[71] Usually placed along the road directly in front of a motel, such signs—and the names displayed on them—were a key part of the building's design. A 1955 book advised motel keepers: "Signs to stop the fast-moving motorist must be big, bold, and high to be seen from afar."[72] The Mount Vernon Motel in Albany, New York, left no doubt as to its architectural reference with the words "Mount Vernon" in white capital letters in place of the building's trademark chinoiserie balustrade.

Motels employed Mount Vernon's architecture to stand out among the plethora of competing lodging establishments. Most of the motels of the 1950s were locally run mom-and-pop operations, and as *Architectural Record* reminded its readers in 1958: "Unlike most businesses, the hotel business makes its money from a building."[73] Architecture was an inexpensive and efficient way for these small businesses to distinguish themselves. Prefiguring Venturi and Scott Brown's *Learning from Las Vegas* without the theory, a 1955 book about planning and

Fig. 45. Mount Vernon Motel, Albany, New York. Undated postcard published by Margo Studio, Rome, New York.

operating a motel, for example, reminded proprietors and their designers that the "whole building is a sign" and that "the facade may be developed as a billboard of distinctive shape and texture."[74] The book's authors illustrated their points with a photograph of the teepee-shaped lobby of the "Wigwam Lodge" and another motel modeled after the Alamo. Professional architects, meanwhile, warned potential motel keepers and designers not to focus on style as a primary means to communicate with their customers; they advised that sound planning and an advantageous location were the keys to success in the highly competitive business. This likely indicated architects' anxieties about the fact that many motels were built quickly and without licensed architects, shutting the profession out of a highly profitable new building type. Architects were especially critical of "side show" architecture that copied historic buildings, dismissing it as uncreative kitsch. Alongside a photograph of a Mount Vernon–inspired motel as an example of the "Southern Mansion" style, *Architectural Forum* preached in 1954: "Architectural allure has always been of essential importance to the successful motel. . . . [M]otelmen have been content to compete for the eye of the motorist by building highly emotional architecture."[75] Whereas architects at the top of the profession had reveled in the experimentation of the Colonial Revival in the early twentieth century, designers devoted to the new mantras of Modernism disdained any direct references to historic buildings.

Yet architecture magazines like *Architectural Forum* also listed "recognition or advertising value" near the top of their lists of things for potential motel owners to think about when starting a new venture. Style was always a central component of this consideration: "Dignified or whimsical, the appearance of the establishment tells in advance what a guest may expect."[76] Trade magazines talked incessantly about the importance of architectural style or "atmosphere" as a means of establishing a distinguishable and readily determined architectural identity from the roadside.[77] Mount Vernon–inspired motels often took the theme to the interiors with Colonial Revival furniture and details to exude a more complete atmosphere as well. Built in 1949, the Mt. Vernon Motor Lodge in Winter Park, Florida, labeled the men's and women's restrooms "George" and "Martha," respectively.[78] As pictured on the Martha Washington Motel's postcard in 1957, a cannon in the front lawn supplemented the "Colonial Atmosphere" of the red brick, white columns, cupola, and chinoiserie balustrade of the Baltimore motel.[79] Others were simply outfitted with Colonial Revival furnishings.[80]

By the mid-1960s, however, the days of mom-and-pop motels fighting to outdo one another with "atmosphere" along the American roadside were fading. As air travel improved and the interstate highway system expanded, the commercial strip shifted, and many motels were no longer as desirably located as they once had been. Franchises and large corporations began to take over smaller motels, standardizing their appearance or replacing them with larger buildings that incorporated new amenities.[81] What had made Mount Vernon such a good model for motels proved a handicap in this transition. While its domestic scale and long piazza had been ideal for smaller, lower buildings, they were not compatible with the larger, boxier hotels that replaced them. Hotel chains eschewed the recognizable architectural features of Mount Vernon or other historical buildings, depending on brand recognition rather than quirky architecture to draw in customers. Even Howard Johnson's abandoned the Colonial style of its orange roof. A small lobby with a bright orange A-frame and abstract, space-age cupola fronted the chain's newly nondescript, Modern buildings. Other hotel chains hired the same architects who had long scoffed at amateurs' designs for retrospective motels, prompting the decline of the Alamo and Mount Vernon form by the 1970s. The English journal *Architect & Building News* used an image of a Mount Vernon–inspired motel in 1970 as "an example of the tawdry banalities of the worst of American motel design."[82] Modernist boxes of reinforced concrete and glass replaced the Mount Vernon motels, forcing travelers to distinguish between corporate brands by the language of logos and signature fonts rather than architectural motifs.

Like the motel, the purpose-built funeral home was a new building type in midcentury America. It similarly needed to create a homey atmosphere that would make customers feel immediately at ease—making Mount Vernon an equally appealing architectural model. By the middle of the twentieth century, the purpose-built funeral home was a relatively new concept. Funeral parlors first became common in American downtowns after the Civil War. With most funerals still taking place in private homes, these spaces usually operated as salesrooms for caskets and other paraphernalia.[83] As embalming became a standard practice by the 1920s, more middle-class Americans sought out funeral parlors for the preparation of corpses and as the location of funeral services.[84] To ease the minds of skeptical customers and to offer an experience that was less obviously commercial, funeral directors began to move their parlors to upscale residential neighborhoods. By converting stately domestic buildings into funeral businesses, they were able to offer homelike atmospheres to clients who just a decade before might have hosted their relatives' funerals in their own living rooms.[85]

Continuing to face criticism for opportunistic profiteering, many funeral directors shifted to building new purpose-built structures after World War II. Simple Colonial or functional modern buildings replaced the luxurious repurposed mansions of the previous decades.[86] With the deaths of hundreds of thousands of Americans in World War II and the Korean War gearing up, the funerary industry took on a particularly patriotic bent in these new buildings: funeral directors marketed their ritualistic preparation and burial of the dead as a preservation of national values.[87]

Capitalizing on the patriotic claims of the industry and the wider popularity of Mount Vernon, the businessman Hubert Eaton built a Mount Vernon replica as the administration building and mortuary at America's most famous and controversial funerary establishment in 1951: Forest Lawn–Hollywood Hills Memorial Park. Ten years later, he built another Mount Vernon mortuary at the chain's Cypress, California, branch. Widely publicized in the popular press and facilitated by the public's greater interest in Washington's home, these buildings were the most public examples of Mount Vernon–inspired funeral establishments to come; they encouraged a national trend in the building type that continues to this day.

Hubert Eaton began his infamous leadership of Forest Lawn Cemetery in Glendale, California, in the early 1910s. His use of Mount Vernon replicas was part of a larger strategy to transform the American cemetery into a more complete funerary experience skillfully aimed at the consumptive patterns of the living. Over fifty years, Eaton transformed the typical picturesque cemetery into a new industry standard and expanded it into a franchise that now includes ten branches across the state. He consolidated a full range of funerary services including the preparation of the body (with options of both embalming and cremation), the hosting of funerals, and burial in a single location. By 1917, Eaton had

Fig. 46. Forest Lawn–Hollywood Hills Memorial Park, California, 1951.

also begun to significantly reimagine the physical arrangement of the cemetery. He replaced all freestanding memorials with plaques flush with the ground and redecorated with a highly controlled artistic program.[88]

Art and architecture were central to Eaton's plan to draw living people to Forest Lawn; he wished Forest Lawn to be a tourist destination as well as a cemetery. Inspired by the sumptuousness and spectacle of the 1915 Panama-Pacific International Exposition (where he might have seen Virginia's replica of Mount Vernon), Eaton began to collect copies of iconic artworks and to commission replicas of famous buildings "redolent of the world's best history and romances."[89] Each sculpture or work of architecture chosen for replication had to "be one surrounded with romantic and historic interest; one associated with a personality famous and well-loved throughout the world."[90] His strategy of replicating highly recognizable works of art and architecture guaranteed an appeal to a broad audience and conveyed a sense of timelessness appropriate for a supposedly eternal resting place.[91] Copies of "immortal works of the world's greatest artists" transferred a sense of culture and importance to the dead buried around them.[92] Eaton acquired copies of Michelangelo's sculptures of Moses and David, as well as a version of Leonardo da Vinci's *The Last Supper* in stained glass. He viewed architecture as another means of "communicating emotion" and began commissioning full-scale replicas of historic buildings in 1918. The first was a version of the English parish church Stoke Poges made famous by Thomas Gray's "Elegy Written in a Country Churchyard." Within a year of its construction the church had become a desirable place for weddings, testifying to its romantic appeal to the living.[93]

By the 1950s, Eaton had expanded to more patriotic themes. He was staunchly antisocialist and professed his political beliefs openly in the cemetery's artistic program, viewing it as an opportunity to both educate the living and uplift the dead. As a monument to the servicemen who died in World War II, he dedicated the "Court of Freedom" at Forest Lawn–Glendale in 1950 with a bronze sculpture of George Washington by John Quincy Adams Ward and a copy of Daniel Chester French's *The Republic* (created for the 1893 World's Columbian Exposition).[94] Eaton also commissioned a twenty-by-thirty-foot replica of John Trumbull's *Declaration of Independence* composed of seven hundred thousand pieces of

Venetian glass.[95] Citing these works and others, *Christian Century* called Forest Lawn–Glendale "America's first politically oriented cemetery."[96] It was a setting for Eaton's views on both how Americans handled death and how they should actively manage their government.

Having already used the figure of George Washington to convey his conservative political beliefs at Forest Lawn–Glendale, Eaton replicated Mount Vernon when he opened a second branch of Forest Lawn in Hollywood in 1951. The side-gabled, two-story white building with a balustraded piazza faced directly onto the roadside at the entrance of the 450-acre cemetery. It held a mortuary, chapel, and flower shop, as well as administrative offices. With this building as a roadside beacon for its greater "colonial theme," the cemetery also included replicas of the First Parish Meeting House in Portland, Maine, made famous by the poet Henry Wadsworth Longfellow (complete with a window depicting the pivotal scene in his poem "The Courtship of Miles Standish"), and of Boston's Old North Church.[97] Customers could choose among burial sites in the fifteen-acre "Court of Liberty" with a monument to Washington at the center and a 162-foot-long mosaic that reproduced scenes from twenty-five famous American paintings and sculptures in order to "teach our children and remind their elders of their most precious heritage, the liberty for which their forefathers died."[98] When Eaton opened another branch of Forest Lawn ten years later in Cypress, California, he once again used Mount Vernon as the model for the cemetery's administration building.

For Eaton, Mount Vernon had a resonance that confirmed the patriotism of the funerary industry, provided an object lesson in American history, and conveyed his own beliefs about the country's illustrious past and tentative future. As an extension of the attempts by many earlier funeral directors to bring a homelike atmosphere to the funeral parlor, Eaton chose the most American of homes to make his customers feel at ease. Placed directly on the road, the buildings also acted as "signs" in much the same way that Mount Vernon motels did in the same decade. The Mount Vernon–inspired mortuaries suggested trustworthiness and tradition to a potentially hesitant audience, while at the same time confirmed the strategy that Eaton was using with other iconic paintings, sculptures, and buildings throughout his cemeteries.

Hubert Eaton's strategies worked: the Forest Lawn memorial parks were terrifically popular, and countless other funerary businesses adapted his techniques—including the idea of replicating Mount Vernon. Regardless of whether or not the press was complimentary, Forest Lawn was unquestionably the most famous funeral establishment in midcentury America. With more than a million visitors a year, more Americans saw the replica of *David* in California than the real thing in Europe.[99] The popular press often compared Forest Lawn to Disneyland in terms of the numbers of visitors, and Eaton counted Walt Disney among his personal friends.[100] Souvenir shops and a guidebook facilitated the tourists' experiences at Forest Lawn's different locations and ensured the clarity of Eaton's vision. Forest Lawn–Hollywood Hills became a special site of pilgrimage as many famous celebrities chose it for their final resting place: notable funerals and burials in and around the Mount Vernon mortuary include those of Bette Davis, Liberace, and more recently Michael Jackson. The continual addition of new works of art and the exploitation of a range of professional advertising techniques encouraged repeat visitation and constant press coverage.[101]

Forest Lawn was made even more famous by a multitude of detractors. Many both within and without the funerary industry dismissed Forest Lawn as unnecessarily luxurious and tasteless; they decried Eaton as the epitome of the greedy funeral director, preying on the vulnerable bereaved. While some found the unabashed sentimentalism of the artistic and architectural programs appealing, others disparaged it as pandering kitsch.[102] In the novel *The Loved One: An Anglo-American Tragedy* of 1948, the British author Evelyn Waugh thinly veiled Forest Lawn as the setting for his satirical look at a vain and ridiculous Hollywood.[103] The folksinger Tom Paxton wrote a song poking fun of the opulent funerals at Forest Lawn in 1970 (John Denver also recorded the song four years later).[104] In her best-selling 1963 book lambasting the American funeral industry, Jessica Mitford used Forest Lawn as the ultimate example of a shamefully greedy and insincere funeral business.[105] Despite the calls for reform by Mitford and others, Forest Lawn continued to be tremendously profitable and a popular tourist destination.[106]

Either copying the buildings at Forest Lawn–Hollywood Hills/Cypress directly or looking to Mount Vernon to assuage lingering mistrust of the funerary industry following Mitford's book, funeral directors across the country began to look to Washington's home as an architectural model for their businesses in the 1960s.[107] The familiar piazza diverted attention from the business's unavoidable commercialism. References to America's most famous residence also confirmed the nature of many funeral homes as family-owned and -operated establishments, suggesting that the director and his family would treat the dead and their families as if they were part of their own. The family-run Karrer-Simpson Funeral Home in Port Huron, Michigan, for example, followed the typical trajectory of American funeral homes over the first half of the twentieth century. After moving from a downtown storefront to a formerly private residence in 1923, the business reestablished itself in a purpose-built, Mount Vernon–inspired facility in 1965.[108] Located directly on a commercial thoroughfare, the two-story building had a long white piazza with square pillars, domestically scaled windows, and inoperable shutters. The DeMarco Funeral home in Monroe Township, New Jersey, was similar. Built in 1979, the structure gestured at Mount Vernon with a central two-story structure complete with a high piazza and one-story wings attached to either side.[109] Decorated with Colonial Revival furniture, the DeMarco Funeral Home recalled the sense of timeless patriotism evoked by Eaton at Forest Lawn–Hollywood Hills.

Toppitzer Funeral Home at Arlington Cemetery in Drexel Hill, Pennsylvania, continued to depend on Hubert Eaton's strategy of replicating Mount Vernon and other historic buildings even more recently.[110] Built in the early 1980s, the building approximated Mount Vernon's piazza, dormers, cupola, and asymmetrical window arrangement. Even the dove-of-peace weathervane, red-shingled hipped roof, rustication, and Venetian window were faithfully copied. The proprietors chose Mount Vernon as the building's inspiration "since Washington's death inspired Americans to create and own mourning art on an important scale."[111] Besides facilities for cremation, consultation, undertaking, and funerals, the building also housed a professionally curated museum of mourning art that included many Washington-related objects. A mausoleum modeled after Thomas Jefferson's Monticello and another with gates identical to those at Christ Church, Philadelphia, carried the historic theme to buildings of internment at the cemetery. With words that could just as easily be those of Hubert Eaton, the funeral home's promotional brochure explained the use of historic buildings: "To be associated with our nation's past, its leaders and their ideals, is congenial to Arlington's desire to perpetuate the history of the families interred here. . . . [L]et us preserve your history along with America's history."[112] But at Toppitzer, like all of the Mount Vernon–inspired funeral homes that came before it, there was no mention of Mount Vernon's role as a southern plantation dependent upon slavery. Long before postmodernism gave theoretical legitimacy to such superficial adaptation of historic styles, the Mount Vernon replicas established that a historic building could be copied while unquestioningly glossing over historical reality.

Facing Change at Mount Vernon, 1970s–1980s

By the early 1970s, Mount Vernon motels and funeral homes peppered the roadside across the country, but fewer Americans were traveling to see the original in Virginia. The numbers of visitors to Mount Vernon began to drop and remained below the highs of the previous two decades. Only in 1976, the U.S. bicentennial year, did numbers reach close to 1964's record-breaking count of 1.3 million tourists; attendance would not surpass that number until 1984.[113] The MVLA blamed lower attendance numbers on a languishing economy, the gas shortage, political unrest in Washington, and the fact that numbers were down at other U.S. house museums.[114] Following the establishment of Disneyland in 1955 and Disney World in 1971, the founding of the National Trust for Historic Preservation in 1949, the passage of the National Preservation Act of 1966, and a rush of new "heritage" museums in the 1960s, Mount Vernon also faced unprecedented competition from both commercial and historic sites.[115] By the nation's two-hundredth birthday, there were other places where Americans could see simulated historical worlds.

The MVLA's worst fear was that the lessons of George Washington's life were too remote to prove useful for the rapidly changing present. The regent Elizabeth Cooke reminded the board in 1970: "These are times of stress, conflict, doubt and violence. More than ever are we bound to preserve and maintain Mount Vernon. Miss Cunningham stressed that under proper regulation it should be open 'to the inspection of all who love the cause of liberty and revere the name

Fig. 47. Toppitzer Funeral Home, Carrier Mausoleums Construction (designers), Arlington Cemetery, Drexel Hill, Pennsylvania, 1980s (photograph 2013).

of Washington.' In fact, it is open to many who know little and care less of Washington, save as a name in our early history, and to many who come merely as a pleasant exception."[116] Believing Washington to be more important than ever in such a tumultuous world, the Association made moves in its preservation and interpretation of Mount Vernon to keep its hero relevant amid the public's waning interest. By the early 1980s, the organization drew criticism despite its efforts. Facing falling numbers and closer scrutiny than it had in at least a century, the MVLA actively attempted to balance the new social history with its idealization of Washington.

Throughout the 1970s and 1980s, the Association remained firmly committed to its mission: the restoration of Mount Vernon to its eighteenth-century appearance.[117] Undertaken with advanced techniques and daring vision, the use of preservation as the primary means of interpreting Mount Vernon was nonetheless conservative and difficult for many Americans to understand and appreciate. The MVLA's most lasting and influential achievement of the period was not defined by what it built or changed, but by what it prevented from happening. Beginning with a fight against the construction of a new water treatment plant in 1961, the Association fiercely advocated for the preservation of the Maryland side of the Potomac River shoreline visible from Mount Vernon.[118] Significant monetary support from the organization and leadership from its board members over the next fifteen years facilitated the purchase of land parcel by parcel, the placement of sections under scenic easements, and the protection of others under the aegis of a new national park. By 1974, the MVLA's "quiet achievements," invisible and unbeknownst to most visitors, nonetheless protected the "eighteenth century enclave from disruptive intrusions, both visual and auditory."[119] The landmark effort extended the MVLA's preservation activities beyond the boundaries of its property and ensured the survival of one of its most important elements.

Just as the vice regents took bold legislative action to save Mount Vernon's view in the period, the MVLA also used the latest in preservation technology to initiate dramatic change in the mansion. Discussion about the repainting of the mansion's interiors began in 1979, when the board realized that it would be "very wrong to put yet another layer on top of the many beneath without first employing the most modern forms of analysis."[120] Much as the repairs to the old greenhouse had prompted its replacement with a reconstruction of the Washington-era building in the 1940s, the wear and tear of millions of visitors on the mansion's interior walls initiated a tremendous shift in the appearance of the building's rooms. Following a yearlong investigation in which the restoration paint specialist Matthew Mosca took more than 2,500 samples "from first floor to cupola," the board determined "the colors of 1799."[121] Mosca employed microscopic examination, chemical manipulation, spectographic analysis, and archival research to determine not only how Washington had originally treated various wall surfaces but also the results of subsequent restoration attempts.[122]

Although Mosca's conclusions were surprising to many, they were perceived as far more authoritative than Ann Pamela Cunningham and Superintendent Dodge's arbitrary paint peeling. The board immediately directed the repainting of the mansion to match Mosca's findings using eighteenth-century techniques for the production and application of paint. The process took an additional three years and "proved to be an opening of Pandora's box of paints" in which the "new, bright, often garish colors shocked [and] repelled" the MVLA's board.[123] Among the most startling changes were the faux-graining of the wall paneling in the central passage and study and the bright, glossy green of the dining room.[124]

Fig. 48. The central passage after paint analysis and restoration, Mount Vernon, 1981. Note the Bastille key in between the two south doors.

While many of the vice regents found the effect of the rooms "not to all tastes," they acquiesced for the sake of accuracy.[125]

The curator, Christine Meadows, also used the repainting of the mansion as an opportunity to apply the inventory more systematically to the house's furnishings and textiles. Meadows had worked at Mount Vernon since 1959, when she was hired after completing her master's degree in history at William and Mary.[126] From the elaborate public rooms of the first floor to the oft-forgotten third-floor bedchambers, Meadows's refurnishing solidified the date of interpretation of the mansion to 1799—the time of Washington's death and the inventory that followed.[127] The press and specialists in the field of American decorative arts praised the MVLA's reinvention of the mansion and application of paint analysis.[128] The bright colors also revised assumptions about the muted tones of the Colonial period: along with similar discoveries at Colonial Williamsburg later in the decade, they prompted a new wave of Colonial Revival decoration in contemporary interior design.[129]

Despite the groundbreaking results of the paint analysis and viewshed preservation, neither effort challenged or significantly changed the MVLA's narrative of the significance of Washington or Mount Vernon. As it had since the 1950s, the Association continued to use restoration and preservation to promote an unquestioningly positive view of Washington and the house as a manifestation of his character. Although the board sought to strip him of his mythical and unapproachable status by making him more human with projects such as the greenhouse and its slave-quarter wings, its goal continued to be to promote Washington as a singularly important historical figure. The MVLA's recognition of the slave quarters as a manifestation of Washington's genius, for example, seemed increasingly out of touch by the end of the 1970s. With the mini-series *Roots* chronicling the violence of slavery on national television in 1977 and most universities churning out studies that challenged the primacy of white, male political figures in American history, the MVLA's Mount Vernon's narrative appeared steadfastly traditional and hierarchical in contrast. The Association's initial attempts to draw new audiences mostly fell flat, and other than a rise at the nation's bicentennial, visitation continued to decline.

In the wake of the new social history, the MVLA saw Washington's own words as a surefire means of reaffirming his significance both to academics and the public. Working with the University of Virginia, the Association launched a new scholarly effort in 1968 that harkened back to Morley Williams's research decades earlier. First proposed by the Virginia state archivist William J. Van Schreeven, the Papers of George Washington was the first attempt to organize and publish Washington's writings comprehensively.[130] Previously, the principal primary source for Washington's correspondence was the twelve-volume set published by the Harvard historian Jared Sparks in the 1820s and 1830s.[131] In more recent decades, the general's biography had undergone serious reevaluation that begged new source material. In an attempt to "debunk" the myths established by Parson Weems and others, some twentieth-century historians had stripped Washington of his humanity, leaving him a dull and dry figure, while others had lambasted him for his political and personal missteps.[132] The Association proclaimed that its commitment to the Papers project (which was largely financial) was to help refute "slanderous misstatements made in jocular malice or perhaps with the more sinister intent of downgrading our country and its history."[133]

Like the historian James Thomas Flexner, who published his Pulitzer Prize–winning biography of Washington in 1974, the Association was also trying to reveal what it believed was a "real" Washington.[134] The regent Elizabeth Cooke wrote in the 1973 annual report: "It is our fervent hope that through our cooperation and the information and inspiration we can give at Mount Vernon a true picture of George Washington will emerge—not as a remote demigod, not as a self-seeking capitalist, but as the real and wonderful person who was, in the words of his young friend Lighthorse Harry Lee, 'First in the hearts of his countrymen' and 'second to none in the humble and endearing scenes of private life.'"[135] The MVLA imagined the Papers of George Washington as a new cache of raw, neutral material from which historians and the public could devise an "authentic" view of the first president. It did not acknowledge that such resources could not guarantee a positive interpretation of his character and deeds, nor did the vice regents refrain from cherry-picking details to serve their own interpretations. In its 1973 annual report, for example, the board printed the Papers' finding of "Washington's constant concern for the well-being of his slaves" with a 1769 letter in which he asked his London factor to send Dutch blankets for "his people."[136] The project's first publication, released between 1976 and 1979, was a six-volume set of Washington's diaries.[137]

While the Association hoped to convince academic circles of Washington's singular importance with the publication of his papers, it offered a heroic and humane Washington to a more popular audience when it agreed to host the sound and light show *The Father of Liberty* in 1976.[138] A birthday gift to the people of the United States from the French government, the show took place on Mount Vernon's bowling green and used the west side of the mansion as a "stage" for the projection of colored and moving lights and a custom narration and score.[139] One hundred thousand people saw the show between the Memorial and Labor Day holidays of 1976 and 1977, after which the Association decided that it was not lucrative enough to warrant the continued demand on the site's physical plant and staff.[140]

Like the Solocast script, the staff had considerable control over the narrative and presentation of the show, even though it was produced outside of the organization.[141] The Association kept the story firmly focused on Washington's personal sacrifices and inspiration for the American and French Revolutions, his relationship with the young Frenchman Lafayette, and Mount Vernon's importance as a physical manifestation of his notable character. The dramatic narrative of the forty-five-minute show began: "Mount Vernon is more than just an estate: Washington's whole life is laid out here, as though on a surveyor's map. This man, summoned to glory and hailed the world over, never forgets his woodland acres, his pastures and ploughed fields, the welfare of his workmen and servants. And if duty calls him first to the battlefields, then to political office, his thoughts will never leave Mount Vernon."[142] In the Bicentennial year, the Association continued to use the now centuries-old Cincinnatus myth to promote a human Washington torn between his sense of responsibility to his country and family—black and white.

The invasiveness of the preparations for *The Father of Liberty* indicated the depth of the Association's desire to be the focus of Washington-related remembrance in the bicentennial year. It physically taxed the historic area more than any previous interpretive program. The preparations were especially shocking considering the attention the board gave to the preservation of the landscape across the Potomac in the same period. The MVLA even considered using fill excavated from the construction of the Washington, D.C., Metro to create stepped seating for the audience on the bowling green.[143] In the end, two hundred lights were installed on freestanding poles, in the trees on either side of the serpentine paths, and in below-grade wells.[144] The Association dug trenches across the bowling green to bury concrete conduits for lights and other electrical equipment.[145] Even though it lasted for only two years and was ultimately declared a financial failure, the sound and light show had a lasting negative effect on the historic area: the trenches dug across the bowling green forever ruined a large swath of land for future archaeological investigation, and the light wells still pepper the otherwise restored eighteenth-century landscape.[146]

Elaborate sound and light show and dramatic new wall colors aside, the Association's devotion to a traditional narrative did not prove as compelling to the public as it had in the decades just after World War II. Operating without a significant endowment, the MVLA looked for new revenue streams in light of languishing attendance. The Association boosted admission fees three times over the course of the 1970s.[147] In 1981, it took over a small concession just outside the Texas Gate and began running the "Mount Vernon Inn" restaurant and an enlarged gift shop (the only other place to buy souvenirs on the site was in the greenhouse).[148] Coupled with rising operating costs, the "critical" situation of falling attendance prompted the board to begin its first capital campaign in 1979 with a goal of raising $10 million.[149] While the endowment significantly changed the possibilities for the scale of the MVLA's projects, it signaled an important shift in concept for the organization itself. For the first time, the board's primary role was no longer to interpret Mount Vernon but to fund-raise. Although the MVLA and individual committees continued to oversee and initiate decisions large and small, the day-to-day carry-through was more often left to a staff of professionals with specific training in the fields of preservation, museum management, and American history. Admission fees and the generosity of individual board members were also no longer Mount Vernon's only support.[150] Corporations and individuals began donating millions of dollars, giving the Association a new and more limited audience to court. At the very moment in which narratives of America's past grew more inclusive, support of the home of its first president became more exclusive.

The capital campaign began quietly in 1979 with the stated purpose of ensuring the MVLA's self-sufficiency from the federal government, keeping admission fees "within the means of all people," and initiating significant improvements (such as a new administrative building).[151] The board established a steering committee to lead the campaign and to advise on raising and managing the largest sum collected by the organization since Ann Pamela Cunningham's nationwide call to arms in the 1850s. Led by Donald T. Regan, who left the chairmanship soon after appointment to serve as President Ronald Reagan's secretary of the treasury, the initial committee consisted entirely of men influential in politics and business. It included present and former CEOs of Safeway, Exxon, and AT&T, as well as the Texas billionaire (and future presidential candidate) H. Ross Perot and the longest-serving chairman of the U.S. Federal Reserve, William McChesney

Martin Jr.[152] The Ronald Reagan fund-raiser and Prudential Life Insurance Company CEO Robert A. Beck replaced Donald T. Regan as chair of the committee. With the guidance of such successful and well-connected advisors, the Association surpassed its goal and raised $11,181,951 in five years with donations from more than 2,774 individuals, foundations, and corporations.[153] While a portion of the funds went into an endowment, the rest made a swift impact. The Association opened a large new library and research center, allowing for the expansion of its educational programming and general operating staff, and undertook a number of projects to improve accessibility and safety in and around the historic area.[154]

In the midst of this important fund-raising campaign, the Mount Vernon Ladies' Association faced the possibility of intense scrutiny. In 1982, the *Washington Post* columnist Dorothy Gilliam published an editorial about Mount Vernon as part of the newspaper's recognition of Black History Month. She evocatively described the pitiful state of the memorial erected in 1929 to the enslaved buried in unmarked graves near Washington's tomb: "Far back in the woods of Mount Vernon, a lone stone monument marks the site where George Washington buried his slaves. It is a modest memorial, apparently too unimportant to be roped off or otherwise distinguished from the other parts of the property. It seems not to matter that the hands of these men and women built the celebrated mansion that was Washington's home. It seems not to matter that these men and women provided the free labor on which the plantation operated."[155] Gilliam put the MLVA's meticulous preservation of the mansion in sharp contrast to the overgrown and ignored cemetery, challenging the Association's very mission. Whereas the MVLA had initially erected the small marker without fanfare or solicitation, its lack of attention to it by the early 1980s elicited public scorn—all in the middle of a visitation crisis and unprecedented fund-raising campaign.

The Association responded immediately to Gilliam's article as if it was a match that could light the operation aflame. Within two weeks, the MVLA cleaned up the cemetery site, constructed a gravel path connecting it to the historic area, and hosted a "reopening" on Washington's birthday.[156] Unlike when it restored the slave quarters at midcentury, the MVLA could not afford to take its time in determining the least controversial way to recognize Mount Vernon's enslaved population.

Gilliam's article did indeed spark the attention of the Fairfax chapter of the National Association for the Advancement of Colored People (NAACP), which raised the issue to the County Board of Supervisors and asked for the reconsideration of the tax-exempt status of the MVLA's Mount Vernon Inn restaurant.[157] After some negotiation, the Board of Supervisors ultimately granted the tax-exempt status on the condition that the Association would "work with the NAACP and come up with an appropriate memorialization."[158] The article and the NAACP's action prompted the MVLA to speed up and switch gears on its efforts to meet the public's rising expectations for social history. Americans might not have been visiting Mount Vernon in droves, but how the MVLA talked about history mattered more than ever. Responding proactively to criticism, the Association finally faced the history of slavery at Mount Vernon.

The all-white board handled each step of the ensuing "delicate situation" with extreme care and the effects were long-lasting and far from superficial.[159] They included the construction of a new monument at the slave cemetery, the establishment of a department of archaeology to research slave life, and the reinterpretation of slavery throughout the site.

The vice regents decided to sponsor a competition for a new slave memorial and created a joint committee with the head of the Fairfax NAACP, Frank Matthews; Judith Burton, a descendant of Washington's enslaved butler, West Ford; and the professor and local activist William Carr.[160] This marked one of the few times in its history that the board invited members of the local community (as opposed to hired consultants) to serve as decision makers for interpretation on the site. Board members were aware that this was a key moment in the public's perception of the organization and that others had accused them of skating over historical reality in the past.[161] Keen to avoid more controversy and well aware of the recent battles over the Vietnam Veterans Memorial, the Association opted to limit the contestants to teams of students from the historically black Howard University.[162] In lieu of a cash prize for the winning team, the MVLA established a $2,500 revolving student loan program at the School of Architecture.[163]

The committee agreed that "the proposed monument should be dignified and evocative of a spirit of reverence" and that it should be "appropriate to Mount Vernon."[164] The committee—and especially the vice regents within the group—did not want the monument to harp on the horrors of slavery or to represent all enslaved peoples; they agreed that this was a place to recognize and memorialize the enslaved laborers at Mount Vernon specifically.[165] The instructions for the competition specified: "The spiritual qualities of the site . . . and inner strength and contributions of the slaves are important design determinants and should be given central consideration. . . . *Socio-political statements and the pain and degradation associated therewith should not be expressed in your designs. Rather, you should transcend those issues and seek to express the courage and strength of a people.* Dignity of design, consideration of site qualities and symbolic expression of the fortitude of slaves are the measures most important. The creation of a quiet place for reflection and relief from the more tourist intense/built-up areas of Mount Vernon is also an important goal of this undertaking."[166] The competition description indicated that the committee did not want the memorial to detract from the laudatory narrative of the historic area but rather to create a new reflective space that recognized the contributions of the enslaved.

In keeping with the committee's hope for a contemplative and respectful design, the impact of construction on the remains buried in the cemetery was "a major concern since the project was first discussed."[167] The MVLA consulted archaeologists and engineers about how to erect a memorial with as little impact on the ground as possible. The committee devised an engineering solution that used a reinforced concrete floating slab foundation, avoiding all but a few footings (and those only two feet deep) to disturb the site.[168]

Thirty teams vied for the opportunity to design the new memorial.[169] Led by senior architecture student David Edge, the winning team's design consisted of an engraved, broken column atop a stone platform raised in three stages. The words "faith," "hope," and "love" engraved on each of the platform's stages signified the "qualities no one could take from these people." The column represented the strength of the enslaved people buried there.[170] The feature's inscription did not evoke the patronizing image of the faithful slave as did the 1929 memorial, but it did define the slave population by its ownership: "In memory of the Afro-Americans who served as slaves at Mount Vernon." Edge and his team designed a brick walk and archway leading to the memorial that echoed the materials and form of the nearby Washington family tomb in order to give the space "the same respect" as Washington's burial place.[171] The MVLA also engraved the date "1929" on the earlier memorial in order to differentiate the effort from the more recent one.[172] The final monument attempted to recognize slavery's hardships through the inspiring survival of its victims.

In her follow-up article after the February 1983 dedication of the new memorial, Dorothy Gilliam wrote: "You could say this long overdue homage is little—and late. But it is a beginning."[173] And indeed the MVLA treated the memorial as such. Pronouncing in its 1982 annual report that "renewed study of the lives of all who lived and worked here has been discussed for several years and research is underway," it began a number of new efforts to interpret slave life throughout the site.[174] In June 1982, within months of Gilliam's initial article, the MVLA released a new pamphlet about slavery at Mount Vernon. Tourists picked up seven thousand in the first two weeks of the pamphlet's availability.[175] Research staff revised

Fig. 49. The winning design team from Howard University for the slave memorial, Mount Vernon, 1983 (photograph 1993). *Left to right:* Dean Harry G. Robinson, David Edge, Glen Rorie, and Adetunji Oyenusi.

interpretive signs and existing brochures to replace those that discussed labor in only passive terms, although references to Washington's ambivalent feelings toward the institution remained.[176] Unlike the quiet reception for the reconstructed slave-quarter wings in the 1960s, this new interpretation was "well received by the public."[177] The board appointed a new Archaeology Study Committee in 1983 with an initial grant of one hundred thousand dollars to investigate the material culture of Mount Vernon's enslaved residents, which developed into the Department of Archaeology by 1987.[178] Collection practices also changed to include objects related to slavery: in 1984, the MVLA acquired a 1754 document from the settlement of Lawrence Washington's estate in which his slaves were divided between George Washington and his widowed sister-in-law.[179]

By recognizing slavery more holistically across the site than it ever had before, the MVLA did not abandon its narrative of George Washington as a great man, nor did it divert its focus entirely away from its preservation of the mansion. Exploring the history of slavery at Mount Vernon added another layer to Washington's humanity, and the MVLA began to willingly open the doors to research that might prove he was more real than ideal. Public pressure sped up and magnified the revelation of Washington as a fuller, more ambiguous figure at Mount Vernon, a change that has proved to be long lasting.

As Americans democratized Mount Vernon along the roadside, the MVLA struggled to produce a narrative that served both its commitment to Washington's memory and the public's growing demand for a more inclusive narrative. Whereas Superintendent Wall told the MVLA's board in 1950 that "you are under no compulsion from without to change your formula," outside criticism thirty years later pushed sustained and substantial change in the Association's recognition of slavery across the site.[180] In the same decades, roadside copies had the luxury of largely avoiding controversy and even context. The Mount Vernon replica had finally succeeded in separating from its model and even the specifics of the Old South myth, existing independently of the more inclusive social and historical significances increasingly demanded of the original.

★ Conclusion

MORE THAN TWO HUNDRED YEARS after the death of George Washington, Mount Vernon remains the country's most famous house and one of its most identifiable symbols. The endurance of its image is a testament to the building's flexibility. Through two centuries of preservation, pilgrimage, and replication, each successive generation has chosen how and what to remember about Mount Vernon. It has been a stage on which Americans act out their idealizations of a graceful past or a screen onto which they project the nation's flaws. It can reference a vaguely imagined world gone by or signify a very particular set of political or social ideals. The variety of strategies has ensured Mount Vernon's longevity into the twenty-first century: in one form or another, Americans have seen and continue to see it everywhere.

Americans remain intensely interested in George Washington's world. Mount Vernon is still the most visited house museum in the nation. To an average of 1 million visitors a year, the Mount Vernon Ladies' Association continues to use the mansion and its landscape to tell "the story of George Washington so that his timeless and relevant life lessons are accessible to the world."[1] It remains a singular example of the American home and a standard-bearer of historic preservation.

In renovated and new buildings along America's roadsides, business owners still rely on Mount Vernon's iconic architecture to communicate quickly and clearly. It remains an especially common trope in residential architecture. Decades after its initial Mount Vernon–inspired model, Garlinghouse uses the building's trademark architectural features in its "Georgian Grace" plan to evoke vague recollections of social elitism and timelessness: an "elegant, move-up home that brings the best of yesterday to today's discerning family. Sturdy brick construction, a towering columned porch, and a formal, central entry are borrowed elements from long ago."[2] Mount Vernon's name—even without its telltale architectural elements—continues to resonate tradition and luxury. Heartland Luxury Homes based in Pittsburgh, Pennsylvania, offers a red-brick Colonial Revival house called "The Mount Vernon" with up to 7,865 finished square feet, a movie theater, and granite countertops.[3] In 2000, Susie Hilfiger (the wife of the fashion mogul Tommy Hilfiger) commissioned the neotraditional architect Allan Greenberg to design a children's playhouse after Mount Vernon. Its tiny Bastille key, furniture, china, and interior wall decoration were all replicated to scale so that children could "learn to love George Washington."[4]

In the wake of an increasing awareness of social history, such projection and even play with Mount Vernon's architecture has become more complicated. Individuals might replicate Mount Vernon's features in their private homes without thinking about the ways in which these buildings glorify the plantation and its supposedly glamorous lifestyle—all supported by enslaved labor. But at Mount Vernon in Virginia, the MVLA is constantly aware of the need for—and expectation of—its interpretation of slavery. Through exhibitions, archaeology, architectural reconstructions, living history, and the mansion tour, visitors learn about the lives of the enslaved everywhere at the Mount Vernon of today. The gulf between the building's image in popular culture and the perceived responsibilities of the MVLA continues to widen.

In each attempt to make Mount Vernon relevant, Americans disclose more about themselves in the present than about days gone by. And of course this is nothing new. Over the past two centuries, the famed piazza has developed an unmatched power to embody Americans' deepest anxieties and sincerest hopes. The need to establish Washington as a national hero engendered the prints of and pilgrimages to Mount Vernon in the eighteenth century. The impulse to save the union galvanized its preservation in the mid-nineteenth century. The desire for sectional reconciliation after a devastating civil war inspired its replicas at the turn of the twentieth century. The hope to sell goods propelled its commercialization in the mid-twentieth century. What Americans project onto Mount Vernon's image will continue to change. And it will be ready for whatever we have for it.

Notes

Abbreviations

ER-MVLA	Early Records of the MVLA, NLSGW
MVLA AR	Annual Report of the Mount Vernon Ladies' Association, NLSGW
MVLA Minutes	Minutes of the Grand Council of the Mount Vernon Ladies' Association, NLSGW
NARA	National Archives and Records Administration, College Park (Archives II Reference Section)
NLSGW	Fred W. Smith National Library for the Study of George Washington at Mount Vernon
PMVLA	Papers of the Mount Vernon Ladies' Association, NLSGW
SEAR	Sesqui-Centennial Exhibition Association Records, City Archives, Philadelphia

Introduction

1. American Village Citizenship Trust, "A Brief History of the American Village," www .americanvillage.org/site/PageServer?pagename=gen_about_history.

2. Tom Walker, conversation with author, 12 August 2013.

3. "Reclaiming American Memory and Identity, Overcoming America's National Amnesia," special issue, *American Village Liberty Journal,* Constitution Day 2012.

4. American Village Citizenship Trust, *Keeping the Republic: The American Village in the Words of Founder Tom Walker* (Montevallo, AL: American Village Citizenship Trust, 2012), 15.

5. American Village Citizenship Trust, "A Brief History of the American Village," www .americanvillage.org/site/PageServer?pagename=gen_about_history.

6. On the history of this perspective, see Ken I. Kersch, "Ecumenicalism through Constitutionalism: The Discursive Development of Constitutional Conservatism in National Review, 1955–1980," *Studies in American Political Development* 25, no. 1 (2011): 1–31. See also Jill Lepore, *The Whites of Their Eyes: The Tea Party's Revolution and the Battle over American History* (Princeton: Princeton University Press, 2010).

7. See Maurice Halbwachs, *The Collective Memory,* trans. Francis J. Ditter Jr. and Vida Yazdi Ditter (New York: Harper and Row, 1980); Eric Hobsbawm and Terence Ranger, *The Invention of Tradition* (Cambridge: Cambridge University Press, 1983); David Lowenthal, *The Past Is a Foreign Country* (Cambridge: Cambridge University Press, 1985); and Michael Kammen, *Mystic Chords of Memory: The Transformation of Tradition in American Culture* (New York: Knopf, 1991).

8. See Charles B. Hosmer Jr., *Presence of the Past: A History of the Preservation Movement in the United States before Williamsburg* (New York: Putnam's Sons, 1965); Patricia West, *Domesticating History* (Washington, DC: Smithsonian Institution Press, 1999); and James M. Lindgren, *Preserving the Old Dominion* (Charlottesville: University Press of Virginia, 1993). The exact date on which the MVLA actually "owned" Mount Vernon is surprisingly difficult to pinpoint. John Augustine Washington III moved out of the house and put it into the women's care before they took possession of the deed. By July 1859, the organization was overseeing repairs on the building ("Repairs at Mt. Vernon: The Work Begun," *Mount Vernon Record,* 2 no. 1 [July 1859]: 19). Ann Pamela Cunningham proclaimed in October 1859 that the MVLA had made its last payment on the purchase price, but liens on the property made it impossible for Washington to technically sell it to the organization (Ann Pamela Cunningham, "Mount Vernon: To the Officers and Members of the Mount Vernon Ladies' Association of the Union," *Mount Vernon Record* 2, no. 4 [October 1859]: 84). The MVLA did not legally acquire the deed to Mount Vernon until 1868, after Washington's death (notes dating 12 May 1868 through 13 May 1869, Box 9, Legal Documents, ER-MVLA). Mount Vernon typically gives the date of possession as 1858—the year that the MVLA made its first payment and John Augustine Washington agreed to sell—but 1859 was the year in which the MVLA started to make changes to the site and proclaimed ownership.

9. See Walter Benjamin, "The Work of Art in the Age of Mechanical Reproduction," (1936; repr. in *Illuminations,* ed. Hannah Arendt, trans. Harry Zohn [New York: Schocken, 1968]), 217–52; Jean Baudrillard, *Simulacra and Simulation,* trans. Sheila Faria Glaser (Ann Arbor: University of Michigan Press, 1994); Jean Baudrillard, *America,* trans. Chris Turner (London: Verso, 1988); and Miles Orvell, *The Real Thing: Imitation and Authenticity in American Culture, 1880–1940* (Chapel Hill: University of North Carolina Press, 1989).

10. Karal Ann Marling, *George Washington Slept Here: Colonial Revivals and American Culture, 1876–1986* (Cambridge: Harvard University Press, 1988); Barry Schwartz, *George Washington: The Making of an American Symbol* (New York: Free Press, 1987); Edward G. Lengel, *Inventing George Washington: America's Founder, in Myth and Memory* (New York: HarperCollins, 2011).

11. See Robert F. Dalzell Jr. and Lee Baldwin Dalzell, *George Washington's Mount Vernon: At Home in Revolutionary America* (New York: Oxford University Press, 1998); Joseph Manca, *George Washington's Eye: Landscape, Architecture, and Design at Mount Vernon* (Baltimore: Johns Hopkins University Press, 2012); and Mac Griswold, *Washington's Gardens at Mount Vernon: Landscape of the Inner Man* (Boston: Houghton Mifflin, 1999).

12. The term "Colonial Revival" is capitalized throughout this book in keeping with the style used in the University of Virginia Press's Buildings of the United States series. This does not imply, however, that the Colonial Revival should be interpreted as an aesthetic movement of architecture that happened in the past. It is an attitude toward early American history that is still very much alive in many facets of the nation's material life today.

1. Prints and Pilgrimage

1. Although Washington called his house the "mansion" and its surrounding land the "mansion house farm," the increasingly interested public usually referred to the building simply as "Mount Vernon" (see George Washington's December 1793 survey of the property as pictured and discussed in Adam T. Erby, "Designing the Beautiful: George Washington's Landscape Improvements, 1784–1787," in *The General in the Garden: George Washington's Landscape at Mount Vernon,* ed. Susan P. Schoelwer [Mount Vernon, VA: NLSGW for the Mount Vernon Ladies' Association, 2015], 20–21).

2. George Washington to David Stuart, 15 June 1790, *The Papers of George Washington Digital Edition,* ed. Theodore J. Crackel et al. (Charlottesville: University of Virginia Press, Rotunda, 2007–).

3. George Washington to William Pearce, 23 November 1794, Electronic Text Center, University of Virginia Library, "The Writings of George Washington from the Original Manuscripts," http://etext.virginia.edu/toc/modeng/public/WasFi34.html.

4. See Dalzell and Dalzell, *George Washington's Mount Vernon;* Griswold, *Washington's Gardens at Mount Vernon;* Mesick, Cohen, Waite Architects, "Mount Vernon Historic Structure Report, Prepared for the Mount Vernon Ladies' Association of the Union, February 1993," NLSGW; and John Milner Associates, Inc., "Mount Vernon Estate and Gardens: Cultural Landscape Study, Prepared for Mount Vernon Ladies' Association, November 2004," NLSGW.

5. See Manca, *George Washington's Eye.*

6. Ibid., 50–52.

7. Erby, "Designing the Beautiful," 32–34.

8. See Carol Borchert Cadou, *The George Washington Collection: Fine and Decorative Arts at Mount Vernon* (New York: Hudson Hills, 2006), 206–7. On Savage, see Louisa Dresser, "Edward Savage, 1761–1817," *Art in America* 40, no. 4 (Autumn 1952): 157–212; and Ellen G. Miles, *American Paintings of the Eighteenth Century* (Washington, DC: National Gallery of Art, 1995), 145–60.

9. See Mantle Fielding, "Edward Savage's Portraits of Washington," *Pennsylvania Magazine of History and Biography* 48, no. 3 (1924): 194–96.

10. *Digital Encyclopedia of George Washington,* s.v. "Palladian Window," by Lydia Mattice Brandt, www.mountvernon.org/research-collections/digital-encyclopedia/article/palladian -window/.

11. List of works exhibited at the Columbian Gallery, New York, 6 April 1802, MVLA Curatorial Files, Mount Vernon.

12. Ibid.; William Dunlap, *A History of the Rise and Progress of The Arts of Design in the United States,* vol. 1 (1834; rev. ed., Boston: C. E. Goodspeed, 1918), 381.

13. "Columbian Gallery," *Gazette of the United States* (Philadelphia), 22 February 1796. See also Harold E. Dickson, *John Wesley Jarvis, American Painter, 1780–1840. With a Checklist of His Works* (New York: New York Historical Society, 1949), 38.

14. Scott E. Casper, "First First Family: Seventy Years with Edward Savage's *The Washington Family,*" *Imprint* 24, no. 2 (Autumn 1999): 2–15.

15. Originally attributed to Francis Guy, these pictures were sold with an attribution of Edward Savage in 1997 (see *Important American Furniture: Including Silver, Folk Art, Prints and Decorative Arts,* Christie's New York auction catalogue [January 1997]: 148–49).

16. See Phoebe Lloyd Jacobs, "John James Barralet and the Apotheosis of George Washington," *Winterthur Portfolio* 12 (1977): 131–32; and Patricia A. Anderson, *Promoted to Glory: The Apotheosis of George Washington* (Northampton, MA: Smith College Museum of Art, 1980). Edwin was closely acquainted with John Wesley Jarvis, an engraving apprentice of Savage who might have even helped to print some of Savage's works (see Dickson, *John Wesley Jarvis,* 43–49).

17. See Wendy C. Wick, *George Washington, An American Icon: The Eighteenth-Century Graphic Portraits* (Washington, DC: Barra Foundation, 1982), 156–57; Jacobs, "John James Barralet," 131; Mark Edward Thistlethwaite, "The Image of George Washington: Studies in Mid-Nineteenth-Century American History Painting" (Ph.D. diss., University of Pennsylvania, 1977), 190, ProQuest (302812461); Harold Holzer, *Washington and Lincoln Portrayed: National Icons in Popular Prints* (Jefferson, NC: McFarland, 1993), 33–36; and Davida Tenenbaum Deutsch, "Washington Memorial Prints," *Antiques* 111, no. 2 (February 1977): 328.

18. Wick, *An American Icon,* 157; Jacobs, "John James Barralet," 131.

19. G. I. Parkyns, *Sketches of Select American Scenery* (Philadelphia: printed by John Ormrod, 1799). See also Eleanor M. McPeck, "George Isham Parkyns: Artist and Landscape Architect, 1749–1820," *Quarterly Journal of the Library of Congress* 30, no. 3 (July 1973): 171–82; I. N. Stokes and Daniel C. Haskell, *American Historical Prints: Early Views of American Cities, etc. from the Phelps Stokes and Other Collections* (New York: New York Public Library, 1932), 39–40; and Robert L. Harley, "George Washington Lived Here: Some Early Prints of Mount Vernon, Part I," *Antiques* 47, no. 3 (March 1945): 104.

20. Adam Erby, associate curator, Mount Vernon, e-mail message to author, 15 March 2015.

21. See E. McSherry Fowble, *Two Centuries of Prints in America, 1680–1880: A Selective Catalogue of the Winterthur Museum Collection* (Charlottesville: University Press of Virginia, 1987), 394.

22. See David Howard and John Ayers, *China for the West: Chinese Porcelain & Other*

Decorative Arts for Export Illustrated from the Mottahedeh Collection, vol. 2 (London: Sotheby Parke Bernet, 1978), 495–96.

23. See Arlene M. Palmer, *A Winterthur Guide to Chinese Export Porcelain* (New York: Crown, 1976), 22–26; and Homer Eaton Keyes, "Lowestoft: Exclusively American," in *Chinese Export Porcelain: An Historical Survey,* ed. Elinor Gordon (New York: Main Street/ Universe, 1977), 115–19.

24. See Jonathan Goldstein, *Philadelphia and the China Trade, 1682–1846: Commercial, Cultural, and Attitudinal Effects* (University Park: Pennsylvania State University Press, 1978).

25. *Chinese Export Porcelain from the Private Collection of Elinor Gordon,* Sotheby's New York auction catalogue (January 2010): 33; Palmer, *A Winterthur Guide,* 132.

26. See Nola O. Hill, "American History on Liverpool and Staffordshire," *Antiques* 64 (October 1953): 290–94.

27. Ellouise Baker Larsen, *American Historical Views on Staffordshire China,* 3rd ed. (New York: Dover, 1975), 18–19, 90–91.

28. See Emily T. Cooperman and Lea Carson Sherk, *William Birch: Picturing the American Scene* (Philadelphia: University of Pennsylvania Press, 2011), 129–59.

29. See Steven P. Petrucelli and Kenneth A. Sposato, *American Banjo Clocks* (Cranbury, NJ: Adams Brown, 1995), ii–iv.

30. See ibid., 99.

31. Rosemarie Zagarri, ed., *David Humphreys' "Life of General Washington" with George Washington's "Remarks"* (Athens: University of Georgia Press, 1991), 40. Washington consistently called the space the "New Room" (see Esther C. White, "The New Room: What's in a Name?," www.mountvernon.org/the-estate-gardens/the-mansion/the-new-room/the-new -room-whats-in-a-name/).

32. Jedidiah Morse, *The American Geography; or, A View of the Present Situation of the United States of America* (Elizabethtown, NJ: Shepard Kollock, 1789), 127–32; Thomas Condie, "Memoirs of George Washington, Esq., Late President of the United States," *Philadelphia Monthly Magazine* 1 (January, February, May, June 1798).

33. Parkyns, *Sketches of Select American Scenery.*

34. See Charlene Mires, *Independence Hall in American Memory* (Philadelphia: University of Pennsylvania Press, 2002), 1–15.

35. William Russell Birch, *The Country Seats of the United States* (1808; repr., Philadelphia: University of Pennsylvania Press, 2009), 43.

36. Ibid., 54.

37. See also Cooperman and Sherk, *William Birch,* 30–34.

38. "Anecdotes of General Washington, Written in 1788," *American Museum* 11, no. 4 (April 1792): 155.

39. "The Fine Arts: For the Port Folio," *Port-Folio* 2, no. 16 (24 April 1802): 127.

40. The terms "neat" and "plain" (especially in concert as a phrase) were often used to

describe the house and worked as a kind of shorthand to refer to a restrained architectural aesthetic that derived from Georgian architecture in England (see Carl R. Lounsbury, *The Courthouses of Early Virginia: An Architectural History* [Charlottesville: University of Virginia Press, 2005], 103; and Manca, *George Washington's Eye*, 3–11).

41. Zagarri, *David Humphreys' "Life of General Washington,"* 35. This quotation is also published in Morse, *The American Geography,* 131; and Thomas Condie, "Memoirs of General Washington, Esq, Late President of the United States," *Philadelphia Monthly Magazine* 1, no. 6 (June 1798): 297.

42. Samuel Knox, "An Ode, Most Respectfully Inscribed to His Excellency, General Washington, on Being Chosen President of the United States," *American Museum* 6, no. 1 (July 1789): 85.

43. Schwartz, *The Making of an American Symbol,* 120–22; Gary Wills, *Cincinnatus: George Washington and the Enlightenment* (New York: Doubleday, 1984), 13; Catherine L. Albanese, *Sons of the Fathers: The Civil Religion of the American Revolution* (Philadelphia: Temple University Press, 1976), 153–54.

44. Schwartz, *The Making of an American Symbol,* 41–44; Wills, *Cincinnatus,* 3–13.

45. On the cult of Washington, see Lawrence J. Friedman, *Inventors of the Promised Land* (New York: Knopf, 1975); Albanese, *Sons of the Fathers;* Schwartz, *The Making of an American Symbol;* Wills, *Cincinnatus;* Daniel J. Boorstin, "The Mythologizing of George Washington," in *George Washington: A Profile,* ed. James Morton Smith (New York: Hill and Wang, 1969), 262–85; and Marcus Cunliffe, *George Washington: Man and Monument* (Boston: Little, Brown, 1958).

46. For the Houdon sculpture, see Wills, *Cincinnatus,* 226–35; and Maurie D. McInnis, "Revisiting Cincinnatus: Houdon's *George Washington,*" in *Shaping the Body Politic: Art and Political Formation in Early America,* ed. McInnis and Louis P. Nelson (Charlottesville: University of Virginia Press, 2011), 128–61.

47. See Wills, *Cincinnatus,* 217–41.

48. Thomas Paine, "An Eulogy on the Life of General Washington, 2 January 1800," in *Eulogies and Orations on the Life and Death of General George Washington, First President of the United States of America* (Boston: printed by Manning and Loring, 1800), 64.

49. "Explanation of the Frontispiece," *Philadelphia Magazine and Review* 1, no. 1 (January 1799): v. The print was based on an illuminated transparency first exhibited in March 1797 (see "Domestic Intelligence," *Literary Museum* [1 February 1797]: 109; and Laura Auricchio, "Two Versions of General Washington's Resignation: Politics, Commerce, and Visual Culture in 1790s Philadelphia," *Eighteenth-Century Studies* 44, no. 3 [Spring 2011]: 383–400). On the print, see Wick, *An American Icon,* 54–58, 133–35; Schwartz, *The Making of an American Symbol,* 138–39; and Thistlethwaite, "The Image of George Washington," 123.

50. "Explanation of the Frontispiece," v.

51. See Isaac Weld Jr., *View of Mount Vernon, Seat of General Washington* (London:

J. Stockdale, 18 December 1798); and Isaac Weld Jr., *Travels through the States of North America, and the Provinces of Upper and Lower Canada, during the Years 1795, 1796, and 1797*, vol. 1, 2nd ed. (London: J. Stockdale, 1799), 92.

52. Jean B. Lee, "Historical Memory, Sectional Strife, and the American Mecca: Mount Vernon, 1783–1853," *Virginia Magazine of History and Biography* 109, no. 3 (2001): 258.

53. See Albanese, *Sons of the Fathers*, 168–71; and Boorstin, "The Mythologizing of George Washington."

54. "Mount Vernon," *Family Magazine* 4 (1836): 281.

55. "Remains of Gen. Washington," *National Register*, 30 March 1816, 65 (emphasis in original).

56. John F. Sears, *Sacred Places: American Tourist Attractions in the Nineteenth Century* (New York: Oxford University Press, 1989), 3–9.

57. See Thomas A. Chambers, *Memories of War: Visiting Battlegrounds and Bonefields in the Early American Republic* (Ithaca: Cornell University Press, 2012), 6–12.

58. Scott E. Casper, *Sarah Johnson's Mount Vernon: The Forgotten History of an American Shrine* (New York: Hill and Wang, 2008), 65.

59. "A Visit to Mount Vernon," *Liberator* 19, no. 29 (20 July 1849): 114.

60. Each of Washington's descendants at Mount Vernon owned slaves.

61. See Jean B. Lee, "Jane C. Washington, Family, and Nation at Mount Vernon, 1830–1855," in *Women Shaping the South: Creating and Confronting Change*, ed. Angela Boswell and Judith McArthur (Columbia: University of Missouri Press, 2005), 30–49; and Lee, "Historical Memory, Sectional Strife, and the American Mecca," 281–86.

62. See Casper, *Sarah Johnson's Mount Vernon*, 29–36; Lee, "Historical Memory, Sectional Strife, and the American Mecca," 282–83.

63. "Mount Vernon—Washington's Tomb," *Zion's Herald* 2, no. 39 (22 September 1824): 4.

64. Samuel Irenaeus Prime, "A Pilgrimage to the Tomb of Washington," *New York Observer and Chronicle* 24, no. 26 (27 June 1846): 1.

65. Barbara J. Mitnick, "Parallel Visions: The Literary and Visual Images of George Washington," in *George Washington: American Symbol*, ed. Mitnick (New York: Hudson Hills, 1999), 63–65; Friedman, *Inventors of the Promised Land*, 68–70. See also James Morton Smith, introduction to *George Washington: A Profile*, ed. Smith (New York: Hill and Wang, 1969), vii–xxiv; and Barry Schwartz, "Social Change and Collective Memory: The Democratization of George Washington," *American Sociological Review* 56, no. 2 (April 1991): 231.

66. See David P. Handlin, *The American Home: Architecture and Society, 1815–1915* (Boston: Little, Brown, 1979), 4–26; Glenna Matthews, *"Just a Housewife": The Rise and Fall of Domesticity in America* (New York: Oxford University Press, 1987), 3–65; Jan Cohn, *The Palace or the Poor House: The American House as a Cultural Symbol* (East Lansing: Michigan State University Press, 1979); Clifford Edward Clark Jr., *The American Family Home, 1800–1960* (Chapel Hill: University of North Carolina Press, 1986), 3–71; and Colleen McDannell, *The*

Christian Home in Victorian America, 1840–1900 (Bloomington: Indiana University Press, 1986). For a leading contemporary example, see Catherine E. Beecher and Harriet Beecher Stowe, *The American Woman's Home; or, Principles of Domestic Science; Being a Guide to the Formation and Maintenance of Economical, Healthful, Beautiful, and Christian Homes* (New York: J. B. Ford, 1869).

67. Messrs Abbott, *The Mount Vernon Reader: A Course of Reading Lessons, Selected with Reference to Their Moral Influence on the Hearts and Lives of the Young* (Boston: Otis, Broaders, 1838).

68. Ibid., vi.

69. Barry Schwartz, "George Washington: A New Man for a New Century," in *George Washington: American Symbol,* ed. Barbara J. Mitnick (New York: Hudson Hills, 1999), 123–27.

70. See Lengel, *Inventing George Washington,* 18–25; Mitnick, "Parallel Visions," 63–65; and Philip Levy, *Where the Cherry Tree Grew: The Story of Ferry Farm, George Washington's Boyhood Home* (New York: St. Martin's, 2013).

71. See Schwartz, "George Washington: A New Man for a New Century"; Barbara J. Mitnick, *The Changing Image of George Washington* (New York: Fraunces Tavern Museum, 1989), 26–39; and Thistlethwaite, "The Image of George Washington," 40–70.

72. See Edward F. Heite, "Chapman Paints the Washington Legend," *Virginia Cavalcade* 17, no. 3 (Winter 1968): 20–29.

73. "The Artist's Studio," *New York Mirror* 12, no. 33 (21 March 1835): 301–2; Edward F. Heite, "Painter of the Old Dominion," *Virginia Cavalcade* 17, no. 3 (Winter 1968): 13; Heite, "Chapman Paints the Washington Legend," 29; William P. Campbell, *John Gadsby Chapman, Painter and Illustrator* (Washington, DC: National Gallery of Art, 1962), 10–12.

74. Chapman's image was used again in *Homes of American Statesmen: With Anecdotal, Personal, and Descriptive Sketches* (New York: Putnam, 1853), 16.

75. Thistlethwaite, "The Image of George Washington," 31–32; Mark Thistlethwaite, "Picturing the Past: Junius Brutus Stearns' Paintings of George Washington," *Arts in Virginia* 25, nos. 2/3 (1985): 12–23.

76. Mitnick, "Parallel Visions," 65.

77. Thistlethwaite, "The Image of George Washington," 40–47. See also William M. S. Rasmussen and Robert S. Tilton, *George Washington: The Man behind the Myths* (Charlottesville: University Press of Virginia, 1999), 80–84.

78. Thistlethwaite, "The Image of George Washington," 126–29; Maurie D. McInnis, "The Most Famous Plantation of All: The Politics of Painting Mount Vernon," in *The Plantation in American Art,* ed. Angela D. Mack and Stephen G. Hoffius (Columbia: University of South Carolina Press, 2008), 86–101.

79. J. Frost, *Pictorial Life of George Washington: Embracing a Complete History of the Seven Years' War, the Revolutionary War, the Formation of the Federal Constitution and the Administration of Washington* (Richmond: Harrold and Murray, 1847), 116–17.

80. See Schwartz, *The Making of an American Symbol,* 124.

81. Charles H. Ruggles to Sarah C. Ruggles, 28 April 1822, qtd. in Jean B. Lee, ed., *Experiencing Mount Vernon: Eyewitness Accounts, 1784–1865* (Charlottesville: University of Virginia Press, 2006), 116–17.

82. See Rubil Morales Vasquez, "Redeeming the Sacred Pledge: The Plans to Bury George Washington in the Nation's Capital," in *Establishing Congress: The Removal to Washington D.C., and the Election of 1800,* ed. Donald Kennon (Athens: Ohio University Press, 2005), 148–89; Blanche M. G. Linden, *Silent City on a Hill: Picturesque Landscapes of Memory and Boston's Mount Auburn Cemetery* (Amherst: University of Massachusetts Press, 2007), 99–101; and Karal Ann Marling, "The United States Capitol as Mausoleum: Or, Who's Buried in Washington's Tomb?," in *A Republic for the Ages: The United States Capitol and the Political Culture of the Early Republic,* ed. Donald R. Kennon (Charlottesville: University Press of Virginia, 1999), 448–66.

83. For Washington's wishes regarding his burial, see George Washington's Last Will and Testament, 9 July 1799, www.mountvernon.org/educational-resources/primary-sources-2 /article/george-washingtons-1799-will-and-testament/.

84. "Extract of a Letter from a New England Traveller, Dated, Mount Vernon, 28 May, 1813," *Literary and Philosophical Repertory* 1, no. 4 (1 May 1813): 308.

85. "Miscellany: An Excursion," *Christian Herald and Seaman's Magazine* 8, no. 15 (15 December 1821): 449. See also "Visit to Mount Vernon, Washington, 28th Dec. 1822," *National Pilot* 2, no. 71 (23 January 1823): 1; L., "Visit to Mount Vernon," *New-England Galaxy and United States Literary Advertiser* 10, no. 482 (5 January 1827): 2; and "Extracts from a Journal," *Juvenile Miscellany* 3, no. 3 (January 1828): 314.

86. "La Fayette [*sic*] at the Tomb of Washington," *National Intelligencer* 1, no. 41 (9 November 1824): 163. For a complete account of Lafayette's visit to the United States, see John Foster, *A Sketch of the Tour of General Lafayette, on His Late Visit to the United States, 1824* . . . (Portland: A. W. Thayer, 1824).

87. "A View of the Sepulchre [*sic*] of Washington," *Saturday Evening Post* 307 (16 June 1827): 2; "The Remains of General Washington," *Banner of the Constitution* 1, no. 32 (7 April 1830): 254.

88. William Strickland, *Tomb of Washington at Mount Vernon* (Philadelphia: Carey and Hart, 1840), 27, 39–40.

89. Ibid., 41–44.

90. Lee, "Historical Memory, Sectional Strife, and the American Mecca," 278.

91. Ibid., 278–88. For period accounts, see "Visit to Mount Vernon, Washington, 25th Dec. 1822," *National Pilot;* "Chronicle," *Niles' Weekly Register* 22, no. 566 (13 July 1822): 320; and "Grave of Washington," *Dwight's American Magazine* 2, no. 44 (1846): 701.

92. Harriet Martineau, "Retrospect of Western Travel," *Albion* 6, no. 12 (24 March 1838): 92.

93. "Purchase of Mt. Vernon," *Horticulturalist and Journal of Rural Art and Rural Taste* 2,

no. 10 (April 1848): 481; "A Visit to Mount Vernon," *Liberator;* "Mount Vernon," *Columbian Lady's and Gentleman's Magazine* 10, no. 2 (February 1849): 87; Robert Criswell, *Godey's Lady's Book* 39 (October 1849): 247; C. H. Brainard, "A Visit to Mount Vernon," *Prisoner's Friend: A Monthly Magazine Devoted to Criminal Reform, Philosophy, Science, Literature, and Art* 1, no. 12 (1 August 1849): 538.

94. "A Visit to Mount Vernon," *Liberator.*

95. H. F. H., "Washington's House," *Ladies' Companion,* January 1840, 103.

96. See "From the Editor," *Trumpet and Universalist Magazine* 19, no. 51 (5 June 1847): 202; and "Purchase of Mt. Vernon," *Horticulturalist and Journal of Rural Art and Rural Taste.*

97. "Review of New Book by Alexander H. Everett," *New-England Galaxy and United States Literary Advertiser* 10, no. 498 (27 April 1827): 2.

98. Ibid.; "Removal of Washington's Remains," *New-England Galaxy and United States Literary Advertiser* 15, no. 750 (25 February 1832): 2; H. F. H., "Washington's House"; "Mount Vernon," *The Columbian Lady's and Gentleman's Magazine;* Criswell, *Godey's Lady's Book.*

99. On Greenough, see Nathalia Wright, *Horatio Greenough: The First American Sculptor* (Philadelphia: University of Pennsylvania Press, 1963).

100. Alexander H. Everett, "Greenough's Statue of Washington," in *A Memorial of Horatio Greenough,* by Henry J. Tuckerman (1853; repr., New York: Benjamin Bloom, 1968), 220; "The Sculptor," *Parley's Magazine* (1 January 1838): 223; "Greenough's Statue of Washington," *Christian Register and Boston Observer* 20, no. 39 (25 September 1841): 156; "Greenough's Statue of Washington," *Monthly Chronicle of Events, Discoveries, Improvements, and Opinions* (September 1841): 460; "Greenough's Statue of Washington," *Boston Cultivator* 3, no. 52 (25 December 1841): 4.

101. See Wills, *Cincinnatus,* 68–74; Richard H. Saunders, *Horatio Greenough: An American Sculptor's Drawings* (Middlebury, VT: Middlebury College Museum of Art, 1999), 13; and Wright, *The First American Sculptor,* 142–59.

102. Georgy Porgy, "Washington," *New York Herald* 56, no. 263 (6 December 1841): 3 (emphasis in original).

103. Leonard Jarvis to Washington Allston, 6 June 1834, qtd. in Wright, *The First American Sculptor,* 129.

104. Declaration by the Washington National Monument Society qtd. in Frederick L. Harvey, *History of the Washington Monument and Washington National Monument Society* (Washington, DC: Government Printing Office, 1903), 25–26. Mills had already created a monument to Washington in Baltimore (see J. Jefferson Miller II, "The Designs for the Washington Monument in Baltimore," *Journal of the Society of Architectural Historians* 23, no. 1 [March 1964]: 19–28).

105. "Description of the Design of the Washington National Monument, to Be Erected at the Seat of the General Government of the United States of America, in Honor of 'The

Father of His Country," and the Worthy Compatriots of the Revolution," qtd. in Harvey, *History of the Washington National Monument,* 26–28.

106. See Kirk Savage, *Monument Wars: Washington, DC, the National Mall, and the Transformation of the Memorial Landscape* (Berkeley: University of California Press, 2009), 76–77; and Kirk Savage, "The Self-Made Monument: George Washington and the Fight to Erect a National Memorial," *Winterthur Portfolio* 22, no. 4 (Winter 1987): 234–36.

107. James Jackson Jarves, *Art-Hints: Architecture, Sculpture, and Painting* (London: Sampson Low, Son, 1855), 308.

2. "Keep It the Home of Washington!"

1. See Edward Everett, *The Mount Vernon Papers* (New York: D. Appleton, 1860), 4.

2. Thomas P. Rossiter, "Mount Vernon, Past and Present: What Shall Be Its Destiny?," *Crayon* 5, no. 9 (September 1858): 243–52. Rossiter visited Mount Vernon in preparation for a small series of paintings begun in 1857, including the massive *Washington and Lafayette at Mount Vernon.*

3. See Steven Conn, "Rescuing the Homestead of the Nation: The MVLA and the Preservation of Mount Vernon," *Nineteenth Century Studies* 11 (1997): 71–93; West, *Domesticating History,* 1–38; and Lee, "Historical Memory, Sectional Strife, and the American Mecca," 293–300.

4. A group of Bostonians re-created the Benjamin Franklin birthplace, complete with interiors, in 1858 (see Jane C. Nylander, *Our Own Snug Fireside: Images of the New England Home, 1760–1860* [New York: Knopf, 1993], 15–18).

5. Lori D. Ginzberg, *Women and the Work of Benevolence: Morality, Politics, and Class in the Nineteenth-Century United States* (New Haven: Yale University Press, 1990).

6. On invalidism in the nineteenth century, see Lorna Duffin, "The Conspicuous Consumptive: Woman as an Invalid," in *The Nineteenth-Century Woman: Her Cultural and Physical World,* ed. Sara Delamont and Duffin (London: Croom Helm, 1978), 26–56; and Erika Ingelin Rozinek, "'We All Take Our Turn': Invalidism in American Culture, 1850–1910" (master's thesis, University of Delaware, 2003), ProQuest (250188820).

7. Qtd. in Grace King, *Mount Vernon on the Potomac* (New York: Macmillan, 1929), 19–22.

8. See Conn, "Rescuing the Homestead of the Nation," 71–78.

9. Cong. Globe., 33rd Cong., n.s. 4 (1853); "Mount Vernon," *New York Times,* 12 January 1854.

10. "Mount Vernon—to the Rescue!," *Mobile Tribune* (8 March 1854), reprinted in *An Appeal for the Future Preservation of the Home and Grave of Washington* (Philadelphia: T. K. and P. G. Collins, Printers, 1855), 20–21.

11. Americana, "Appeal to the Ladies of Philadelphia," *Philadelphia Evening Bulletin* (18 September 1854), reprinted in *An Appeal for the Future Preservation of the Home and Grave of Washington* (Philadelphia: T. K. and P. G. Collins, Printers, 1855), 4–5.

12. See "A Southern Matron," "To the Ladies of the South, for *The Enquirer*," undated clipping in Scrapbook 2, Box 14, Bound Manuscripts, 1853–1876, ER-MVLA.

13. Letter from a Southern Matron, *Pennsylvania Inquirer*, 10 April 1856, clipping in Scrapbook 2, Box 14, Bound Manuscripts, 1853–1876, ER-MVLA; Mount Vernon scrapbook kept by Anna Cora Ritchie, Box 4–5, ER-MVLA; Ann Pamela Cunningham to John Gilmer, 13 January 1855, ER-MVLA. See also Elizabeth R. Varon, *We Mean to Be Counted: White Women and Politics in Antebellum Virginia* (Chapel Hill: University of North Carolina Press, 1998), 126–27; and West, *Domesticating History*, 1–38.

14. "To the Daughters of Washington," *Southern Literary Messenger* 21, no. 5 (May 1855): 318 (my emphasis).

15. "The Ladies' Mount Vernon Association," *Godey's Lady's Book and Magazine* 51 (August 1855): 177.

16. "To the Daughters of Washington."

17. "The 'Monthly Report' to the Mount Vernon Association of the Union," *Southern Literary Messenger* 21, no. 9 (September 1855): 575. Because of Ann Pamela Cunningham's friendship with a number of Philadelphia women, the Pennsylvania state committee was one of the earliest to form after she extended her appeal to women nationwide (see "From Cape May, Correspondence of the Pennsylvania Inquirer," 28 July 1855, clipping in Box 10, Printed and Photographic, 1848–1875, ER-MVLA; and "A Meeting of National Interest," 18 October 1855, clipping from Pennsylvania newspaper in Scrapbook 2, Box 14, Bound Manuscripts, 1853–1876, ER-MVLA).

18. "An Act to Incorporate the MVLA of the Union and to Authorize the Purchase of a Part of Mount Vernon, passed March 17, 1856," Box 10, Printed and Photographic, 1848–1875, ER-MVLA.

19. "The Southern Matron's letter to Virginia, addressed to Mr. Gilmer, Corresponding Secretary of the Mt. Vernon Association," *Southern Literary Messenger* 21, no. 5 (May 1855): 318.

20. "Editor's Table," *Godey's Lady's Book and Magazine* 51 (August 1855): 177.

21. "Purchase of Mount Vernon—Cheering Prospects," clipping from a New York newspaper featuring an article reprinted from the *Richmond Enquirer* (27 March 1857) in Scrapbook 2, Box 14, Bound Manuscripts, 1853–1876, ER-MVLA; "Mount Vernon," undated clipping in New York Scrapbook, 1858–1859, Box 4–6, ER-MVLA. See also Casper, *Sarah Johnson's Mount Vernon*, 71–72; and Edward P. Alexander, *Museum Masters: Their Museums and Their Influence* (Walnut Creek, CA: AltaMira, 1995), 180–81.

22. John Augustine Washington to John A. Gilmer, 26 July 1854, Folder "1854 July 14–Oct. 4 Corres. between John A. Gilmer from *Richmond Whig*," Box 10, Printed and Photographic, 1848–1875, ER-MVLA.

23. "Purchase of Mount Vernon—Cheering Prospects." See also "Mr. John A. Washington

and the Ladies Mount Vernon Association—The Ladies Movement All Right," *New York Herald* undated clipping in Scrapbook 2, Box 14, Bound Manuscripts, 1853–1876, ER-MVLA.

24. See Edward Everett," *Historical Magazine* 9, no. 3 (March 1865): 72.

25. *Digital Encyclopedia of George Washington,* s.v. "Edward Everett (1794–1865)," by Lydia Mattice Brandt, www.mountvernon.org/educational-resources/encyclopedia/edward-everett#. The exact amount raised by Everett's lectures was $50,042.48. Many sources claim that he raised upward of $68,000, but this is an aggregate sum, including proceeds from the lectures as well as donations he solicited (see Cunningham, "Mount Vernon: To the Officers and Members of the MVLA," 84).

26. Edward Everett, "The Character of Washington," *Oration on the Character of Washington by Hon. Edward Everett* (New York: Little, Brown for the MVLA, 1913), 24–25.

27. See Ronald F. Reid, "Edward Everett's 'The Character of Washington,'" *Southern Speech Journal* 22 (1957): 144–56.

28. These debates are detailed in West, *Domesticating History,* 18–26; and Varon, *We Meant to Be Counted,* 130–34.

29. "Mount Vernon Association," undated clipping in Mount Vernon scrapbook kept by Anna Cora Ritchie, Box 4–5, ER-MVLA.

30. "Constitutions and By-Laws of the Ladies Mount Vernon Association of the United States of America," approved by Virginia governor Henry A. Wise, 5 January 1858, Box 10, ER-MVLA.

31. The MVLA paid Washington eighteen thousand dollars toward the purchase price on 6 April 1858, after the passage of the act of incorporation by the Virginia state legislature (see Cunningham, "Mount Vernon: To the Officers and Members of the MVLA," 84).

32. See Act of Incorporation of the MVLA, 19 March 1858, Box 10, ER-MVLA; John Augustine Washington to Ann Pamela Cunningham, 13 March 1858, qtd. in *Catalogue of the Centennial Exhibition Commemorating the Founding of the Mount Vernon Ladies' Association of the Union, 1853–1953* (Mount Vernon: MVLA, 1953), 27. See also West, *Domesticating History,* 25.

33. Ann Pamela Cunningham to John Augustine Washington, 12 March 1858, and John Augustine Washington to Ann Pamela Cunningham, 19 March 1858, published in "Mount Vernon to Be Purchased by the Ladies," *Daily Richmond Enquirer,* 3 April 1858, Folder "1858 June Newspaper article on Madame LeVert and the MVLA," Box 10, Printed and Photographic, 1848–1875, ER-MVLA.

34. Agreement between John Augustine Washington and MVLA, 6 April 1858, Box 9, ER-MVLA.

35. Ann Pamela Cunningham to Margaret Comegys, n.d., Book 2, Box "Correspondence (Bound Manuscripts: Letterbooks, Extracts, 1858–1876)," ER-MVLA; "Mount Vernonism," *New York Times,* 25 December 1858.

36. This encouraged a sense of healthy competition among the states and the vice regents as each hoped to demonstrate their devotion to Washington (see Abba Isabella Little, "Appeal of the Mount Vernon Association, to the Ladies of the State of Maine," *Mount Vernon Record* 1, no. 4 [October 1858]: 1).

37. See "Facts for Consideration," *Mount Vernon Record* 1, no. 4 (October 1858): 26; and Anna Cora Ritchie, "The Purchase of Mt. Vernon," *Mount Vernon Record* 1, no. 3 (September 1858): 19.

38. For examples, see "Home of the Washington Family on the Rappahannock," *Mount Vernon Record* 1, no. 5 (November 1858): 1; "Head-Quarters at Cambridge," *Mount Vernon Record* 1, no. 9 (March 1859): 1; "Washington, Franklin, and Christ Church, Philada.," *Mount Vernon Record* 2, no. 5 (November 1859): 106; "The Title to Mount Vernon," *Mount Vernon Record* 1, no. 11 (May 1859): 1; and "Washington Irving," *Mount Vernon Record* 1, no. 7 (January 1859): 61.

39. After the first volume of the *Mount Vernon Record* was completed in June 1859, the Association's publisher, Devereux and Co., did advertise a bound volume of the first year's newsletters with a "tinted frontispiece view of Mt. Vernon" (see "Now Read, Volume 1, Mt. Vernon Record," *Mount Vernon Record* 2, no. 2 [August 1859]: 29).

40. Undated clipping in Folder "1859 July Clipping from a Penna. paper on purchase of Mount Vernon," Box 10, Printed and Photographic, 1848–1875, ER-MVLA. See also "The Mount Vernon Fund—$158,333 already paid!," *Philadelphia Press,* 29 March 1859, clipping in Box 10, Printed and Photographic, 1848–1875, ER-MVLA. This article was also reprinted in the *Mount Vernon Record* 1, no. 1 (May 1859): 178.

41. The entire run of articles written by Everett for the *New York Ledger* was compiled, along with a handful of letters explaining the agreement, in Everett, *The Mount Vernon Papers.*

42. Hale used the journal to promote causes other than the MVLA's, despite the publisher's intent to keep the magazine neutral (see Patricia Okker, *Our Sister Editors: Sarah J. Hale and the Tradition of Nineteenth-Century American Women Editors* [Athens: University of Georgia Press, 1995], 51). On Hale's patriotism and her use of *Godey's* to promote it, see Joseph Michael Sommers, "*Godey's Lady's Book:* Sarah Hale and the Construction of Sentimental Nationalism," *College Literature* 37, no. 3 (Summer 2010): 43–61.

43. See "The Ladies' Mount Vernon Association," *Godey's Lady's Book and Magazine* 55 (July 1857): 81; "The MVLA of the Union," *Godey's Lady's Book and Magazine* 52 (June 1856): 557; "The Ladies' Mount Vernon Association," *Godey's Lady's Book and Magazine* 55 (October 1857): 369; and "Editor's Table: The Purchase of Mount Vernon," *Godey's Lady's Book* (June 1859): 560.

44. Benson J. Lossing to Mary Hamilton, 29 June 1858, ER-MVLA.

45. B. J. Lossing, *Pictorial Field-Book of the Revolution,* vol. 2 (New York: Harper Brothers,

1852), 414–19. See Harold E. Mahan, *Benson Lossing and Historical Writing in the United States: 1830–1890* (Westbrook, CT: Greenwood, 1996), 53–68. For more on Lossing, see David D. Van Tassel, "Benson J. Lossing: Pen and Pencil Historian," *American Quarterly* 6, no. 1 (Spring 1954): 32–44.

46. Benson J. Lossing, "Arlington House, the Seat of G. W. P. Custis, Esq.," *Harper's New Monthly Magazine* 7, no. 40 (September 1853): 434–54; Certification of Benson J. Lossing by George Washington Parke Custis, 24 March 1853, Microfilm Reel 4, Mount Vernon Washington Manuscripts, 1831–1870, NLSGW. Custis and Lossing's relationship led Custis's daughter, Mary Custis Lee, to ask Lossing to edit her father's memoirs for publication after his death at Arlington House in 1857 (see Benson J. Lossing, *Recollections and Private Memoirs of Washington, by His Adopted Son, George Washington Parke Custis, with a Memoir of the Author, by His Daughter; and Illustrative and Explanatory Notes* [Philadelphia: J. W. Bradley, 1861], 119–20; and Mary Custis Lee to Benson J. Lossing, 22 October 1858, Unowned Manuscripts, NLSGW).

47. A list of the members of New York's "Advisory Committee of Gentlemen" was published in the *Mount Vernon Record* 1, no. 3 (September 1858): 1. Lossing met with Ann Pamela Cunningham personally (see Mary Hamilton to Ann Pamela Cunningham, 23 April 1859, ER-MVLA; and Joseph Henry to Nancy Halsted, 17 March 1870, ER-MVLA). Mrs. Lossing raised more than five hundred dollars for the New York State committee (see Cash Book of the MVLA of the Union, New York, Box "MVLA Early Records," ER-MVLA).

48. B. J. L., "A Visit to Mount Vernon," undated clipping from Poughkeepsie, NY, newspaper in Box 10, Printed and Photographic, 1848–1875, ER-MVLA; "A Visit to Mount Vernon," *Harper's Weekly* 2, no. 79 (3 July 1858): 420–21; Benson J. Lossing to John Augustine Washington, 2 August 1858, Historic Manuscript Collection, NLSGW; Benson J. Lossing, *Mount Vernon and Its Associations, Historical, Biographical, and Pictorial* (New York: W. A. Townsend, 1859).

49. The first American architectural history is generally thought to be Louisa C. Tuthill, *History of Architecture from the Earliest Times: Its Present Condition in Europe and the United States* (Philadelphia: Lindsay and Blakiston, 1848). See Sarah Allaback, "Louisa Tuthill, Ithiel Town, and the Beginnings of Architectural History Writing in America," in *American Architects and Their Books to 1848,* ed. Kenneth Hafertepe and James F. O'Gorman (Amherst: University of Massachusetts Press, 2001), 199–216.

50. Lossing, *Mount Vernon and Its Associations,* 137. Charles Cecil Wall speculated that Lossing based this early chronology of the house on family tradition (see Wall, "Notes on the Early History of Mount Vernon," *William and Mary Quarterly,* 3rd ser., 2, no. 2 [April 1945]: 184–85).

51. John Augustine Washington to Benson J. Lossing, 14 August 1858, Unowned Manuscripts, NLSGW; Certification of Benson J. Lossing by George Washington Parke Custis.

52. After some of these articles were lost during the Civil War, Lossing's book served as a vital record of Washingtonia. Mount Vernon's curatorial staff continues to use Lossing's engravings in its restoration efforts (see Adam T. Erby, "George Washington's New Room: An American Vision," *Antiques & Fine Art Magazine* 13, no. 3 [Autumn 2014]: 118–25).

53. "*Mount Vernon and Its Associations, Historical, Biographical, and Pictorial* by Benson J. Lossing," *North American Review* 90, no. 186 (January 1860): 281–82. See also Mary Hamilton to Ann Pamela Cunningham, 23 April 1859, ER-MVLA.

54. Cunningham, "Mount Vernon: To the Officers and Members of the MVLA," 84.

55. *Mount Vernon Record* 2, no. 1 (July 1859): 1.

56. Cunningham, "Mount Vernon: To the Officers and Members of the MVLA of the Union," 84 (emphasis in original).

57. Conn, "Rescuing the Homestead of a Nation." See also James M. Lindgren, "'A New Departure in Historic, Patriotic Work': Personalism, Professionalism, and Conflicting Concepts of Material Culture in the Late Nineteenth and Early Twentieth Centuries," *Public Historian* 18, no. 2 (Spring 1996): 41–60.

58. "Mount Vernon," *Michigan Farmer* 2, no. 23 (9 June 1860): 182; "Mount Vernon," *Monthly Religious Magazine and Independent Journal* 24, no. 4 (October 1860): 229–31. See also "Trip to Mount Vernon," 11 October 1859, undated clipping in Box 10, Printed and Photographic, 1848–1875, ER-MVLA; "Honor to the Illustrious Dead," *North American Review* 87, no. 182 (January 1859): 52.

59. See Cunningham, "Mount Vernon: To the Officers and Members of the MVLA of the Union," 84.

60. Sarah Tracy to Margaretta Morse, 20 December 1860, ER-MVLA.

61. Ibid. Because of a tax snafu, the MVLA did not technically acquire the deed until after the war, and then from John Augustine Washington III's descendants (notes dating 12 May 1868 through 13 May 1869, Box 9, Legal Documents, ER-MVLA).

62. See Dorothy Troth Muir, *Presence of a Lady: Mount Vernon, 1861–1868* (Mount Vernon, VA: printed by Mount Vernon Publishing, 1946).

63. See West, *Domesticating History*, 32–34.

64. Sarah Tracy to Philoclea Eve, 22 August 1865, ER-MVLA. See also Sarah Tracy to Margaret Comegys, 1 July 1861, ER-MVLA; and Sarah Tracy to Anna Cora Ritchie, 22 January 1864, ER-MVLA.

65. Sarah Tracy to Ann Pamela Cunningham, 17 June 1861, ER-MVLA.

66. "Notes from the Capital," *Independent* 13, no. 676 (14 November 1861): 1.

67. Sarah Tracy to Margaret Comegys, 9 October 1861 and 29 June 1863, ER-MVLA.

68. "Mount Vernon to Be Confiscated," *New York Times,* 28 September 1861; "Mount Vernonism." The newspaper also picked up on a scandal involving Devereux and Co., the printer of the *Mount Vernon Record,* which was indicted for stealing thousands of dollars from a number of different clients.

69. Col. Forney, "The Mount Vernon Swindle—Miss Ann Pamela Cunningham a Secession Spy," *Western Reserve Chronicle* 45, no. 46 (2 July 1861): 1.

70. Manuscript reply by Mrs. Comegys to charges against Miss C. viz "Living at Mt. V.," Book 2, Box "Correspondence (Bound Manuscripts: Letterbooks, Extracts, 1858–1876)," ER-MVLA. See also Sarah Tracy to Margaret Comegys, 1 July 1861, ER-MVLA.

71. See Sarah Tracy to Margaretta Morse, 20 December 1860, ER-MVLA.

72. Sarah Tracy to Ann Pamela Cunningham, 1 December 1860, ER-MVLA.

73. Excerpt from "Lettres sur les Estats-Unis" by Prince Napoleon, published in Paris in 1862 about his 1861 trip to Mount Vernon, Binder "Early Descriptions, 1842–," Black Binder Collection, NLSGW; George W. Clymans of Fairfax Seminary, typescript of "A Visit to Mount Vernon," 11 May 1865, Folder "Object Information," W-16 Harpsichord Object Files, MVLA Curatorial Files, Mount Vernon. Cunningham would not have been able to walk up and down the stairs unaided, necessitating her use of the first-floor spaces.

74. Sarah Tracy to Ann Pamela Cunningham, 1 December 1860 ER-MVLA.

75. Ibid. In this letter, Tracy is most likely referring to the place's African American residents (Philip Herrington, conversation with the author, September 2015).

76. Sarah Tracy to Anna Cora Ritchie, 22 January 1864, ER-MVLA; Mary Hamilton to Margaret Comegys, 10 March 1864, ER-MVLA.

77. "An Act to Incorporate the MVLA of the Union."

78. The Association claimed that the government did not provide them with a reason for prohibiting the boat from stopping at the Mount Vernon wharf (see copy of letter to Hon. Edwin M. Staunton, Secretary of War, November 1863, in a scrapbook kept by Mary Hamilton, Box 4–6, ER-MVLA. See also Casper, *Sarah Johnson's Mount Vernon,* 84).

79. Copy of letter from Mary Hamilton to Hon. Edwin M. Staunton.

80. "Copy of appeal to Congress for compensation to the Mt. V. L. Asso: for Losses during the Blockade of about two + half years ceasing May 1865," Box 9, ER-MVLA.

81. Sarah Tracy to Philoclea Eve, 22 August 1865, ER-MVLA.

82. "The Home of Washington," *Maine Farmer* 33, no. 34 (3 August 1865): 4. The condition of the tomb and exterior of the house also brought considerable criticism, as did the very fact that the MVLA charged an entrance fee (see C. A. Hopkinson to Sarah Tracy, 28 November 1865, ER-MVLA; and "The Home of Washington," *Maine Farmer,* 4).

83. Sarah Tracy to Philoclea Eve, 22 August 1865, ER-MVLA.

84. The Association reconnected with Sarah Hale, for example (see Abby Wheaton Chase to Sarah Tracy, 1 November 1865, ER-MVLA; and "Editor's Table," *Godey's Lady's Book and Magazine* 72, no. 368 [April 1866]: 72–75). On Hamilton's suggestion, see Sarah Tracy to Margaret Comegys, 16 February 1865, ER-MVLA; George Riggs to Margaret Comegys, 24 February 1865, ER-MVLA; Ann Pamela Cunningham to Sarah Tracy, 10 July 1865, ER-MVLA; and "Mount Vernon," *Harper's Weekly* 2, no. 20 (20 February 1869): 114.

85. "Editor's Table," *Godey's Lady's Book and Magazine* 72, no. 368 (April 1866): 72–75.

86. Mires, *Independence Hall in American Memory,* 73–113.

87. See Steven Conn, *Museums and American Intellectual Life, 1876–1926* (Chicago: University of Chicago Press, 1998).

88. See Teresa Lynn Barnett, "The Nineteenth-Century Relic: A Pre-History of the Historical Artifact" (Ph.D. diss., University of California, Los Angeles, 2008), ProQuest (304658273); and Elizabeth Stillinger, *The Antiquers: The Lives and Careers, the Deals, the Finds, the Collections of the Men and Women Who Were Responsible for the Changing Taste in American Antiques, 1850–1930* (New York: Knopf, 1980), 4–16.

89. For efforts to preserve buildings as tourist attractions before Mount Vernon, see Whitney Ann Martinko, "Progress through Preservation: History on the American Landscape in an Age of Improvement, 1785–1860" (Ph.D. diss., University of Virginia, 2012), 160–84.

90. Dorothy C. Barck, "The First Historic House Museum," *Journal of the Society of Architectural Historians* 14, no. 2 (May 1955): 30–32; Richard Caldwell, *A True History of the Acquisition of Washington's Headquarters at Newburgh by the State of New York* (Middletown, NY: Stivers, Slauson and Boyd, 1887); Richard Guy Wilson, *The Colonial Revival House* (New York: Abrams, 2004), 29–32; Hosmer, *Presence of the Past,* 35–37.

91. Caldwell, *A True History of the Acquisition of Washington's Headquarters,* 24.

92. Beverly Gordon, *The Saturated World: Aesthetic Meaning, Intimate Objects, Women's Lives, 1890–1940* (Knoxville: University of Tennessee Press, 2006). See also Abigail Carroll, "Of Kettles and Cranes: Colonial Revival Kitchens and the Performance of National Identity," *Winterthur Portfolio* 43, no. 4 (2009): 335–64.

93. Gordon, *The Saturated World,* 72–76.

94. Beverly Gordon, *Bazaars and Fair Ladies: The History of the American Fundraising Fair* (Knoxville: University of Tennessee Press, 1998), 59–76; Stillinger, *The Antiquers,* 8–9; Carroll, "Of Kettles and Cranes," 349–51; Rodris Roth, "The New England, or 'Old Tyme,' Kitchen Exhibit at Nineteenth-Century Fairs," in *Colonial Revival in America,* ed. Alan Axelrod (New York: Norton, 1985), 159–73.

95. See Frank Norton, *Frank Leslie's Historical Register of the Centennial Exposition* (New York: Frank Leslie's Publishing, 1877), 87; James D. McCabe, *The Illustrated History of the Centennial Exhibition, Held in Commemoration of the One Hundredth Anniversary of American Independence* (Philadelphia: National Publishing Company, 1876), 646; *What Ben Beverly Saw at the Great Exposition* (Chicago: Centennial, 1876), 54; Roth, "The New England, or 'Old Tyme,' Kitchen Exhibit," 160–73; Gordon, *Bazaars and Fair Ladies,* esp. 74–6; and Marling, *George Washington Slept Here,* 25–52.

96. Stillinger, *The Antiquers,* 13–16; Carroll, "Of Kettles and Cranes," 335–64.

97. Mary Hamilton's then-niece (she would become her stepdaughter once Hamilton married her sister's husband after her death) was one of the leaders in the New York Sanitary Commission.

98. See Nancy Halsted to Lily Berghmans, 13 April 1875, ER-MVLA; MVLA Minutes 1875, 7; "Mount Vernon," *Harper's Weekly* 4, no. 22 (22 April 1876): 323.

99. Marling, *George Washington Slept Here,* 38–52.

100. "A Lady Washington Tea Party," *Harper's Bazaar* 9, no. 13 (25 March 1876): 198. On the merits (or lack thereof) of the painting, see "George Washington's Levees," *Independent* 17, no. 881 (19 October 1865): 4; and "The Spring Exhibition of the Academy," *Independent* 21, no. 1066 (6 May 1869): 2.

101. See Michael K. Brown, "The Mount Vernon Ladies: Victorian Perceptions of Eighteenth Century Taste" (master's thesis, University of Delaware, 1977), NLSGW.

102. "Washington's Home Going to Ruin," *New York Observer and Chronicle* 47, no. 4 (18 January 1869): 30; George W. Clymans of Fairfax Seminary, typescript of "A Visit to Mount Vernon," 11 May 1865, Folder "Object Information," W-16 Harpsichord Object Files, MVLA Curatorial Files, Mount Vernon.

103. "Mount Vernon," *Harper's Weekly* (1876), 323. General Nathaniel Michler was also busy overseeing changes to the White House ("The White House," *Philadelphia Inquirer,* 19 November 1868).

104. W. M. Brasher to Nancy Halsted, 26 June 1869, ER-MVLA; "Washington's Home Going to Ruin," 30.

105. Ann Pamela Cunningham to Nancy Halsted, 23 March 1869, ER-MVLA. The greenhouse was expanded again in 1881 (see MVLA AR, 1881; "The Mount Vernon Regents," *Washington Post,* 12 June 1881).

106. Sarah Tiffey to Ann Pamela Cunningham, 1 July 1869 and 3 July 1869, ER-MVLA.

107. Sarah Tiffey to Nancy Halsted, 30 August 1869 and 11 September 1869, ER-MVLA; Sarah Tiffey to Ann Pamela Cunningham, 2 September 1869, 4 September 1869, 20 September 1869, and 22 September 1869, ER-MVLA; Ann Pamela Cunningham to Nancy Halsted, 3 September 1869, ER-MVLA.

108. Thomas Reinhart, architectural historian at Mount Vernon, conversation with author, 22 July 2014.

109. Ella B. Washington, "A Day and Night at Mount Vernon," *Appleton's Journal of Literature, Science and Art* 5, no. 109 (1871): 488–90.

110. Sarah Tiffey to Ann Pamela Cunningham, 3 July 1869, ER-MVLA. See also Brown, "The Mount Vernon Ladies," 16.

111. Ann Pamela Cunningham to Nancy Halsted, 3 September 1869, ER-MVLA.

112. John Augustine Washington died 13 September 1861 in West Virginia while serving as lieutenant colonel under Robert E. Lee.

113. Sarah Tiffey to Ann Pamela Cunningham, 30 August 1869, ER-MVLA; Casper, *Sarah Johnson's Mount Vernon,* 115–16.

114. Ann Pamela Cunningham to Nancy Halsted, 3 September 1869, ER-MVLA.

115. See Elswyth Thane, *Mount Vernon Is Ours: The Story of Its Preservation* (New York: Duell, Sloan and Pearce, 1966), 375; and Casper, *Sarah Johnson's Mount Vernon,* 113–14.

116. Ann Pamela Cunningham's plan was to solicit money from wealthy individuals, such as Corcoran and the Vanderbilts (Ann Pamela Cunningham to Nancy Halsted, 4 March 1870, ER-MVLA).

117. Sarah Tiffey to Ann Pamela Cunningham, 1 July 1869, ER-MVLA.

118. Nancy Halsted to Doctor Colfax, 8 July 1869, ER-MVLA; Nancy Halsted to Editor, 12 May 1869, ER-MVLA.

119. Mary Goodrich to Ann Pamela Cunningham, 5 July 1859, ER-MVLA; MVLA Minutes 1868, 7.

120. Sarah Tiffey to Nancy Halsted, 16 July 1869, ER-MVLA; Nancy Halsted to Doctor Colfax, 8 July 1869, ER-MVLA.

121. Nancy Halsted to James S. Grinnell, 4 May 1869, ER-MVLA; Nancy Halsted to Professor Joseph Henry, 28 April 1869, ER-MVLA.

122. Series of hand-transcribed letters, Folder "1869, June 24 Tiffey to Genl Halsted, 1869, June 29 Genl Halsted to Tiffey, 1869, July 16 Tiffey to Nancy Halsted," ER-MVLA; Nancy Halsted to Doctor Colfax, 8 July 1869, ER-MVLA.

123. Nancy Halsted to Doctor Colfax, 8 July 1869, ER-MVLA.

124. Mary Custis Lee to John Augustine Washington III, copy of a letter dated February 1859, Folder "Object Information," W-16 Harpsichord Object Files, MVLA Curatorial Files, Mount Vernon.

125. Lossing, *Mount Vernon and Its Associations* (1859), 267.

126. MVLA AR 1870, 4.

127. "History of the Maine Vice-Regency by Mrs. Sweat," p. 123, Box 15, ER-MVLA; MVLA AR 1872, 11.

128. "History of the Maine Vice-Regency by Mrs. Sweat," p. 109, Box 15, ER-MVLA.

129. Susan Hudson to Margaret Sweat, 25 July 1872, ER-MVLA.

130. See "History of the Maine Vice-Regency by Mrs. Sweat," p. 109, Box 15, ER-MVLA; and D. P. Smith to Benson J. Lossing, 29 June 1874, ER-MVLA.

131. "Meeting of the Board of Visitors," undated clipping pasted in "History of the Maine Vice-Regency by Mrs. Sweat," Box 15, ER-MVLA.

132. MVLA Minutes 1873, 11–12.

133. Mary McMakin to Colonel J. McHenry Hollingsworth, 17 October 1872, ER-MVLA; Elizabeth Mason to Colonel J. McHenry Hollingsworth, 3 September 1872, ER-MVLA; Susan Hudson to Margaret Sweat, 25 July 1872, ER-MVLA; "History of the Maine Vice-Regency by Mrs. Sweat," p. 149, Box 15, ER-MVLA.

134. "History of the Maine Vice-Regency by Mrs. Sweat," p. 150, Box 15, ER-MVLA.

135. Ann Pamela Cunningham, "To the Council of the Ladies' Mt. Vernon Association of June, 1874," in MVLA Minutes 1874, 5 (emphasis in original).

136. Irving Whitall Lyon, *The Colonial Furniture of New England: A Study of the Domestic Furniture in Use in the Seventeenth and Eighteenth Centuries* (Boston: Houghton, Mifflin, 1891).

137. "History of the Maine Vice-Regency by Mrs. Sweat," p. 167, Box 15, ER-MVLA.

138. MVLA Minutes 1895, 81–82. Upon her resignation, Ann Pamela Cunningham designated the Pennsylvania vice regent, Lily Berghmans, as her replacement. The MVLA officially elected Berghmans as regent the next year.

139. "History of the Maine Vice-Regency by Mrs. Sweat," p. 215, Box 15, ER-MVLA.

140. For examples, see MVLA AR 1889, 30–31; MVLA AR 1890, 17; MVLA AR 1891, 23; and MVLA AR 1892, 13.

141. Nancy Halsted to Benson J. Lossing, 5 August 1873, Box 1, Benson Lossing Papers, NLSGW; MVLA AR 1867, 4.

142. Nancy Halsted to Lily Berghmans, 5 January 1875 and 13 April 1875, ER-MVLA; MVLA AR 1875, 4; Nancy Halsted to Benson J. Lossing, 7 September 1874, 5 August 1873, and 27 March 1875, Box 1, Benson Lossing Papers, NLSGW; Nancy Halsted to Colonel J. McHenry Hollingsworth, 18 December 1875, ER-MVLA.

143. "History of the Maine Vice-Regency by Mrs. Sweat," p. 123, Box 15, ER-MVLA; MVLA AR 1872, 11. Ann Pamela Cunningham had begun calling for an endowment years earlier (see Ann Pamela Cunningham to Nancy Halsted, 4 March 1870, ER-MVLA).

144. "The Mount Vernon Regents," *Washington Post,* 24 May 1883.

145. MVLA AR 1887, 28.

146. Susanna W. Gold, "Imagining Memory: Re-Presentations of the Civil War at the 1876 Centennial Exhibition" (Ph.D. diss., University of Pennsylvania, 2004), 19, ProQuest (305143145).

147. Wedding cake trade card, Box "vol. 20, Large Centennial Scrapbook," Centennial Exhibition #1544, Historical Society of Pennsylvania, Philadelphia.

148. "The Centennial Exposition," *New York Observer and Chronicle* 54, no. 45 (9 November 1876): 358; William Chandler Raymond, *Curiosities of the U.S. Patent Office* (Syracuse: W. C. Raymond, 1888), 122–24; "Godey's Arm Chair," *Godey's Ladies Book and Magazine* 93, no. 555 (September 1876): 289; McCabe, *Illustrated History,* 553–54; Gold, "Imagining Memory," 103–12; Kenneth W. Dobyns, *The Patent Office Pony: A History of the Early Patent Office* (Fredericksburg: Sergeant Kirkland's Museum and Historical Society, 1994), 188.

149. MVLA AR 1877, 15–16.

150. Ibid., 7.

151. See "Alice in Washington," *Godey's Lady's Book and Magazine* 92, no. 552 (June 1876): 525; "Mount Vernon," *Harper's Weekly* (1876), 323; and "Mount Vernon," *Harper's Weekly* 2, no. 28 (28 February 1874): 202.

152. MVLA AR 1890, 31; MVLA AR 1891, 27.

153. MVLA Minutes 1891, 66; MVLA Minutes 1894, 80. See also Wilbur H. Simonson,

"The Mount Vernon Memorial Highway," *American City* 43, no. 4 (October 1930): 85. Visitor totals are taken from one May MVLA council meeting to the next.

154. MVLA Minutes 1893, 26.

155. Ibid. This was a problem even before the extended hours were instituted (see MVLA Minutes 1891, 27).

156. "Mount Vernon," *Harper's Weekly* 7, no. 3 (3 July 1886): 430. On employee uniforms, see MVLA AR 1879, 4

157. MVLA AR 1884, 16.

158. MVLA AR 1890, 24; MVLA Minutes 1895, 39. This route is very similar to that used in the mansion today.

159. Elizabeth B. Johnston, *1876 Visitor's Guide to Mount Vernon* (Washington, DC: Gibson Printers, 1876).

160. Engravings in the first illustrated edition included pictures of Christ Church in Alexandria, the old tomb, the New Room mantelpiece, the harpsichord, the west and east facades, and a view of Fort Washington (Elizabeth B. Johnston, *Visitor's Guide to Mount Vernon,* 3rd ed. [Washington, DC: Gibson Printers, 1879]).

161. The MVLA's original plan was to put the coat-of-arms for each state above each door, but this was given up after the coats-of-arms proved too large (Lily Berghmans Laughton to Margaret Comegys, 15 December 1875, ER-MVLA; MVLA AR 1881, 8). Although the state signs came down in 1902, individual vice regents continued to identify with particular rooms until they stopped sleeping in the mansion during their annual meetings in the 1920s (MVLA Minutes 1902, 80; MVLA Minutes 1926, 91; Abby G. Baker, "The Restoration of Mount Vernon," *Munsey's Magazine,* September 1905, 669; Carol Borchert Cadou, senior vice president, Historic Preservation & Collections at Mount Vernon, conversation with author, 22 July 2014). The guidebook listed rooms by state until the mid-1920s.

162. Edward Everett, *The Life of George Washington* (New York: Sheldon, 1860), 286–317; Benson J. Lossing, *The Home of Washington; or Mount Vernon and Its Associations, Historical, Biographical, and Pictorial* (Hartford, CT: A. S. Hale, 1871), 400–410. Interestingly, Lossing omitted the listing of Washington's slaves in his reprinting of the inventory. For an explanation of the inventory's provenance, see the introduction by Worthington Chauncey Ford in *Inventory of the Contents of Mount Vernon 1810* (Cambridge, MA: University Press, 1909), v–ix.

163. Nancy Halsted to Susan Hudson, 8 November 1875, ER-MVLA; MVLA AR 1885, 16; J. Q. Throckmorton, "Mount Vernon, Past and Present," *Peterson's Magazine* 88, no. 5 (November 1885): 393–99; Cadou, conversation with author, 22 July 2014.

164. See "The George Washington Papers: Provenance and Publication History," http://memory.loc.gov/ammem/gwhtml/gwabout.html.

165. MVLA Minutes 1883, 25–26; undated clipping in Folder "Pickens, Mrs. Frances W., Vice-Regent for South Carolina," Vice Regents' Files, NLSGW; MVLA AR 1885, 21.

166. Pamphlet, "Charleston, S.C. and Mount Vernon, 22–23 February 1884," Folder "Pickens, Mrs. Frances W., Vice-Regent for South Carolina," Vice Regents' Files, NLSGW; MVLA AR 1884, 16. Emmart and Quarterly had completed other restoration work in the house before Pickens hired the firm for the dining room.

167. Emmart and Quarterly to Lucy Pickens, 31 October 1883, Folder "Mansion Interior," Box 3, Restoration Files, NLSGW.

168. Susan Hudson to Colonel J. McHenry Hollingsworth, 13 August 1873 and 20 August 1873, ER-MVLA. The sideboard in the dining room during Washington's period is one drawn by Lossing at Arlington House but has since been lost (see Lossing, *Mount Vernon and Its Associations,* 303).

169. In the later 1870s, the room featured a handful of pictures and a placard listing all the subscribers who had given money to the restoration of the south porch (see *Mount Vernon Guide,* 3rd ed. rev. [Baltimore: Our Fireside, 1877], n.p.).

170. MVLA AR 1883, 18.

171. "Mount Vernon," *Harper's Weekly* (1886), 430

172. MVLA AR 1882, 16; MVLA AR 1889, 33.

173. The large case in the central passage, for example, was removed after the space was restored in 1898 (Harrison H. Dodge to Justine Townsend, 7 July 1898, Folder "Passage," Box 3, Restoration Files, NLSGW).

174. See Elizabeth B. Johnston, *Visitor's Guide to Mount Vernon,* 18th ed (Washington DC: Gibson Brothers, 1892), 27.

175. MVLA Minutes 1873, 9; MVLA Minutes 1902, 62, 76–77.

176. Johnston, *1876 Visitor's Guide to Mount Vernon,* 14.

177. Obituary (11 January 1890), clipping in Folder "Mrs. Samuel J. Broadwell, Vice Regent for Ohio," Vice Regents' Files, NLSGW.

178. Ibid.

179. MVLA Minutes 1879, 4–5

180. MVLA Minutes 1878, 8.

181. A. J. Wedderburn, *Mount Vernon Guide* (Alexandria: Office of Our Fireside, 1876), 18; Elizabeth Lytle Broadwell, "Report of Vice Regent of Ohio," in MVLA Minutes 1879, 12–13; Johnston, *Visitor's Guide to Mount Vernon* (1879), 18. Although the harpsichord was not listed in the inventory, the MVLA had always known via family history that it belonged in the small front parlor.

182. Relic Book vol. 2, MVLA Curatorial Files, Mount Vernon; MVLA Minutes 1879, 5. The flute was recently purchased from the West Virginia vice regent and Washington relative Ella B. Washington. Later investigations revealed that Washington did not play the flute or any other instrument (see Memo "the Music Room," 23 March 1949, Folder "Little Parlor," Box 3, Restoration Files, NLSGW).

183. Relic Book vol. 2, MVLA Curatorial Files, Mount Vernon.

184. Ibid.

185. *Inventory of the Contents of Mount Vernon 1810,* 2–3; Relic Book vol. 2, MVLA Curatorial Files, Mount Vernon.

186. This was a suggestion of Susan Hudson as early as 1873, although the labels might not have been affixed until later in the decade (see Susan Hudson to Colonel J. McHenry Hollingsworth, 13 August 1873 and 20 August 1873, ER-MVLA; and Emma Ball to Colonel J. McHenry Hollingsworth, 17 May 1877, ER-MVLA).

187. Elizabeth B. Johnston, *Visitor's Guide to Mount Vernon,* 13th ed. (Washington, DC: Gibson Brothers, Printers, 1886), 25; Bertha Gerneaux Davis, "Mount Vernon, the Home of Washington," *Christian Advocate,* 17 February 1898, 263. My evaluation of the furniture is based on a 22 July 2014 conversation with Adam Erby, associate curator at Mount Vernon.

188. MVLA AR 1889, 10.

189. MVLA AR 1879, 6

190. After Broadwell stepped down as Ohio vice regent in 1890, Mary Pendleton Abney filled the position from 1893 until 1897. Elizabeth Campbell took over Ohio's position on the board from 1897 until 1902.

191. Relic Book vol. 1, MVLA Curatorial Files, Mount Vernon; MVLA, *An Illustrated Handbook of Mount Vernon, The Home of Washington* (L. Windsor House, 1905), n.p.

192. Relic Book vol. 2, MVLA Curatorial Files, Mount Vernon; MVLA AR 1891, 4; MVLA Minutes 1891, 9.

193. MVLA AR 1877, 5.

194. MVLA Minutes 1911, 84; MVLA Minutes 1914, 27. When the piece was acquired in 1912, the Association originally displayed it in Washington's bedroom (see Harrison H. Dodge to John C. Lewis, 20 May 1912, Folder "Acquisition Information, W-760 Mary Ball Washington Desk," MVLA Curatorial Files, Mount Vernon; and MVLA, *An Illustrated Handbook of Mount Vernon, The Home of Washington* [Mount Vernon, VA: Mount Vernon Ladies' Association, 1921], 12). It has been on loan to the Mary Ball Washington House since.

195. Susan P. Schoelwer, curator at Mount Vernon, conversation with author, 16 July 2014.

196. Colonel Jehiel Brooks to the regent and vice regents of the MVLA, 16 February 1859, Box RM-478, ER-3017, ER-MVLA; Martha Mitchell to Susan Johnson Hudson, 13 June 1873, ER-MVLA.

197. Nancy Halsted to Benson J. Lossing, 5 August 1873, Box 1, Benson Lossing Papers, NLSGW; Nancy Halsted to Colonel J. McHenry Hollingsworth, 18 December 1875, ER-MVLA.

198. Nancy Halsted to Lily Berghmans, 5 January 1875 and 13 April 1875, ER-MVLA; Nancy Halsted to Benson J. Lossing, 5 August 1873, 7 September 1874, and 27 March 1875, Box 1, Benson Lossing Papers, NLSGW; MVLA Minutes 1875, 4; Nancy Halsted to Colonel J. McHenry Hollingsworth, 18 December 1875, ER-MVLA; MVLA Minutes 1876, 3; "Mount Vernon," *Harper's Weekly* (1876), 323.

199. Nancy Halsted to Colonel J. McHenry Hollingsworth, 18 December 1875, ER-MVLA; Nancy Halsted to Benson J. Lossing, 5 August 1873, Box 1, Benson Lossing Papers, NLSGW; Nancy Halsted to Lily Berghmans, 5 January 1875, ER-MVLA. Halsted and Taylor chose to use Rossiter's memory of the porch over Lossing's after Corcoran expressed his preference for it. Sarah Tracy and Upton Herbert, however, might have known these features were not original; the two had discussed Mount Vernon's history with John Augustine Washington III and West Ford, who told them that the summerhouse, another feature rebuilt in this period under Halsted's direction, was not original to the Washington era (Memo to the Director from John H. Rhodehamel, 9 December 1980, Folder "Summerhouse," Box 6, Restoration Files, NLSGW).

200. MVLA Minutes 1877, 10; Mesick, Cohen, Waite Architects, "Mount Vernon Historic Structure Report," 134, NLSGW.

201. Wilson, *Colonial Revival House,* 36–38.

202. Nancy Halsted to Colonel J. McHenry Hollingsworth, 6 January 1876, ER-MVLA; MVLA Minutes 1876, 3; MVLA Minutes 1877, 11.

203. MVLA AR 1889, 10, 18; Nancy Halsted to Hollingsworth, 6 January 1876, ER-MVLA.

204. "Our Lithographic Illustrations," *Building News,* 21 September 1877, 278 and plate.

205. John Augustine Washington might have introduced the arch, although Sarah Johnson told Harrison H. Dodge in the 1890s that the MVLA had done the work (Harrison H. Dodge to Justine Townsend, 7 July 1898, and Harrison H. Dodge to Rebecca Flandrau, 8 June 1898, Folder "Passage," Box 3, Restoration Files, NLSGW; Thomas Reinhart, architectural historian at Mount Vernon, conversation with author, 24 July 2014).

206. "The Mount Vernon Regents," *Washington Post,* 26 May 1882; MVLA Minutes 1882, 6; Walter M. Macomber, "Report and Recommendations for Restoration of First Floor Stair Hall Ceiling Beam," 30 July 1951, Folder "Building Committee–General," PMVLA.

207. Mires, *Independence Hall in American Memory,* 141–43.

208. Harrison H. Dodge to Susan Hudson, 24 June 1898, and Harrison H. Dodge to Justine Townsend, 7 July 1898, Folder "Passage," Box 3, Restoration Files, NLSGW; T. Mellon Rogers to Ellen Harrison, 17 May 1897, Folder "Building Committee (2)," PMVLA. Washington had indeed painted the room a light color before graining it during later innovations (Reinhart, conversation with author, 24 July 2014).

209. Harrison H. Dodge to H. A. Ogden, 12 January 1899, Folder "Passage," Box 3, Restoration Files, NLSGW; MVLA Minutes 1899, 10.

210. Harrison H. Dodge to Elizabeth Rathbone, 8 October 1898, 21 October 1898, and 22 November 1898, Folder "Passage," Box 3, Restoration Files, NLSGW.

211. Clare Edwards, MVLA vice regent for Connecticut, in conversation with author, 31 May 2014.

212. Sarah Tracy to Ann Pamela Cunningham, 9 September 1865, ER-MVLA.

213. Sarah Tracy to Ann Pamela Cunningham, 26 April 1866, ER-MVLA. From January through December 1874, photography sales generated $605.98 out of $9,987.09 in total receipts (Ledger of J. Mv. H. Hollingsworth in account with Mt. Vernon Association, July 1872, Box "MVLA Early Records," ER-MVLA).

214. Folder "1876 Dec, Certificate of Publication of the suit of MVLA vs. Armstrong and others to prohibit photographing MV, 8–29," Box "Early Records, Feb 1876–Feb 1877," ER-MVLA. See also MVLA Minutes 1877, 16–17.

215. MVLA AR 1878, 6.

216. MVLA AR 1880, 7.

217. "At Mount Vernon," *Harper's Bazaar* 26, no. 19 (13 May 1893): 378; Bertha Gerneaux Davis, "Mount Vernon: The Home of Washington," *Christian Advocate,* 17 February 1898, 263.

218. MVLA AR 1891, 10

219. Ibid., 36

220. MVLA Minutes 1898, 41, 75

221. MVLA Minutes 1900, 10.

3. Replicas, Replicas, Replicas

1. On the American home in this period, see Clark, *The American Family Home,* 130–70.

2. Sarah M. Lockwood, "The Grace of Old Fashions in Furniture," *Garden & Home Builder* 45 (March/August 1927): 473.

3. See Neil Harris, "Period Rooms and the American Art Museum," *Winterthur Portfolio* 46, no. 2/3 (Summer/Autumn 2012): 117–38; Melinda Young Frye, "The Beginnings of the Period Room in American Museums: Charles P. Wilcomb's Colonial Kitchens, 1896, 1906, 1910," in *The Colonial Revival in America,* ed. Alan Axelrod (New York: Norton, 1985), 217–40; Dianne H. Pilgrim, "Inherited from the Past: The American Period Room," *American Art Journal* 10, no. 1 (May 1978): 7–10; Stillinger, *The Antiquers,* 149–54; and Hosmer, *Presence of the Past,* 212–16. See also Carroll, "Of Kettles and Cranes."

4. MVLA Minutes 1894, 80; MVLA Minutes 1924, 37.

5. Abby Gunn Baker, "The Preservation of Mount Vernon," *Century Magazine* 79, no. 4 (February 1910): 487; MVLA Minutes 1895, 9, 37–38; MVLA Minutes 1891, 8, 34–35.

6. "In the Kitchen Garden, Mount Vernon, Va., the Home of Washington," *American Architect* 118, no. 2348 (22 December 1920): 822. See also "The Editor Looks About—Sightseeing at Home," *Country Life* 53 (April 1928): 44; "Mount Vernon Revisited," *Atlantic Monthly* 98 (December 1906): 860.

7. Mitchell qtd. in Baker, "The Preservation of Mount Vernon," 483–84.

8. MVLA Minutes 1900, 34–35; Harrison H. Dodge, *Mount Vernon: Its Owner and Its Story* (Philadelphia: Lippincott, 1932), 175–76.

9. Baker, "The Preservation of Mount Vernon," 485; Roger Warden, "Safeguarding Mount Vernon," *Technical World Magazine*, February 1915, 892–83; MVLA Minutes 1895, 29; MVLA Minutes 1892, 36–39; Worth E. Shoults, "The Home of the First Farmer of America," *National Geographic Magazine* 53, no. 5 (May 1928): 627–68; MVLA Minutes 1925, 45; Dodge, *Mount Vernon,* 175–83.

10. MVLA Minutes 1916, 69–70.

11. See MVLA Minutes 1905, 62.

12. *Inventory of the Contents of Mount Vernon.*

13. MVLA Minutes 1911, 50, 74; MVLA Minutes 1913, 62–63; MVLA Minutes 1914, 71–73; MVLA Minutes 1915, 56–57; MVLA Minutes 1916, 78–79.

14. Mesick, Cohen, Waite Architects, "Mount Vernon Historic Structure Report," 136, NLSGW; MVLA Minutes 1895, 10, 19.

15. MVLA AR 1912, 30.

16. See Harrison Howell Dodge, "Washington at Mount Vernon," *Youth's Companion,* 17 February 1910, 83.

17. "Colonel Dodge of Mount Vernon," *Federal Architect* 7 (1936): 26–27.

18. See Phyllis Anderson, "'If Washington Were Here Himself, He Would Be on My Side': Charles Sprague Sargent and the Preservation of the Mount Vernon Landscape," in *Design with Culture: Claiming America's Landscape Heritage,* ed. Charles A. Birnbaum and Mary V. Hughes (Charlottesville: University of Virginia Press, 2005), 39–56.

19. See N. H. Ellsworth, "Mount Vernon in May," *House Beautiful* 45, no. 5 (May 1919): 288; Francis E. Leupp, "The Old Garden at Mount Vernon," *Century Magazine* 72, no. 1 (May 1906): 73–79. On the role of historical archaeology in landscape architecture, see Elizabeth Hope Cushing, *Arthur A. Shurcliff: Design, Preservation, and the Creation of the Colonial Williamsburg Landscape* (Amherst: University of Massachusetts Press, 2014).

20. See May Brawley Hill, *Grandmother's Garden: The Old-Fashioned American Garden, 1865–1915* (New York: Abrams, 1995).

21. MVLA Minutes 1911, 12. See also Mildred Stapley, "The Home of George Washington, Country Gentleman," *Country Life in America* 26 (May 1914): 39–41.

22. Nancy Halsted to James S. Grinnell, 4 May 1869, ER-MVLA; Nancy Halsted to Joseph Henry, 28 April 1869, ER-MVLA; Brown, "The Mount Vernon Ladies," 25.

23. MVLA Minutes 1889, 26.

24. MVLA Minutes 1891, 42, 80.

25. Ibid., 86.

26. MVLA Minutes 1899, 46; MVLA Minutes 1911, 48; MVLA Minutes, 1918, 30; MVLA Minutes 1920, 43, 82.

27. Milton Bennett Medary Jr. was most likely hired at the recommendation of Ellen Harrison, vice regent for Pennsylvania. Medary had recently finished the Washington Memorial Chapel at Valley Forge, a project largely funded by donations brought in by Harrison's husband (see Barbara MacDonald Powell, "The Most Celebrated Encampment: Valley Forge in American Culture, 1777–1983" [Ph.D. diss., Cornell University, 1983], 127–29, ProQuest [303274108]).

28. MVLA Minutes 1921, 16; MVLA Minutes 1929, 18–19, 44–45.

29. Harriet Comegys to Milton Medary, 19 November 1921, Folder "Salt House," Box 5, Restoration Files, NLSGW; Harrison H. Dodge to Harriet Comegys, 4 November 1920, Folder "Museum," Box 4, Restoration Files, NLSGW.

30. MVLA Minutes 1921, 76, 81.

31. MVLA Minutes 1889, 16; MVLA Minutes 1890, 11, 43–44.

32. Milton Medary to Harriet Comegys, 1 May 1922, and Milton Medary to Comegys, 3 May 1922, Folder "Salt House," Box 5, Restoration Files, NLSGW.

33. Harriet Comegys to Milton Medary, 2 May 1922, Folder "Salt House," Box 5, Restoration Files, NLSGW.

34. MVLA Minutes 1922, 28, 83. The building is interpreted today as a salt house and was probably made a carpenter's shop in the nineteenth century by Superintendent Hollingsworth (Charles Cecil Wall, Memorandum "Carpenter Shop, 15 February 1935," Folder "Salt House," Box 5, Restoration Files, NLSGW).

35. Walter M. Macomber, Memorandum "Salt House Restoration–1966," and Milton Medary to Harriet Comegys, 4 May 1922, Folder "Salt House," Box 5, Restoration Files, NLSGW.

36. Excerpts from Harrison H. Dodge's daily diaries, Folder "Salt House," Box 5, Restoration Files, NLSGW; MVLA Minutes 1922, 28; MVLA Minutes 1923, 14, 18, 50–51.

37. MVLA Minutes 1924, 69; MVLA Minutes 1925, 45; MVLA Minutes 1926, 49; Isaac Hathaway Francis to Zantzinger, Borie, & Medary, 16 June 1925, Milton Medary to Harriet Comegys, 19 June 1925, and Milton Medary to Comegys, 20 August 1925, Folder "Salt House," Box 5, Restoration Files, NLSGW.

38. MVLA Minutes 1928, 71–72, 77–78; Harrison H. Dodge to Milton Medary, 23 May 1928, and Harrison H. Dodge to Milton Medary, 9 June 1928, Folder "Museum (2)," Box 4, Restoration Files, NLSGW.

39. MVLA Minutes 1921, 55, 60–61; Milton Medary to Harriet Comegys, 2 December 1921, and Harriet Comegys to Milton Medary, 21 March 1922, Folder "Salt House," Box 5, Restoration Files, NLSGW; Harriet Comegys to Milton Medary, 15 March 1922, Folder "Museum (2)," Box 4, Restoration Files, NLSGW.

40. For a survey of attitudes toward and interest in Colonial American architecture before the Civil War, see W. Barksdale Maynard, "'Best, Lowliest Style!' The Early-Nineteenth-Century Rediscovery of American Colonial Architecture," *Journal of the Society of Architectural Historians* 59, no. 3 (September 2000): 338–57.

41. "Colonial Houses and Their Uses to Art," *American Architect and Building News* 3, no.

107 (12 January 1878): 12. See also Arthur Little, *Early New England Interiors* (1878); Walter Knight Sturges, "Arthur Little and the Colonial Revival," *Journal of the Society of Architectural Historians* 32, no. 2 (May 1973): 147–63.

42. See Vincent Scully, *The Shingle Style* (New Haven: Yale University Press, 1955); William B. Rhoads, *The Colonial Revival* (New York: Garland, 1977); William B. Rhoads, "The Discovery of America's Architectural Past, 1874–1914," in *The Architectural Historian in America,* ed. Elisabeth Blair MacDougall (Washington, DC: National Gallery of Art, 1990): 23–39; and Wilson, *The Colonial Revival House.*

43. John Stewardson, "Architecture in America: A Forecast," *Lippincott's Monthly Magazine,* January 1896, 132.

44. J. C. Halden et al., *The Georgian Period, Being Measured Drawings of Colonial Work,* vol. 6 (American Architect and Building News Co., 1900), 44–48 and plates 33–35; Mesick, Cohen, Waite Architects, "Mount Vernon Historic Structure Report," 136, 138–39, NLSGW. The three plates include a tracing of the plan by Samuel Vaughan, drawings of the west facade and of the north dependency, a plan, and details of the pedimented doorway and a variety of molding profiles.

45. *American Architect and Building News* 61, no. 1182 (20 August 1898): 57; Wilson, *The Colonial Revival House,* 39–40.

46. Stapley, "The Home of George Washington, Country Gentleman," 39.

47. Paul Wilstach, *Mount Vernon: Washington's Home and the Nation's Shrine* (New York: Doubleday, Page, 1916).

48. See Talbot Faulkner Hamlin, *The American Spirit in Architecture* (New Haven: Yale University Press, 1926); Fiske Kimball, *American Architecture* (New York: Bobbs-Merrill, 1928); Lewis Mumford, *Sticks and Stones: A Study of American Architecture and Civilization* (New York: Boni and Liveright, 1927); and Thomas E. Tallmadge, *The Story of Architecture in America* (New York: Norton, 1927).

49. Wilstach, *Mount Vernon,* 22–25, 55–56, 125–26, 140–42. See also Fiske Kimball, *Domestic Architecture of the American Colonies and of the Early Republic* (New York: Scribner's Sons, 1922), 284.

50. In 1922, Warren D. Brush published an alternative theory that suggested that Washington had raised the roof of the house as part of the first round of alterations (see Warren D. Brush, "The Building of Mount Vernon Mansion," *House Beautiful* 51, no. 2 [February 1922]: 130–31, 162+).

51. Wilstach, *Mount Vernon,* 24; "Review," *Dial* 730 (30 November 1916): 471.

52. Wilstach, *Mount Vernon,* 75.

53. Ibid., 276.

54. Ibid., 23.

55. See John Maas, "Architecture and Americanism or Pastiches of Independence Hall," *Historic Preservation* 22, no. 2 (April–June 1970): 17–25.

56. Alla Harman Rogers, *History of Mount Vernon: America's Patriotic Shrine* (Washington, DC: National Art Service Co., 1928), n.p.

57. See Nina Silber, *The Romance of Reunion: Northerners and the South, 1865–1900* (Chapel Hill: University of North Carolina Press, 1993).

58. Some scholars have termed this the "Southern Colonial Revival" (see Wilson, *The Colonial Revival House*, 50–63; and Rhoads, *The Colonial Revival*, 112–15).

59. See William M. S. Rasmussen and Robert S. Tilton, *Old Virginia: The Pursuit of a Pastoral Ideal* (Charlottesville, VA: Howell, 2003); David W. Blight, *Race and Reunion: The Civil War in American Memory* (Cambridge: Belknap Press of Harvard University Press, 2001), 4; David W. Blight, *Beyond the Battlefield: Race, Memory, and the American Civil War* (Amherst: University of Massachusetts Press, 2002), 120–52; Silber, *The Romance of Reunion*; and Wilson, *The Colonial Revival House*, 50–63.

60. See Catherine Bishir, "Landmarks of Power: Building a Southern Past, 1885–1915," in *Southern Built: American Architecture, Regional Practice* (Charlottesville: University of Virginia Press, 2006), 254–93; Steven Hoelscher, "The White-Pillared Past: Landscapes of Memory and Race in the American South," in *Landscape and Race in the United States,* ed. Richard H. Schein (New York: Routledge, 2006), 39–48; Robert Gamble, "The White-Columned Tradition: Classical Architecture and the Southern Mystique," in "Classical Tradition in the South," special issue, *Southern Humanities Review* (1977): 41–59; and Angela D. Mack and Stephen G. Hoffius, eds., *The Plantation in American Art* (Columbia: University of South Carolina Press, 2008).

61. C. W. Coleman, "A Virginia Plantation," *Chautauquan: A Weekly Newsmagazine* 9, no. 7 (April 1889): 412.

62. Constance Cary Harrison, "The Homes and Haunts of Washington," *Century Illustrated Magazine* 35, no. 1 (November 1887): 3.

63. T. J. Mackey, "George Washington: The Citizen, the Soldier, the Statesman, the Patriot," *Peterson's Magazine* 6, no. 7 (July 1895): 679.

64. For the Lost Cause, see Gaines M. Foster, *Ghosts of the Confederacy: Defeat, the Lost Cause, and the Emergence of the New South* (New York: Oxford University Press, 1987); Gary W. Gallagher and Alan T. Nolan, eds., *The Myth of the Lost Cause and Civil War History* (Bloomington: Indiana University Press, 2000); Fitzhugh Brundage, ed., *Where These Memories Grow: History, Memory, and Southern Identity* (Chapel Hill: University of North Carolina Press, 2000); and Cynthia Mills and Pamela Simpson, eds., *Monuments to the Lost Cause: Women, Art and the Landscapes of Southern Memory* (Knoxville: University of Tennessee Press, 2003).

65. Rhoads, *The Colonial Revival*, 126; Montgomery Schuyler, "State Buildings at the Fair," *Architectural Record* 3 (July–September 1893): 56.

66. See Susan Prendergast Schoelwer, "Curious Relics and Quaint Scenes: The Colonial Revival at Chicago's Great Fair," in *The Colonial Revival in America,* ed. Alan Axelrod (New York: Norton, 1985), 184–216.

67. Rhoads, *The Colonial Revival*, 127; Board of World's Fair Managers of Pennsylvania, *Catalogue of the Exhibits of the State of Pennsylvania and of Pennsylvanians at the World's Columbian Exposition* (Philadelphia: Clarence M. Busch, 1893), 13.

68. On the "softened" Lost Cause of the 1890s, see Foster, *Ghosts of the Confederacy,* 104–44; and Blight, *Race and Reunion,* 277–84.

69. See *The Dream City: A Portfolio of Photographic Views of the World's Columbian Exposition* (St. Louis: N. D. Thompson, 1893), n.p.

70. Mary Mann Page Newton, *Colonial Virginia: A Paper Read before the Historical Congress at Chicago* (Richmond: West, Johnston, 1893), 15.

71. "The Columbian Exposition," *Richmond Times,* 16 July 1891; "Virginia at Chicago," *Washington Post,* 16 July 1891.

72. "Grand Colonial Ball," *Washington Post,* 10 January 1892. For the DAR at the World's Columbian Exposition, see Jeanne Madeline Weimann, *The Fair Women: The Story of the Woman's Building, World's Columbian Exposition, Chicago 1893* (Chicago: Academy Chicago, 1981), 504; and Wanda Corn, *Women Building History: Public Art at the 1893 Columbian Exposition* (Berkeley: University of California Press, 2011).

73. John S. Wise, *The End of an Era* (Boston: Houghton, Mifflin, 1902), 218. On Beale, see M. Sheffey-Petters, "Mrs. Lucy Preston Beale: A Lady of Charming Manners and Diplomatic Address," broadside reprinted from the *Charlottesville Daily Progress,* 14 January 1893, Special Collections, University of Virginia; B. D. F., "Mrs. Lucy Preston Beale," *American Monthly Magazine* 3, no. 3 (September 1893): 269–73; and John A. Logan and Mary Simmerson Cunningham Logan, *The Part Taken by Women in American History* (Wilmington: Perry-Nalle, 1892), 460.

74. Beale was elected a vice-president general of the DAR on 24 February 1893 ("Official Proceedings of the Second Continental Congress," *American Monthly Magazine* 2, no. 6 [June 1893]: 673; B. D. F., "Mrs. Lucy Preston Beale").

75. MVLA Minutes 1893, 37; Harrison H. Dodge to Emma Ball, 18 November 1892, Microfilm Reel 2, Superintendent's Letters, NLSGW; J. A. G., "Mount Vernon and the Mount Vernon Association," *American Monthly Magazine* 2, no. 5 (May 1893): 530.

76. MVLA Minutes 1892, 52; "The World's Fair," *Richmond Times,* 29 July 1892. On Rogers, see "Capt. Edgerton S. Rogers," *Inland Architect and News Record* 38, no. 4 (November 1901): 32; and "Capt. Edgerton Rogers Dead," *Richmond Times,* 20 August 1901.

77. MVLA Minutes 1893, 37.

78. Edgerton Stewart Rogers, "Details: Sketches by Edgerton S. Rogers, archt.," *Inland Architect and News Record* 21 (April 1893): plate following p. 42.

79. Rossiter Johnson, ed., *A History of the World's Columbian Exposition* (New York: D. Appleton, 1897), 485.

80. Moses P. Handy, *The Official Directory of the World's Columbian Exposition, May 1st to October 30th* (Chicago: W. B. Conkey, 1893), 100.

81. Ibid.

82. Virginia State Legislature, Board of World's Fair Managers of Virginia, *Communication from the Governor Inclosing the Report of the World's Fair Commissioner*, November 1893, S. Doc. 16, 10–28.

83. Ibid., 10–16.

84. Ibid., 10–15.

85. See Robert E. Bonner, "Americans Apart: Nationality in the Slaveholding South" (Ph.D. diss., Yale University, 1997), 304–17, ProQuest (304383734); and Blight, *Race and Reunion*, 259–61.

86. Mary Stuart Smith and William F. Pumphrey donated objects to both exhibits (see William E. Pumphrey, *Catalogue of Valuable and Rare Collections of Confederate Miscellany* . . . [Richmond: n.p., n.d.]; and "The Monument to General Robert E. Lee, Part IV," *Southern* 17 [January–December 1889]: 264).

87. See Malinda W. Collier, John M. Coski, Richard C. Cote, Tucker H. Hill, and Guy R. Swanson, *White House of the Confederacy: An Illustrated History* (Richmond: Cadmus Marketing, 1993); John M. Coski, "A Century of Collecting: The History of the Museum of the Confederacy," *Museum of the Confederacy Journal* 74 (1996): 2–24; John M. Coski and Amy R. Feely, "A Monument to Southern Womanhood: The Founding Generation of the Confederate Museum," in *A Woman's War: Southern Women, Civil War, and the Confederate Legacy*, ed. Edward D. C. Campbell Jr. and Kym S. Rice (Charlottesville: University Press of Virginia, 1996), 130–63; Reiko Margarita Hillyer, "Designing Dixie: Landscape, Tourism, and Memory in the New South, 1870–1917" (Ph.D. diss., Columbia University, 2007), 276–331, ProQuest (304861970); and Reiko Hillyer, "Relics of Reconciliation: The Confederate Museum and Civil War Memory in the New South," *Public Historian* 33, no. 4 (November 2011): 35–62.

88. Confederate Memorial Literary Society, *Catalogue of the Confederate Museum, of the Confederate Memorial Literary Society, Corner Twelfth and Clay Streets, Richmond, Virginia* (Richmond: Ware and Duke, Printers, 1905), 16–95. See also Coski and Feely, "A Monument to Southern Womanhood," 146–47.

89. Handy, *The Official Directory*, 100.

90. Virginia State Legislature, *Communication*, 39.

91. "Virginia's Exhibit: The Mother of Civilization," *Oshkosh Daily Northwestern*, 14 October 1893. For the role of women in the Lost Cause, see Sarah E. Gardner, *Blood & Irony: Southern White Women's Narratives of the Civil War, 1861–1937* (Chapel Hill: University of North Carolina Press, 2004).

92. Handy, *The Official Directory*, 100.

93. Hubert Howe Bancroft, *The Book of the Fair* (Chicago: Bancroft, 1893), 789–90.

94. Casper, *Sarah Johnson's Mount Vernon*, 187–92.

95. "Virginia's Exhibit"; "Tell of Early Days: Interesting Furnishings for the Fair's Mount Vernon," *Chicago Daily Tribune*, 14 May 1893.

96. "Virginia's Exhibit."

97. On the concept of the faithful slave, see Blight, *Race and Reunion,* 273–75; James C. Cobb, *Away Down South: A History of Southern Identity* (New York: Oxford University Press, 2005), 78–80; and Micki McElya, *Clinging to Mammy: The Faithful Slave in Twentieth-Century America* (Cambridge: Harvard University Press, 2007).

98. McElya, *Clinging to Mammy,* 15–37; Maurice M. Manring, "Aunt Jemima Explained: The Old South, The Absent Mistress, and the Slave in a Box," *Southern Cultures* 2, no. 1 (Fall 1995): 19–44.

99. Robert W. Rydell, "'Darkest Africa': African Shows at America's World's Fairs, 1893–1940," in *Africans on Stage: Studies in Ethnological Show Business*, ed. Bernth Lindfors (Bloomington: Indiana University Press, 1999), 135–55; Gertrude M. Scott, "Village Performance: Villages at the Chicago World's Columbian Exposition, 1893" (Ph.D. diss., New York University, 1991), 283–86, ProQuest (9134689); Rosemary Bank, "Representing History: Performing the Columbian Exposition," *Theatre Journal* 54 (2002): 589–606.

100. "For Panama Exposition," *Richmond Times Dispatch,* 15 March 1914; Virginia State Legislature, Panama-Pacific International Exposition Commission, *Communication from the Governor of Virginia Transmitting the Report of the Panama-Pacific International Exposition Commission,* February 1916, S. Doc. 10., 2.

101. See Edward H. Hurlbut, "Features of the Panama-Pacific Exposition," *Overland Monthly and Out West Magazine* 66, no. 5 (November 1915): 379–87; and Frank Morton Todd, *The Story of the Exposition: Being the Official History of the International Celebration Held at San Francisco in 1915 to Commemorate the Discovery of the Pacific Ocean and the Construction of the Panama Canal,* vol. 3 (New York: G. P. Putnam's Sons, 1921), 367.

102. James A. Buchanan, *History of the Panama-Pacific International Exposition* (San Francisco: Pan-Pacific Press Association, 1916), 328; "Will Show Heirlooms," *Washington Post,* 10 January 1915.

103. See Charles K. Bryant to Dr. F. J. V. Skiff, 16 May 1914, Folder 59.18, Carton 59, Panama-Pacific International Exposition Records, Bancroft Library, University of California, Berkeley.

104. See Report by Commissioners Baker, Holt, and Lewis to Governor Stuart, 15 February 1916, Folder 143.30, Carton 143, Panama-Pacific International Exposition Records, Bancroft Library, University of California, Berkeley.

105. Dated and handwritten will of Edgerton Stewart Rogers, 24 February 1899, Richmond Circuit Court, Richmond. Rogers, Poindexter, and Bryant were also all members of the Ashby Light Horse Guard, a militia of young privileged white men that regrouped after Reconstruction as a social organization (see John A. Cutchins, *A Famous Command: The Richmond Light Infantry Blues* [Richmond: Garrett and Massie, 1934]; Andrew Morrison, ed., *The City on the James: Richmond, Virginia, The Chamber of Commerce Book* [Richmond:

George W. Engelhardt, 1893], 58; and "Troopers Parade and Banquet," *Richmond Dispatch,* 12 March 1893). For a discussion of Poindexter's work and his partnership with Bryant, see Kerri Elizabeth Culhane, "'The Fifth Avenue of Richmond': The Development of the 800 and 900 Blocks of West Franklin Street, Richmond, Virginia, 1855–1925" (master's thesis, Virginia Commonwealth University, 1997), ProQuest (304406157).

106. Todd, *The Story of the Exposition,* 3:354; "With Exposition Plans for the Old Dominion," *Los Angeles Times,* 13 June 1914.

107. The MVLA was under the impression that the replica would not copy Mount Vernon at full scale, though there is no evidence that Bryant's Virginia Building was a reduced version. It also granted permission after Virginia had already decided to replicate Mount Vernon (see MVLA Minutes 1914, 32).

108. On replicas at world's fairs, see Marling, *George Washington Slept Here,* 156–59; Rhoads, *The Colonial Revival,* 125–41; and Maas, "Architecture and Americanism," 17–19.

109. See Frye, "The Beginnings of the Period Room in American Museums," 217–40.

110. "Will Show Heirlooms."

111. "Old Virginia on View," *Washington Post,* 20 December 1914; Buchanan, *History of the Panama-Pacific International Exposition,* 328.

112. Buchanan, *History of the Panama-Pacific International Exposition,* 328.

113. Todd, *The Story of the Exposition,* 3:354–55; Buchanan, *History of the Panama-Pacific International Exposition,* 328.

114. "Will Show Heirlooms"; Frances A. Groff, "Lovely Woman at the Exposition," *Sunset Magazine* 34, no. 5 (May 1915): 888; Report by the Commissioners, Folder 143.30, Carton 143, Panama-Pacific International Exposition Records, Bancroft Library, University of California, Berkeley.

115. Upon the death of Jefferson Davis's beloved daughter Winnie, Heth also accepted the presidency of the Southern Relief Society, an organization benefiting Confederate veterans and their families (see "New Home of the Southern Relief Society," *Washington Post,* 1 April 1906).

116. Heth was acting within the general realm of Colonial Revival performance and historic preservation (see David Glassberg, *American Historical Pageantry: The Uses of Tradition in the Early Twentieth Century* [Chapel Hill: University of North Carolina Press, 1990], 10–199; Thomas Andrew Denenberg, *Wallace Nutting and the Invention of Old America* [New Haven: Yale University Press, 2003], 45–122; and Beverly Gordon, "Costumed Representations of Early America: A Gendered Portrayal, 1850–1940," *Dress* 30 [2003]: 3–20).

117. See Blight, *Race and Reunion,* 284–91; and Lindgren, *Preserving the Old Dominion,* 181–84.

118. See Mark Alan Hewitt, *The Architect and the American Country House, 1890–1940* (New Haven: Yale University Press, 1990), 1–14; and Richard Guy Wilson, *Harbor Hill:*

Portrait of a House (New York: Norton, 2008), 6–13. See also Clive Aslet, *The American Country House* (New Haven: Yale University Press, 1990).

119. See Joan Ockman, ed., *Architecture School: Three Centuries of Educating Architects in North America* (Cambridge: MIT Press, 2012).

120. See Richard Guy Wilson, "Scientific Eclecticism," in Richard Guy Wilson, Dianne H. Pilgrim, and Richard N. Murray, *The American Renaissance, 1876–1917* (New York: Brooklyn Museum, 1979), 57–62; Richard Guy Wilson, *McKim, Mead & White, Architects* (New York: Rizzoli, 1983), 43–63; and Richard W. Longstreth, "Eclecticism in American Architecture," *Winterthur Portfolio* 17, no. 1 (Spring 1982): 55–82.

121. Frank Miles Day, preface to *American Country Houses of Today* (New York: Architectural Book Publishing, 1912), v. See also Longstreth, "Academic Eclecticism in American Architecture."

122. Frank E. Wallis, "The Colonial House," in *Architectural Styles for Country Houses,* ed. Henry H. Saylor (New York: Robert M. McBride, 1919), 20. This essay was also published as "What and Why Is Colonial Architecture?," *House and Garden* 16, no. 6 (December 1909): 189–92, vi–vii.

123. Hewitt, *The Architect and the American Country House,* 38–42, 69–71. See also Aymar Embury II, ed., *The Livable House: Its Plan and Design,* vol. 1 (New York: Moffat Yard, 1917), 35–81.

124. Henry H. Saylor, introduction to *Architectural Styles for Country Houses,* ed. Saylor (New York: Robert M. McBride, 1919), 2.

125. James F. O'Gorman, "Hill-Stead and Its Architect," in *Hill-Stead: The Country Place of Theodate Pope Riddle,* ed. O'Gorman (New York: Princeton Architectural Press, 2010), 43–81. See also Lisa Pfueller Davidson and Julia A. Sienkewicz, "Hill-Stead (Alfred Atmore Pope home and estate)," Historic American Buildings Survey (HABS CT-472); Wilson, *The Colonial Revival House,* 64–73.

126. Davidson and Sienkewicz, "Hill-Stead," 73–74; O'Gorman, "Hill-Stead and Its Architect," 68–69; Hewitt, *The Architect and the American Country House,* 160–61.

127. Barr Ferree, "Notable American Homes—'Hill Stead,' the Estate of Alfred Atmore Pope, Esq., Farmington, Conn.," *American Homes and Gardens* 7, no. 2 (February 1910): 47.

128. Henry H. Saylor, "The Best Twelve Country Houses in America: The Home of James L. Breese," *Country Life in America* 27 (March 1915): 48.

129. See Samuel G. White, *The Houses of McKim, Mead & White* (New York: Rizzoli, 1998), 238–42.

130. Barr Ferree, *American Estates and Gardens* (New York: Munn, 1904), 173.

131. *Architecture* 25, no. 1 (15 January 1912): 3.

132. Saylor, "The Best Twelve Country Houses in America," 46–49.

133. McKim, Mead & White, *A Monograph of the Work of McKim, Mead & White,* vol. 3 (New York: Architectural Book Publishing, 1915), plate 270. See also Richard Cheek, *Selling*

the Dwelling: The Books That Built America's Houses, 1775–2000 (New York: Grolier Club, 2013), 146–49.

134. See Frank Wallis, "The Colonial Renaissance: Houses of the Middle and Southern Colonies," *White Pine Series of Architectural Monographs* 2, no. 1 (February 1916): 3.

135. On the "genealogy" of this group of architects, see Hewitt, *The Architect and the American Country House,* 25–31.

136. Wilhelm Miller, "Mount Vernon as Washington Would Have Had It," *Country Life in America* 26 (June 1914): 49–52, 88–90; "George Washington: Country Gentleman," *Country Life* 41, no. 2 (December 1921): 35–41; Paul Wilstach, "George Washington as a Planter and Country Gentleman," *Country Life in America* 30 (June 1916): 31–33; Paul Wilstach, "The Country Home of George Washington," *Country Life in America* 29 (April 1916): 23–26; Paul Wilstach, "Domestic Life at Mount Vernon," *Country Life in America* 30 (May 1916): 35–37; Paul Wilstach, "Social Life at Mount Vernon in Washington's Day," *Country Life in America* 30 (September 1916): 29–31.

137. Hewitt, *The Architect and the American Country House,* 46–47.

138. John Russell Pope, *The Architecture of John Russell Pope,* vol. 3 (New York: 1925), plates 1–5; "House, Robert J. Collier, Wickatunk, N.J.," *Architecture* 36, no. 1 (July 1917): plates 114–20.

139. James F. Garrison, *Mastering Tradition: The Residential Architecture of John Russell Pope* (New York: Acanthus, 2004), 68.

140. Dwight Pitcaithley, "Abraham Lincoln's Birthplace Cabin: The Making of an American Icon," in *Myth, Memory, and the Making of the American Landscape,* ed. Paul A. Shackel (Gainesville: University Press of Florida, 2001), 240–54.

141. "The Georgian House," *American Architect* 117, no. 2298 (7 January 1920): 4–6.

142. Samuel Howe, *American Country Houses of To-day* (New York: Architectural Book Publishing, 1915), 251–61.

143. See *American Architect* 108, no. 2066 (28 July 1915); *Architecture* 41, no. 4 (April 1920): plates 53–57; and Howe, *American Country Houses of To-day,* 240–46.

144. See Hewitt, *The Architect and the American Country House,* 48–51. See also Peter Pennoyer and Anne Walker, *The Architecture of Delano & Aldrich* (New York: Norton, 2003); and Mark A. Hewitt, "William Adams Delano and the Muttontown Enclave," *Antiques* 132, no. 2 (August 1987): 316–27.

145. Delano and Aldrich also designed a house with the Mount Vernon piazza for Cornelius Vanderbilt Whitney in Old Westbury in 1941.

146. See Howe, *American Country Houses of Today,* 240.

147. Ibid.

148. C. Matlack Price, "Painting the Outside of the House," *House Beautiful* 43, no. 3 (February 1918): 127.

149. Advertisement for the Southern Pine Association, New Orleans, Louisiana, *House Beautiful* 42 (August 1917), n.p.

150. For examples, see house for Frederick T. Steinway in Great Neck, New York, by Patterson and Dula in *Architecture* 35, no. 4 (April 1917): plate 60; house for W. Warner Harper in Chestnut Hill, Pennsylvania, in Howe, *American Country Houses of To-Day,* 302–3; house for Honorable Lathrop Brown in St. James, New York, by Peabody, Wilson and Brown in *Architectural Forum* 33 (September 1920): 89–92; Pond Hollow Farm in Old Westbury, New York, by Peabody, Wilson and Brown in *Architecture* (1914); Meadow Farm in Glen Cove, New York, by Davis, McGrath and Keissling in *Architectural Review* (1918); house for Francis Skiddy Von Stade Sr. by Cross and Cross in Old Westbury in *Architecture* (1915); Valley House by Warren and Clark in Old Brookville, New York, in *Architecture* (1919). See also Guy Lowell's Piping Rock Club in *American Architect & Architecture* (1912) and *Country Life* (1920). See Hewitt, *The Architect and the American Country House.*

151. "Report of the Jury Award," *White Pine Series of Architectural Monographs* 3, no. 4 (August 1917): 3–7.

152. Henry H. Saylor, ed., *Inexpensive Homes of Individuality,* rev. ed. (New York: McBride, Nast, 1915), 16.

153. On the Mount Vernon–inspired women's prison, see Alfred Hopkins, "Prisons and Prison Building," *Architectural Forum* 28 (May 1918): 189–93; and Alfred Hopkins, *Prisons and Prison Building* (New York: Architectural Book Publishing, 1930), plate 10. Hopkins also designed a country house based on Mount Vernon (see "Colonial House for Mr. Raymond S. Clark, Alfred Hopkins, Architect," *Architecture and Building* 46, no. 5 [May 1914]: 203–4).

154. See Kammen, *Mystic Chords of Memory,* 299–309.

155. William B. Rhoads, "Roadside Colonial: Early American Design for the Automobile Age, 1900–1940," *Winterthur Portfolio* 21, no. 2/3 (Summer–Autumn 1986): 133–52; Kammen, *Mystic Chords of Memory,* 310–74.

156. Kammen, *Mystic Chords of Memory,* 310–74.

157. See L. Earle Rowe, "A Wing Devoted to American Art," *Bulletin of the Metropolitan Museum of Art,* November 1922, 3.

158. Wilson, *The Colonial Revival House,* 90.

159. See Marling, *George Washington Slept Here,* 176–82.

160. See Wendy Kaplan, "R. T. H. Halsey: An Ideology of Collecting American Decorative Arts," *Winterthur Portfolio* 17, no. 1 (Spring 1982): 43–53; William B. Rhoads, "The Colonial Revival and the Americanization of Immigrants," in *The Colonial Revival,* ed. Alan Alexrod (New York: Norton, 1985), 341–61; William B. Rhoads, "The Colonial Revival and American Nationalism," *Journal of the Society of Architectural Historians* 35, no. 4 (December 1976): 239–54.

161. R. T. H. Halsey qtd. in Kaplan, "R. T. H. Halsey," 49.

162. "Y.W.C.A. at Sesqui Will Be Dedicated," *Philadelphia Evening Public Ledger,* 14 June 1926, clipping in Scrapbook 9, SEAR.

163. "In the Old Market Place," 13 August 1926, clipping in High Street Record Book 5, Committee of 1926 Sesquicentennial Collection, Historic Strawberry Mansion, Philadelphia; "'400' Aid Workmen at Sesqui," *Philadelphia Daily News,* 10 June 1926, clipping in Scrapbook 9, SEAR; "Philadelphia Plays Hostess," *Woman's Press* 20, no. 6 (June 1926): 420.

164. "Mt. Vernon House," *Philadelphia Inquirer,* 19 June 1926, clipping in Scrapbook 9, SEAR.

165. Joanna J. Meyerowitz, *Women Adrift: Independent Wage Earners in Chicago, 1880–1930* (Chicago: University of Chicago Press, 1988). See also Daphne Spain, *How Women Saved the City* (Minneapolis: University of Minnesota Press, 2001), 14–27.

166. Karen Sue Mittelman, "'A Spirit That Touches the Problems of Today': Women and Social Reform in the Philadelphia Young Women's Christian Association, 1920–1945" (Ph.D. diss., University of Pennsylvania, 1987), 25–40, ProQuest (303595070); Spain, *How Women Saved the City,* 89–91; Sarah Heath, "Negotiating White Womanhood: The Cincinnati YWCA and White Wage-Earning Women, 1918–1929," in *Men and Women Adrift: The YMCA and YWCA in the City,* ed. Nina Mjagkij and Margaret Spratt (New York: New York University Press, 1997), 89–94; and J. Stanley Lemons, *The Woman Citizen: Social Feminism in the 1920s,* 2nd ed. (Charlottesville: University Press of Virginia, 1990), 137–38.

167. See Mary S. Sims, *The Natural History of a Social Institution: The Young Women's Christian Association* (New York: Woman's Press, 1936), 88.

168. "Beulah Kennard, On Entertaining Visitors," undated clipping in High Street Record Book 5, Committee of 1926 Sesquicentennial Collection, Historic Strawberry Mansion, Philadelphia.

169. The Room Registry Department registered 7,699 people. See undated report, High Street Record Book 8, Committee of 1926 Sesquicentennial Collection, Historic Strawberry Mansion, Philadelphia; Mrs. George H. Earle Jr., "Mt. Vernon House," report dated March 1927, Folder 12, Box 7, Records of the YWCA of Philadelphia, Metropolitan Collection, Urban Archives, Temple University, Philadelphia.

170. "Beulah Kennard, On Entertaining Visitors"; *Y.W.C.A. of Philadelphia Mount Vernon House on the Grounds of the Sesqui-Centennial, Broad Street and Pattison Avenue,"* pamphlet, Box "Wr 692 v. 2, the Sesqui-Centennial," Philadelphia Ephemera Collection, Historical Society of Pennsylvania, Philadelphia.

171. "Women's Work at the Sesquicentennial," undated report, High Street Record Book 8, Committee of 1926 Sesquicentennial Collection, Historic Strawberry Mansion, Philadelphia; "Beulah Kennard, On Entertaining Visitors."

172. Marion Vincent to Mary Johns Hopper, 28 August 1926, Microfilm Reel 210, YWCA of the USA Records, Sophia Smith Collection, Smith College, Northampton. The total attendance for the Sesquicentennial was 6,408,289. The Mount Vernon House cafeteria served

302,719 patrons (see undated and untitled report in High Street Record Book 8, Committee of 1926 Sesquicentennial Collection, Historic Strawberry Mansion, Philadelphia; and E. L. Austin and Odell Hauser, *The Sesqui-Centennial International Exposition* [Philadelphia: Current Publications, 1929], 26).

173. Daphne Spain, conversation with author, 12 November 2010.

174. Earle, "Mt. Vernon House."

175. Minutes for the 28 June 1926 meeting of the Philadelphia Metropolitan YWCA held at Mount Vernon House, Folder 6, Box 2, Records of the YWCA of Philadelphia, Metropolitan Collection, Urban Archives, Temple University, Philadelphia.

176. "Beulah Kennard, On Entertaining Visitors"; Earle, "Mt. Vernon House."

177. Earle, "Mt. Vernon House"; "Philadelphia Plays Hostess."

178. Courtney Fint, "Jackson's Mill State 4-H Camp Historic District," National Register of Historic Places nomination, 2005.

179. The T-shaped configuration of the building was common to camp dining halls beginning in this period (see Abigail A. Van Slyck, "Kitchen Technologies and Mealtime Rituals: Interpreting the Food Axis at American Summer Camps, 1890–1950," *Technology and Culture* 43, no. 4 [October 2002]: 685–91).

180. Thomas Wessel and Marilyn Wessel, *4-H: An American Idea 1900–1980* (Chevy Chase, MD: National 4-H Council, 1982), 1–42.

181. Orville Merton Kile, "An Adventure in Citizenship," *McClure's Magazine* 55, no. 4 (June 1923): 62. See also Wessel and Wessel, *4-H*, 42–43; Franklin M. Reck, *The 4-H Story: A History of 4-H Club Work* (Ames: Iowa State College Press, 1951), 199–200; and Abigail A. Van Slyck, *A Manufactured Wilderness: Summer Camps and the Shaping of American Youth, 1890–1960* (Minneapolis: University of Minnesota Press, 2006).

182. Courtney Fint, "The American Summer Youth Camp as a Cultural Landscape," in *Cultural Landscapes: Balancing Nature and Heritage in Preservation Practice,* ed. Richard Longstreth (Minneapolis: University of Minnesota Press, 2008), 74.

183. On Kendrick, see Guy H. Stewart, *A Touch of Charisma: A History of the 4-H Club Program in West Virginia* (n.p., 1969), 22–30; *History of the Maryland 4-H Club All Stars, 1921–1948* (4-H Club, 1949), 14–17.

184. Reck, *The 4-H Story,* 200; Kile, "An Adventure in Citizenship," 62. See also Stewart, *A Touch of Charisma,* 38–41.

185. See Fint, "Jackson's Mill State 4-H Camp Historic District," 28–29.

186. W. H. Kendrick, *The Four-H Trail* (Boston: Richard G. Badger, 1926), 110.

187. Ibid., 55.

188. Fint, "Jackson's Mill State 4-H Camp Historic District," 23.

189. Michael Meador, *Historic Jackson's Mill: A Walking Tour* (Parsons, WV: McClain Printing, 1991), 30–35.

190. For more on the rustic architecture of summer camps, see W. Barksdale Maynard,

"'An Ideal Life in the Woods for Boys': Architecture and Culture in the Earliest Summer Camps," *Winterthur Portfolio* 34, no. 1 (Spring 1999): 3–29.

191. Kendrick, *The Four-H Trail,* 109–10.

192. Reck, *The 4-H Story,* 201; Stewart, *A Touch of Charisma,* 77–78.

193. Proposal sent by William H. Kendrick to Henry Ford, 17 February 1930, Jackson's Mill Archives.

194. Kendrick, *The Four-H Trail,* 55; Chad Proudfoot, program coordinator, Cultural Resources, Jackson's Mill, conversation with author, November 2014.

195. Courtney Fint, conversation with author, November 2014.

196. On the plan for Jackson's Mill, see Fint, "The American Summer Youth Camp as a Cultural Landscape," 78–80.

197. See Harold Robert Shurtleff, *The Log Cabin Myth: A Study of the Early Dwellings of the English Colonists in North America,* ed. Samuel Eliot Morison (Gloucester, MA: P. Smith, 1967).

198. Carmen V. Harris, "States' Rights, Federal Bureaucrats, and Segregated 4-H Camps in the United States, 1927–1969," *Journal of African American History* 93, no. 3 (Summer 2008): 362–88.

199. See Rodney S. Collins, "West Virginia 4-H Camp for Negros; Camp Washington-Carver," National Register of Historic Places nomination, 1980.

200. "Rumanian [*sic*] Exhibit Opens," *Philadelphia Inquirer,* 28 June 1926, clipping in Scrapbook 10, SEAR; "Y.W.C.A. House at Sesqui Has Rumanian [*sic*] Exhibit," *Philadelphia Record,* 28 June 1926, clipping in Scrapbook 10, SEAR; "150,000 Expected at Sesqui Today," *Public Ledger and North American,* 15 September 1926, clipping in Scrapbook 12, SEAR; "Beulah Kennard, On Entertaining Visitors"; "Tea for N. E. A. Delegates," *Philadelphia Public Ledger and North American,* 30 June 1926, clipping in Scrapbook 10, SEAR.

201. Mittelman, "A Spirit That Touches the Problems of Today," 145–52.

202. See Amy Thompson McCandless, *The Past in the Present: Women's Higher Education in the Twentieth-Century American South* (Tuscaloosa: University of Alabama Press, 1999), 121–58.

203. W. Elliott Dunwoody, "Greater Wesleyan College," *Wesleyan Alumnae* 1, no. 2 (April 1927): 53. Although the college first hired the New York firm Ludlow and Peabody to work up a scheme for the new campus, Walker and Weeks were hired by December 1925 (see minutes for Executive Committee for 23 January 1924 and 1 December 1925, Willet Memorial Library, Wesleyan College, Macon). On Walker and Weeks, see Eric Johannesen, *A Cleveland Legacy: The Architecture of Walker and Weeks* (Kent, OH: Kent State University Press, 1999).

204. Much like many of their Beaux-Arts–minded peers, Walker and Weeks had designed a country house based on Mount Vernon a few years prior to starting work on Wesleyan. In 1917, Walker designed Circle W. Farm, a country house for Walter C. White, founder of the White Sewing Machine Company and White Motor Company, in Gates Mills, Ohio (see

Johannesen, *A Cleveland Legacy,* 18–21; and Dan Ruminski and Alan Dutka, *Cleveland in the Gilded Age: A Stroll down Millionaires' Row* [Charleston, SC: History Press, 2012], 123–55).

205. See Kenneth H. Thomas, "Wesleyan College Historic District," National Register of Historic Places nomination, 2004; "Seven Units Near Completion at Wesleyan," *Watchtower* 5, no. 5 (20 October 1927).

206. William F. Quillian, *A New Day for Historic Wesleyan* (Nashville: Publishing House M. E. Church, South, ca. 1928), 9. On Wesleyan's early years, see Samuel Luttrell Akers, *The First Hundred Years of Wesleyan College, 1836–1936* (Macon, GA: Beehive, 1976).

207. "Dr. Quillian Opens Courses of Lectures," *Watchtower* 4, no. 2 (30 September 1926).

208. *Official Circular of Information for the Use of Students, 1928–1929, Wesleyan College* (Atlanta: Foote and Davies, 1928), 21–35, Willet Memorial Library, Wesleyan College, Macon.

209. "A Beautiful Dignity," *Watchtower* 4, no. 2 (30 September 1926).

210. "Future Home of Wesleyan Reflects Beauty of Old South," *Watchtower* 5, no. 18 (23 February 1928).

211. *Bulletin of Wesleyan College, Macon, Georgia, Catalogue 1926–1927,* ser. 2, no. 10 (February 1927), 25, Willet Memorial Library, Wesleyan College, Macon.

212. *Atlanta Constitution,* 17 July 1917.

213. On Brown, see Robert M. Craig, *Atlanta Architecture: Art Deco to Modern Classic, 1929–1959* (Gretna, LA: Pelican, 1995).

214. *Lanier University Bulletin: Fourth Annual Catalog Number, 1920–21* 4, no. 1 (June 1920), 17, Hargett Rare Book and Manuscript Library, University of Georgia, Athens.

215. Thomas G. Dyer, "The Klan on Campus: C. Lewis Fowler and Lanier University," *South Atlantic Quarterly* 77, no. 4 (Autumn 1978): 453–69.

216. See Nancy Maclean, *Behind the Mask of Chivalry: The Making of the Second Ku Klux Klan* (New York: Oxford University Press, 1994); Rory McVeigh, *The Rise of the Ku Klux Klan: Right-Wing Movements and National Politics* (Minneapolis: University of Minnesota Press, 2009); and Kenneth T. Jackson, *The Ku Klux Klan in the City, 1915–1930* (New York: Oxford University Press, 1967).

217. *Lanier University Bulletin,* 19; Clement Charlton Moseley, "The Political Influence of the Role of Ku Klux Klan in Georgia," *Georgia Historical Quarterly* 57 (1973): 235–55; Kesavan Sudheendran, "Community Power Structure in Atlanta: A Study in Decision Making, 1920–1939" (Ph.D. diss., Georgia State University, 1982), ProQuest (303269138).

218. *Lanier University Bulletin,* 32. It is not clear when Simmons was hired, but he was certainly on the faculty by 1920 (see "Mass Meeting Today at Atlanta Theater," *Atlanta Constitution,* 13 June 1920).

219. "Relations of Races Discussed at Rally," *Atlanta Constitution,* 14 June 1920.

220. C. Lewis Fowler, *The Ku Klux Klan: It's [sic] Origin, Meaning and Scope of Operation* (Atlanta, 1922), 8.

221. "Lanier University Now Making Plans for Great Future," *Atlanta Constitution*, 23 September 1917; "Lanier Given Site Valued at $250,000," *Atlanta Constitution*, 14 November 1917.

222. "Work on the Buildings at Lanier Starts Soon," *Atlanta Constitution*, 14 January 1918.

223. "Lanier Now Planning South-Wide Campaign," *Atlanta Constitution*, 30 January 1918. For biographies of these men, see *New Georgia Encyclopedia*, www.georgiaencyclopedia.org.

224. Lucian Lamar Knight, *Georgia's Landmarks, Memorials and Legends*, vol. 1 (Atlanta: Byrd Printing, 1913), 507.

225. "Lanier University News," *Atlanta Constitution*, 10 February 1918; "Begin New Buildings at Lanier University," *Atlanta Constitution*, 27 April 1919; "Lanier University Drive Opens Today," *Atlanta Constitution*, 8 July 1919.

226. "Simmons Heads Lanier University," *Atlanta Constitution*, 19 August 1921.

227. "Forrest Tells Aims of Ku Klux College," *New York Times*, 12 September 1921.

228. Advertisement for Lanier University, *Atlanta Constitution*, 13 September 1921.

229. "Forrest Announces Plans for University of America," *Atlanta Constitution*, 5 February 1922.

230. "Lanier University Buys Large Tract," *Atlanta Constitution*, 18 September 1921.

231. Ibid.; *The Ku-Klux Klan, Hearings before the Committee on Rules, House of Representatives, Sixty-Seventh Congress, First Session* (Washington, DC: Government Printing Office, 1921), 110; "Big Site Bought for Klan Million-Dollar College," *Atlanta Constitution*, 2 February 1922; "Lanier University Will Be Abandoned," *Atlanta Constitution*, 13 July 1922.

232. Frank Bohn, "The Ku Klux Klan Interpreted," *American Journal of Sociology* 30, no. 4 (January 1925): 385–407; Dyer, "The Klan on Campus," 467–69.

4. Battles of "Authenticity"

1. See David Gebhard, "The American Colonial Revival in the 1930s," *Winterthur Portfolio* 22, no. 2/3 (Summer/Autumn 1987): 109–48; and Marling, *George Washington Slept Here*, 325–64.

2. "Welcome the Honored Guest with Mount Vernon . . . ," advertisement for Mount Vernon Brand Straight Rye Whiskey, 1939, National Distillers Products Corporation, Folder "Publicity (Old)–1937–1945," PMVLA.

3. On the primacy of Gilbert Stuart's *Athenaeum Portrait*, see Adam Greenhalgh, "'Not a Man but a God': The Apotheosis of Gilbert Stuart's Athenaeum Portrait of George Washington," *Winterthur Portfolio* 41, no 4 (Winter 2007): 269–303.

4. Charles Cecil Wall to N. Cook, 9 October 1937, Folder "Policy–Misc.," PMVLA.

5. Charles Cecil Wall to Robert Barry, 27 February 1939, Folder "Publicity (Old)–1937–1945," PMVLA.

6. Timothy Davis, "The American Parkway as Colonial Revival Landscape," in *Re-creating the American Past: Essays on the Colonial Revival,* ed. Richard Guy Wilson, Shaun Eyring, and Kenny Marotta (Charlottesville: University of Virginia Press, 2006), 151–53; Timothy Mark Davis, "Mount Vernon Memorial Highway and the Evolution of the American Parkway" (Ph.D. diss., University of Texas at Austin, 1997), ProQuest (304414413).

7. MVLA Minutes 1931, 88–91, 108; MVLA Minutes 1933, 14–15; MVLA Minutes 1934, 14.

8. MVLA Minutes 1936, 12.

9. MVLA Minutes 1929, 45–46; "Barreled Sunlight" advertisement, *Country Life* 58 (May 1930): 81.

10. The MVLA endured a very public accusation that the organization was prospering mightily off of visitors' admission fees in the 1910s (see House of Delegates of Virginia, "Grounds of Legal Objection to the Bill and the Joint Resolution in Reference to the Mount Vernon Ladies' Association of the Union" [Richmond, 1912]).

11. Harrison H. Dodge to P. A. Manker, 29 June 1932, Folder "Rep. of Bldgs," PMVLA.

12. Charles Bascom Slemp qtd. in Frances Parkinson Keyes, "Tricolor and Stars and Stripes Float Together over the Greatest Show on Earth," *Good Housekeeping* 93, no. 5 (November 1931): 199.

13. Charles Bascom Slemp to Henry L. Stimson, telegram, 11 September 1930, Folder "Building of US and Site at Paris," Box 1, Entry 1316, RG 43, NARA; Louis Hall to Charles Bascom Slemp, memorandum, 6 September 1930, Folder "Mr. Charles Bascom Slemp, letters to and from to Dec. 31, 1930," Box 1, Entry 1317, RG 43, NARA; House, Committee on Foreign Affairs, *A Joint Resolution to Increase the Amount Authorized to Be Appropriated for the Expenses of Participation by the United States in the International Exposition of Colonial and Overseas Countries to Be Held at Paris, France, in 1931,* 71st Cong., 3rd sess., 9 December 1930, 2.

14. Charles Bascom Slemp to Henry L. Stimson, 24 September 1930, Folder "Charles Kirkpatrick Bryant, Architect," Box 2, Entry 1315, RG 43, NARA.

15. Alexander C. T. Geppert, *Fleeting Cities: International Expositions in Fin-de-Siècle Europe* (London: Palgrave Macmillan, 2010), 190–91; Patricia Morton, *Hybrid Modernities: Architecture and Representation at the 1931 Colonial Exposition, Paris* (Cambridge: MIT Press, 2000), 234–51; Dana S. Hale, *Races on Display: French Representations of Colonized Peoples, 1886–1940* (Bloomington: Indiana University Press, 2008), 141–51.

16. William Adams Delano to Charles Bascom Slemp, 2 October 1930, Folder "Charles Kirkpatrick Bryant, Architect," Box 2, Entry 1315, RG 43, NARA.

17. Resolution of the Washington Exposition of 1932, Inc., passed by the Board of Alderman, 21 February 1928, Folder 1, Box WJJ-230, Mayor James J. Walker Papers, Municipal Archives, New York City.

18. United States George Washington Bicentennial Commission, *Report of the United States George Washington Bicentennial Commission,* vol. 5 (Washington, DC: United States George Washington Bicentennial Commission, 1932), 2.

19. Ibid., 472–73.

20. Marling, *George Washington Slept Here,* 325–64.

21. James Hosmer Penniman, "Washington Proprietor of Mount Vernon," in *History of the George Washington Bicentennial Celebration,* Literature Series, vol. 1 (Washington, DC: United States George Washington Bicentennial Commission, 1932), 95.

22. Charles K. Bryant to Herbert Hoover, 1 September 1930, Folder "Charles Kirkpatrick Bryant, Architect," Box 2, Entry 1315, RG 43, NARA; Senate, *Commission of the United States of America, the International Colonial and Overseas Exposition at Paris, Exposition of Overseas Countries Held at Paris, 1931,* 72nd Cong., 1st sess., 1932, S. Doc. 94, 4; "Mount Vernon at Paris Exposition," *Washington Post,* 1 February 1931.

23. See Gustav Meissner to Charles Bascom Slemp, 10 August 1931, Folder "French Colonial Exposition Correspondence Aug.–Sept. 1931," Box 1, Entry 1317, RG 43, NARA; House, Committee on Foreign Affairs, *A Joint Resolution to Increase the Amount Authorized,* 3; William Adams Delano to Charles Bascom Slemp, 2 October 1930, Folder "Charles Kirkpatrick Bryant, Architect," Box 2, Entry 1315, RG 43, NARA; "Mail Order Co.'s Have Poor Year," *Wall Street Journal,* 1 January 1931; "Mass-Produced Houses in Review," *Fortune* 7, no. 4 (April 1933): 52–54; Boris Emmet and John E. Jeuck, *Catalogues and Counters: A History of Sears, Roebuck and Company* (Chicago: University of Chicago Press, 1950), 522–23.

24. Jacques Gréber to Charles Bascom Slemp, 9 May 1931, Folder "Landscaping," Box 11, Entry 1316, RG 43, NARA.

25. House, Committee on Foreign Affairs, *A Joint Resolution to Increase the Amount Authorized,* 3–4.

26. "Mt. Vernon Replica for Paris," undated clipping in Folder "Mt. Vernon, Replicas of," PMVLA.

27. Emmet and Jeuck, *Catalogues and Counters,* 108, 226–28. See also Amanda Cooke and Avi Friedman, "Ahead of Their Time: The Sears Catalogue Prefabricated Houses," *Journal of Design History* 14, no. 1 (2001): 53–70; Katherine Cole Stevenson and H. Ward Jandl, *Houses by Mail: A Guide to Houses from Sears, Roebuck and Company* (Washington, DC: Preservation Press, 1986); Robert Schweitzer and Michael W. R. Davis, *America's Favorite Homes: Mail-Order Catalogues as a Guide to Popular Early 20th-Century Houses* (Detroit: Wayne State University Press, 1990), 61–75.

28. Schweitzer and Davis, *America's Favorite Homes,* 66; Dolores Hayden, *Building Suburbia: Green Fields and Urban Growth, 1820–2000* (New York: Knopf, 2003), 103–5; Emmet and Jeuck, *Catalogues and Counters,* 227–28, 268–69; Cooke and Friedman, "Ahead of Their Time," 67–68.

29. "Sears Aids Home Modernization," *Wall Street Journal,* 6 October 1930; "Sears, Roebuck to Build Houses," *New York Times,* 19 January 1930; "Sears Will Expand Home Construction," *Wall Street Journal,* 22 January 1932. See also Emmet and Jeuck, *Catalogues and Counters,* 448–49, 525–26; and Stevenson and Jandl, *Houses by Mail,* 22.

30. See Gebhard, "The American Colonial Revival in the 1930s," 119–20.

31. See "Quality Production Reaches the Home Builder," *Business Week,* 26 March 1930, 25–26.

32. Charles K. Bryant to Charles Bascom Slemp, n.d., Folder "Charles Kirkpatrick Bryant, Architect," Box 2, Entry 1315, RG 43, NARA; "Report of the Activities of the Commission, Aug. 28, 1930–Nov. 30, 1930," Folder "State Department," Box 18, Entry 1316, RG 43, NARA.

33. Press release from Charles K. Bryant, Architect, n.d., Folder "Electrical Fixture," Box 4, Entry 1316, RG 43, NARA.

34. Mary Moss Wellborn to Charles Bascom Slemp, 24 November 1930, Folder "Wellborn–Mary Moss," Box 19, Entry 1316, RG 43, NARA.

35. Charles Bascom Slemp to General William E. Horton, 3 April 1931, Folder "Charles Bascom Slemp, Hon. C. Blascom" [*sic*] (3 of 4), Box 17, Entry 1316, RG 43, NARA.

36. Charles Bascom Slemp to Gustav Meissner, 21 February 1931, and Charles Bascom Slemp to Gustav Meissner, 28 February 1931, Folder "Contractors—Sears, Roebuck and Company" (1 of 2), Box 3, Entry 1316, RG 43, NARA.

37. "Report by the United States Colonial and Overseas Exposition to Hon. Henry L. Stimson, 22 September 1930," Folder "State Department," Box 18, Entry 1316, RG 43, NARA.

38. "G. R. Artists to Duplicate Mt. Vernon," *Grand Rapids Herald,* 9 November 1930; House, Committee on Foreign Affairs, *A Joint Resolution to Increase the Amount Authorized,* 5; memorandum of telephone conversation between Slemp and Mr. Wallace (Grand Rapids Furniture Association), 25 November 1930, Folder "Furniture for Mt. Vernon Mansion" (3 of 5), Box 8, Entry 1316, RG 43, NARA.

39. "Furnishing Mt. Vernon as Restored May Develop into Community Enterprise," *Grand Rapids Herald,* 14 November 1930. On Grand Rapids furniture, see Christian G. Carron, *Grand Rapids Furniture: The Story of America's Furniture City* (Grand Rapids: Public Museum of Grand Rapids, 1998); James Stanford Bradshaw, "Grand Rapids, 1870–1880: Furniture City Emerges," *Michigan History* 55, no. 4 (Winter 1971): 321–42; and Sam Burchell, *A History of Furniture: Celebrating Baker Furniture, 100 Years of Fine Reproductions* (New York: Abrams, 1991), 136–37.

40. Charles Bascom Slemp to George Harrison Phelps, 10 November 1930, and Frances Rogers to Charles H. Burke, n.d., Folder "Furniture for Mt. Vernon Mansion" (5 of 5), Box 8, Entry 1316, RG 43, NARA; Frances Rogers to Charles Bascom Slemp, 23 October 1930, Folder "Building of US and Site at Paris," Box 1, Entry 1316, RG 43, NARA.

41. Tom Kindel to George Harrison Phelps, 21 November 1930, Folder "Furniture for Mt. Vernon Mansion" (3 of 5), Box 8, Entry 1316, RG 43, NARA.

42. "The Paris Reproduction of Washington's Home," undated newspaper clipping in Folder "Mt. Vernon, Replicas of," PMVLA.

43. Marling, *George Washington Slept Here,* 331–33.

44. Typewritten lists of excerpts from the Philippines Registration Book and Porto [*sic*] Rican Registration Book, Folder "r.e. International Colonial & Overseas Expositions," Box 11, Series 1, Papers of Charles Bascom Slemp, Special Collections, University of Virginia

Library, Charlottesville; translated newspaper clipping, "The Colonial Exposition at Paris: America without skyscrapers" (July 1931) in Folder "Correspondence File" (3 of 3), Box 19, Entry 1316, RG 43, NARA.

45. Paul Reynauld qtd. in "French Exposition Leaders Honored by American Club," *New York Herald* (Paris), 27 June 1931, clipping in Scrapbook "Charles Bascom Slemp (1931, Paris Exposition)," Box 70, Series 1, Additional Papers of Charles Bascom Slemp, Special Collections, University of Virginia Library, Charlottesville.

46. Keyes, "Tricolor and Stars and Stripes," 199.

47. Frances Rogers to Mrs. John Dickinson Sherman, 19 May 1933, Folder "Bi-Centennial Committee," PMVLA; Frances Rogers to Charles K. Bryant, 8 January 1931, Folder "Building of US and Site at Paris," Box 1, Entry 1316, RG 43, NARA.

48. MVLA Minutes 1931, 19; Frances Rogers to Charles Bascom Slemp, 23 October 1930, Folder "Building of US and Site at Paris," Box 1, Entry 1316, RG 43, NARA.

49. Charles Bascom Slemp to Harrison H. Dodge, 17 January 1931, and Charles H. Burke to Frances Rogers, 27 October 1930, Folder "Building of US and Site at Paris," Box 1, Entry 1316, RG 43, NARA.

50. MVLA Minutes 1930, 22.

51. MVLA Minutes 1931, 53; Harrison H. Dodge to Alice Richards, 4 May 1931, Superintendent's Monthly Letters to the Regent, NLSGW.

52. Charles K. Bryant to Harrison H. Dodge, 9 March 1932, and Daniel M. Curran to Harrison H. Dodge, 2 February 1932, Folder "Rep. of Bldgs," PMVLA.

53. Alice Richards to Mary Deventer, 9 March 1932, Folder "Publications–Mount Vernon and Its Preservation," PMVLA.

54. Harrison H. Dodge to Louise Strantz, 9 January 1932, Harrison H. Dodge to Alice Griggs, 31 October 1931, and Harrison H. Dodge to P. A. Manker, 29 June 1932, Folder "Rep. of Bldgs," PMVLA. On projects to make models of Mount Vernon in the classroom, see Beula Mary Wadsworth, "Making Mount Vernon Seem Real," *School Arts* 33 (January 1934): 310–13, x–xi.

55. Harold Abbott to John H. Passmore, 7 May 1934, Folder "Policy–Misc.," PMVLA. See also Alice Richards to Harriet Carpenter, 14 April 1934, Folder "Fair–Chicago," PMVLA; Alice Richards to Mary Van Deventer, 9 March 1932, Folder "Publications–Mount Vernon and Its Preservation by Page," PMVLA.

56. George Wharton Pepper to Alice Richards, 29 February 1932, Folder "Mt. Vernon, Replicas of," PMVLA.

57. John W. Davis to Alice Richards, 18 March 1932, Folder "Mount Vernon, Replicas of," PMVLA.

58. "Backs Bryant Park for Historic Shrine," *New York Times,* 3 February 1932; "Bicentennial Seen as Help in Crisis," *New York Times,* 22 March 1932; "Washington Fete Seen as Aid to Business," *American,* 25 January 1932, clipping in Scrapbook "January 1932," Grover Whalen Papers, Municipal Archives, New York City.

59. Alice Richards to Mary Van Deventer, 9 March 1932, Folder "Publications–Mount Vernon and Its Preservation by Page," PMVLA; Alice Richards to Nathan Straus Jr., 6 March 1932, and Nathan Straus Jr. to Alice Richards, 8 March 1932, Folder "Mt. Vernon, Replicas of," PMVLA.

60. See "New York's Old Federal Hall as It Was in Washington's Day," *New York Times,* 24 April 1932.

61. "Explains Washington Copies," *New York Herald Tribune,* 11 April 1932, clipping in Scrapbook "April 1–31," Grover Whalen Papers, Municipal Archives, New York City; "'Washington' Rides amid Din of Wall St. in Pomp of Old Days," *New York Times,* 1 May 1932; "Washington Shrine Presented to City," *New York Times,* 9 May 1932; "Mayor Accepts Mt. Vernon for City as Its Dedication Follows Patriotic Parade," *Brooklyn Standard Union,* 9 May 1932, clipping in Scrapbook "May 1–31," Grover Whalen Papers, Municipal Archives, New York City.

62. Gustav Meissner to Charles Bascom Slemp, 16 February 1932, Folder "r.e. International Colonial & Overseas Exposition," Box 11, Series 1, Papers of Charles Bascom Slemp, Special Collections, University of Virginia Library, Charlottesville; "Washington Shrine in Brooklyn Fought," *New York Times,* 21 February 1932. On the house more recently, see Jean Rafferty, "Washington Never Slept Here, but He'd Recognize the Place," *New York Times,* 5 December 2013.

63. "Whalen Explains Admission Fee to Mt. Vernon Replica," *Brooklyn Eagle,* 28 May 1932, clipping in Scrapbook "May 23–July 5, 1932," Grover Whalen Papers, Municipal Archives, New York City.

64. "Prospect Park Favored for 'Mt Vernon,'" *Evening Journal,* 13 February 1932, clipping in Scrapbook "February 1932," Grover Whalen Papers, Municipal Archives, New York City; "2,000 in Brooklyn See 'Mount Vernon,'" *New York Times,* 2 May 1932.

65. "Boxwood Planted by Washington in 1761 Is Set out at 'Mt. Vernon' in Prospect Park," *New York Times,* 27 April 1932; "Boxwood Planted by Washington to Be Sent Here," *Brooklyn Eagle,* 27 April 1932, clipping in Scrapbook "April 1–31," Grover Whalen Papers, Municipal Archives, New York City.

66. "Doors Opened Defying Rain at 'Mt. Vernon,'" *Brooklyn Eagle,* 2 May 1932, clipping in Scrapbook "May 1–31," Grover Whalen Papers, Municipal Archives, New York City; "Straus Fights Plan to Keep Mt. Vernon," *New York Times,* 15 June 1932; Mary Moss Wellborn to Charles Bascom Slemp, 22 October 1932, Folder "Personal and Political Correspondence, RE Wellborn, Mary Moss, 1931–36," Box 17, Papers of Charles Bascom Slemp, Special Collections, University of Virginia Library, Charlottesville.

67. "Big Cultural Evening at Bryant Park," *News,* 6 August 1932, and Joseph Cookman, "Bryant Park Plans Opera to Pay Sears, Roebuck," *Evening Post,* 22 July 1932, clippings in Scrapbook "July 27–August ? 1932," Grover Whalen Papers, Municipal Archives, New York City; "Doubt over Fate of Federal Hall," *New York Times,* 16 November 1932; "'Mt. Vernon' Here Fails to Reopen," *New York Times,* 14 June 1933.

68. See Merrill D. Peterson, *The Jefferson Image in the American Mind* (New York: Oxford University Press, 1960), 330–76.

69. See Richard Guy Wilson, "Building on the Foundations: The Historic Present in Virginia Architecture, 1870–1990," in *The Making of Virginia Architecture,* by Charles E. Brownell, Calder Loth, William M. S. Rasmussen, and Wilson (Charlottesville: University Press of Virginia, 1992), 82, 86–87.

70. Sears Archives, www.searsarchives.com/homes/1927-1932.htm.

71. Aladdin Readi-Cut Homes, *Annual Sales Catalog* (1941), 15, www.cmich.edu/library /clarke/ResearchResources/Michigan_Material_Local/Bay_City_Aladdin_Co/Documents /1941_annual_sales_catalog.pdf.

72. See Daniel D. Reiff, *Houses from Books: The Influences of Treatises, Pattern Books, and Catalogs in American Architecture, 1738–1950* (University Park: Pennsylvania State University Press, 2000), 196–202, 254, 375.

73. Aladdin Readi-Cut Homes, *Annual Sales Catalog* (1941), 15.

74. Ibid., 41.

75. See Reiff, *Houses from Books,* 204–5

76. L. F. Garlinghouse Co., Inc., *Garlinghouse All American Homes* (1940), 19, https:// archive.org/details/GarlinghouseAllAmericanHomes.

77. Gordon-Van Tine Co., *Book of Homes* (1932), 2, https://archive.org/details/building technologyheritagelibrary?&and[]=gordon-van.

78. *Ladies' Home Journal,* October 1937; Ladies' Home Journal, *Mount Vernon Rooms,* booklet (Curtis, 1937).

79. See Leland Roth, "Getting the Houses to the People: Edward Bok, the *Ladies' Home Journal,* and the Idea House," *Perspectives in Vernacular Architecture* 4 (1991): 187–96; Kathryn Dethier, "The Spirit of Progressive Reform: The *Ladies' Home Journal* House Plans, 1900–1902," *Journal of Design History* 6, no. 4 (1993): 247–61.

80. Ladies' Home Journal, *Mount Vernon Rooms.*

81. Ibid.

82. John Fistere to Charles Cecil Wall, 13 October 1937, Folder "Publicity (Old–1937–1945)," PMVLA.

83. Press release for the Colonial Village dated 22 June 1934, Folder 1-3641, Box 129, Series 1, Century of Progress Records, Special Collections, University of Illinois at Chicago.

84. "Old Colonial Room Shown," *Chicago Herald and Examiner,* 1 July 1934; "Rare Antiques at Mt. Vernon," *Chicago Herald and Examiner,* 29 July 1934; undated press release for the Colonial Village, Folder 1-3641, Box 129, Series 1, Century of Progress Records, Special Collections, University of Illinois at Chicago; Contract between the Colonial Village, Inc. and Mrs. B. B. Dahlquist, 4 May 1934, Folder 1-3639, Box 129, Series 1, Century of Progress Records, Special Collections, University of Illinois at Chicago; "Antique Show Operator Dies at Age of 88," *Chicago Daily Tribune,* 27 August 1963; *Proceedings of the 44th Continental*

Congress of the National Society of the Daughters of the American Revolution, Washington, DC, April 15–20, 1935 (N.p., 1935), 451-42; Louis E. Laflin Jr., *Fair-Minded: A Guide to the Century of Progress, 1934* 2, no. 2 (August 1934): 182–83.

85. Report dated 1933, Folder 15-157, Box 13, Series 15, Century of Progress Records, Special Collections, University of Illinois at Chicago. See also Lisa D. Schrenk, "From Historic Village to Modern Pavilion: The Evolution of Foreign Architectural Representation at International Expositions in the 1930s," *National Identities* 1, no. 3 (1999): 287–311.

86. Harriet Carpenter to Alice Richards, 13 April 1934, Folder "Fair–Chicago," PMVLA.

87. Harriet Carpenter to Alice Richards, 21 April 1934, Folder "Fair–Chicago," PMVLA.

88. Mary Moss Wellborn to Charles Bascom Slemp, 24 January 1932, Folder "Personal and Political Correspondence, RE Wellborn, Mary Moss, 1931–36," Box 17, Series 1, Papers of Charles Bascom Slemp, Special Collections, University of Virginia Library, Charlottesville.

89. See Tallmadge, *The Story of Architecture in America;* Thomas H. Taylor Jr., "The Williamsburg Restoration and Its Reception by the American Public: 1926–1942" (Ph.D. diss., George Washington University, 1989), 83–86, ProQuest (303732278).

90. Harriet Carpenter to Alice Richards, 13 April 1934, Folder "Fair–Chicago," PMVLA.

91. Ibid. For Tallmadge's potential sources, see Wilstach, *Mount Vernon;* Halden et al., *The Georgian Period,* vol. 6, plates 33–35; and Glenn Brown, "The Message of Mount Vernon," *Garden and Home Builder* 45 (March–August 1927): 464.

92. For Tallmadge's adaptations of the other historic buildings in the Colonial Village, see Thomas E. Tallmadge, *The Colonial Village: A Reproduction of Early American Life in the 13 Colonies, A Guide to the Buildings of Historical Interest* (Chicago: Century of Progress, 1934), Folder 16–278, Box 19, Series 16, Century of Progress Records, Special Collections, University of Illinois at Chicago.

93. Miss Scott's notes from a meeting held on 30 April 1934, Folder "Fair–Chicago," PMVLA; MVLA Minutes 1935, 27.

94. Harriet Carpenter to Alice Richards, 13 April 1934, Folder "Fair–Chicago," PMVLA.

95. Alice Richards to Harriet Carpenter, 7 May 1934, Folder "Fair–Chicago," PMVLA.

96. Harriet Carpenter to Mrs. Washington, 23 June 1934, and Harriet Carpenter to Harrison H. Dodge, 16 July 1934, Folder "Carpenter, Mrs. George A., 1925–1937" (2 of 3), Vice Regents' Files, NLSGW; Frederick Dalrymple to Harriet Carpenter, 1 August 1934, Folder "Mary Mason Scott," Vice Regents' Files, NLSGW; MVLA Minutes 1934, 82; MVLA Minutes 1935, 56–57.

97. MVLA Minutes 1935, 27, 56–57.

98. Morley Jeffers Williams to Earl S. Putnam, 3 March 1938, Folder "Williams, Morley J. Correspondence 1937–1938," Morley Jeffers Williams Collection, NLSGW; George Wharton Pepper to Alice Richards, 29 February 1932, Folder "Mt. Vernon, Replicas of," PMVLA.

99. George Pepper to Alice Richards, 29 February 1932, Folder "Mt. Vernon, Replicas of," PMVLA.

100. See James M. Lindgren, "'A New Departure in Historic, Patriotic Work'" *Public Historian* 18, no. 2 (Spring 1996): 41–60; Daniel Bluestone, "Academics in Tennis Shoes: Historic Preservation and the Academy," *Journal of the Society of Architectural Historians* 58, no. 3 (September 1999): 300–307; and Hosmer, *Presence of the Past,* 153–259.

101. West, *Domesticating History,* 93–128; Hosmer, *Presence of the Past,* 153–92.

102. Alice Richards to Morley Jeffers Williams, 6 February 1936, Folder "Williams, Morley J. Misc Papers: Office Expenses, Budgets, Reports & Corres.," Morley Jeffers Williams Collection, NLSGW. On Williams, see Thomas E. Beaman Jr., "The Archaeology of Morley Jeffers Williams and the Restoration of Historic Landscapes at Stratford Hall, Mount Vernon, and Tryon Palace," *North Carolina Historical Review* 79, no. 3 (July 2002): 347–72.

103. See Charles B. Hosmer Jr., "The Colonial Revival in the Public Eye: Williamsburg and Early Garden Restoration," in *The Colonial Revival in America,* ed. Alan Axelrod (New York: Norton, 1985), 52–70.

104. "Colonel Dodge Will Be Buried in State Today," *Washington Post,* 21 May 1937; "Colonel Dodge of Mount Vernon," 26–27.

105. Morley Jeffers Williams, "Restoration at Stratford," *Landscape Architecture* 23 (April 1933): 175–77; MVLA Minutes 1932, 12; Beaman, "The Archaeology of Morley Jeffers Williams," 355–58.

106. Morley Jeffers Williams, "The Evolution of the Design of Mount Vernon," *Landscape Architecture* 22 (April 1932): 165.

107. Alice Richards to Morley Jeffers Williams, 6 February 1936, Folder "Williams, Morley J. Misc Papers: Office Expenses, Budgets, Reports & Corres.," Morley Jeffers Williams Collection, NLSGW; Morley Jeffers Williams to Bradford Williams, 21 December 1937, Folder "Williams, Morley J. Correspondence 1937–1938," Morley Jeffers Williams Collection, NLSGW; MVLA Minutes 1934, 11–12; MVLA Minutes 1936, 11–12.

108. Hopkins would go on to lead the restoration of many important early Virginia gardens and work with Arthur Shurcliff at Colonial Williamsburg. Morley Jeffers Williams to Bradford Williams, 21 December 1937, Folder "Williams, Morley J. Correspondence 1937–1938," Morley Jeffers Williams Collection, NLSGW; Morley Jeffers Williams to Harriet Towner, 22 October 1937, Folder "Williams, Morley J. Corres. Sent to Vice-Regents, 1931, 1935–1939," Morley Jeffers Williams Collection, NLSGW.

109. Morley Jeffers Williams to Caroline Brown, 22 October 1937, and Morley Jeffers Williams to Romayne Warren, 22 March 1938, Folder "Williams, Morley J. Corres. Sent to Vice-Regents, 1931, 1935–1939," Morley Jeffers Williams Collection, NLSGW; Morley Jeffers Williams to Henry I. Brock, 22 March 1938, Folder "Williams, Morley J. Correspondence 1937–1938," Morley Jeffers Williams Collection, NLSGW.

110. "Former Master of Mt. Vernon Charles Cecil Wall Dies at 91," *Washington Post,* 4 May 1995.

111. Williams succinctly explained his approach in Williams, "The Evolution of the Design of Mount Vernon," 165–77.

112. Morley Jeffers Williams to Harriet Towner, 1 September 1937 and 22 October 1937, Folder "Williams, Morley J. Corres. Sent to Vice-Regents, 1931, 1935–1939," Morley Jeffers Williams Collection, NLSGW; Mesick, Cohen, Waite Architects, "Mount Vernon Historic Structure Report," 142–49.

113. Morley Jeffers Williams to Romayne Warren, 22 March 1938, Folder "Williams, Morley J. Corres. Sent to Vice-Regents, 1931, 1935–1939," Morley Jeffers Williams Collection, NLSGW.

114. Morley Jeffers Williams to Wilmarth S. Lewis, 3 March 1938, Folder "Williams, Morley J. Correspondence 1937–1938," Morley Jeffers Williams Collection, NLSGW.

115. MVLA Minutes 1936, 8–9, 19; Beaman, "The Archaeology of Morley Jeffers Williams," 358–62; Dennis J. Pogue, "Archaeology at George Washington's Mount Vernon: 1931–1937," File Report 1 (March 1988), 18–20, NLSGW.

116. Morley Jeffers Williams to Caroline Brown, 11 February 1938, and Morley Jeffers Williams to Louise Loughborough, 24 January 1939, Folder "Williams, Morley J. Corres. Sent to Vice-Regents, 1931, 1935–1939," Morley Jeffers Williams Collection, NLSGW.

117. Morley Jeffers Williams to Bertha Lord, 14 April 1938, Folder "Williams, Morley J. Corres. Sent to Vice-Regents, 1931, 1935–1939," Morley Jeffers Williams Collection, NLSGW.

118. Henry I. Brock, "Mt. Vernon: Domain of a 'Planned Economy,'" *New York Times,* 20 February 1938; Morley Jeffers Williams to Emma Little, 22 January 1938, and Morley Jeffers Williams to Wilbur C. Hall, 23 March 1938, Folder "Williams, Morley J. Correspondence 1937–1938," Morley Jeffers Williams Collection, NLSGW. An article was published in *American Collector* the year before that laid out many of Williams's conclusions about the development of the mansion, but it was not particularly succinct or well-illustrated (see Thomas H. Ormsbee, "Mount Vernon Was Enlarged, Not Built," *American Collector* 6 [June 1937]: 4–5, 16).

119. Williams was not the first to figure this out (see Brush, "The Building of Mount Vernon Mansion").

120. Brock, "Mt. Vernon: Domain of a 'Planned Economy.'"

121. Morley Jeffers Williams, "Washington's Changes at Mount Vernon Plantation," *Landscape Architecture* 28 (January 1938): 62–73. Williams also presented a longer version of the paper to the 39th Annual Meeting of the American Society of Landscape Architects.

122. Williams, "Washington's Changes at Mount Vernon," 66.

123. "The Portfolio: The Mansion House, Mount Vernon, Virginia, Seat of General George Washington," *American Architect and Architecture,* February 1938, 41–52.

124. Morley Jeffers Williams to Lillian Wheeler, 29 October 1937, Folder "Williams, Morley J. Corres. Sent to Vice-Regents, 1931, 1935–1939," Morley Jeffers Williams Collection, NLSGW.

125. See "Frances Benjamin Johnston: Her Photographs of Our Old Buildings," *Magazine of Art* 30 (September 1937): 548–55; Maria Elizabeth Ausherman, *The Photographic Legacy of Frances Benjamin Johnston* (Gainesville: University Press of Florida, 2009), 124–221; and Annie D. Peterson, "Crusader with a Camera," *Historic Preservation* 32 (January 1980): 17–20.

126. Morley Jeffers Williams to Caroline Brown, 11 February 1938, Folder "Williams, Morley J. Corres. Sent to Vice-Regents, 1931, 1935–1939," Morley Jeffers Williams Collection, NLSGW.

127. For example, see "Mount Vernon: Five Historic Interiors," *House and Garden* 78 (July 1940): 22–23.

128. "Mt. Vernon Restored," *New York Times,* 25 July 1931.

129. MVLA Minutes 1932, 11, 69.

130. Memo from the Library of Congress to Harrison H. Dodge, 14 November 1934, Folder "Piazza," Box 3, Restoration Files, NLSGW; MVLA Minutes 1934, 74.

131. Morley Jeffers Williams to Elizabeth Hitz, 20 October 1938, Folder "Williams, Morley J. Corres. Sent to Vice-Regents, 1931, 1935–1939," Morley Jeffers Williams Collection, NLSGW.

132. MVLA Minutes 1936, 34.

133. Morley Jeffers Williams to Elizabeth Hitz, 20 October 1938, Folder "Williams, Morley J. Corres. Sent to Vice-Regents, 1931, 1935–1939," Morley Jeffers Williams Collection, NLSGW.

134. MVLA Minutes 1929, 82, 66.

135. MVLA Minutes 1929, 32; MVLA Minutes 1932, 11, 53; MVLA Minutes 1933, 11–13, 15; MVLA Minutes 1934, 11; MVLA Minutes 1936, 8.

136. Memorandum Report for the Chairman of the Mansion Committee, 6 April 1940, Folder "Building Committee–Mansion (Corres. 1936–1940)," PMVLA.

137. MVLA Minutes 1929, 36, 48–49, 67.

138. United States George Washington Bicentennial Commission, "Wallpaper of Washington's Bedroom," *Special News Releases Relating to the Life and Time of General Washington,* vol. 1 (Washington, DC: United States George Washington Bicentennial Commission, 1931); Henry Burn to Harrison H. Dodge, 17 March 1931, 29 March 1931, 5 April 1932, and "FCH" to Charles Cecil Wall, 26 November 1937, Folder "Public Relations Policy RE Reproductions–Wallpaper," PMVLA; Harrison H. Dodge to Alice Griggs, 2 November 1931, Folder "Rep. of Bldgs," PMVLA.

139. Morley Jeffers Williams to Charlotte Woodbury, 29 March 1938, Folder "Williams, Morley J. Correspondence 1937–1938," Morley Jeffers Williams Collection, NLSGW.

140. Charles Cecil Wall to Horace Hotchkiss, 22 May 1950, Folder "Public Relations Policy RE Reproductions–Wallpaper," PMVLA; MVLA Minutes 1949, 72–73; Lonnelle Aikman, "Mount Vernon Lives On," *National Geographic Magazine* 104 (November 1953): 679.

141. Esther C. White, "Reconstruction Dilemmas at George Washington's Blacksmith

Shop," in *The Reconstructed Past,* ed. John H. Jameson Jr. (Lanham, MD: AltaMira Press, 2004), 80–81; Pogue, "Archaeology at George Washington's Mount Vernon."

142. MVLA Minutes 1936, 8–9, 19.

143. Morley J. Williams, "Proposed Green House Restoration," undated drawing, Folder "Greenhouse," Box 3, Restoration Files, NLSGW.

144. MVLA Minutes 1941, 89; MVLA Minutes 1942, 29–31.

145. Charles Cecil Wall to Walter Mayo Macomber, 24 May 1946, Folder "Architect for Restoration, Correspondence–Reports 1946–60," PMVLA; MVLA Minutes 1947, 74.

146. MVLA Minutes 1936, 10, 48–49.

147. *Inventory of the Contents of Mount Vernon,* 1; MVLA Minutes 1931, 72.

148. MVLA AR 1954, 30.

149. MVLA Minutes 1931, 71–72; MVLA Minutes 1932, 10; Marian Sadtler Carson, "Washington's American Carpet at Mount Vernon," *Antiques* 51 (February 1947): 118–19; MVLA AR 1947, 17.

150. "Kitchen Garden at Mount Vernon," *House and Garden* 98 (July 1950): 80–83; Beaman, "The Archaeology of Morley Jeffers Williams," 361.

151. Report of the Mansion Committee, May 1940 Council Meeting, Folder "Building Committee (3)," PMVLA.

5. "In This Changing and Troubled World"

1. MVLA AR 1952, 10; Charles Cecil Wall to Hope Powel, 2 October 1952, Superintendent's Monthly Reports, 1948–1952, NLSGW.

2. "Here Lived a Hero," *Saturday Evening Post* 228 (2 July 1955): 26–27; editors of the *Saturday Evening Post, The Face of America* (Philadelphia: Curtis, 1957), 62–63.

3. Dorothy Gilliam, "Remembrance," *Washington Post,* 6 February 1982.

4. See John A. Jackle, *The Tourist: Travel in Twentieth-Century America* (Lincoln: University of Nebraska Press, 1985), 185–98.

5. Charles Cecil Wall qtd. in Judith Crist, "Man of Mount Vernon," *Scholastic* 64 (21 April 1954): 6.

6. On the aesthetic focus of most house museums in the period, see Stuart D. Hobbs, "Exhibiting Antimodernism: History, Memory, and the Aestheticized Past in Mid-Twentieth-century America," *Public Historian* 23, no. 3 (Summer 2001): 39–61.

7. MVLA Minutes 1929, 15, 46, 62.

8. MVLA AR 1952, 19.

9. MVLA Minutes 1941, 89; MVLA Minutes 1942, 30.

10. Walter Mayo Macomber to Harriet Towner, 13 May 1941, Folder "Greenhouse," Box 2, Restoration Files, NLSGW.

11. Walter Mayo Macomber, Report to the Buildings Committee of the MVLA, 11 December 1941, PMVLA.

12. MVLA Minutes 1942, 30.

13. See MVLA Minutes 1946, 92; and MVLA Minutes 1949, 40.

14. MVLA Minutes 1947, 74; MVLA AR 1949, 33–35.

15. MVLA Minutes 1951, 92–94; MVLA AR 1955, 13–21; MVLA Minutes 1958, 27–29.

16. MVLA Minutes 1962, 25; MVLA AR 1966, 11–14; Ruth Davidson, "News from Mount Vernon," *Antiques* 92 (August 1967): 176.

17. MVLA Minutes 1950, 10, 94–97.

18. MVLA Minutes 1946, 61.

19. MVLA AR 1952, 42–43; Charles Cecil Wall, "A Program for Restoration and Development," 5 November 1947, Folder "Buildings Committee, 1942–1952," PMVLA; G. Moffett King to John Beverley Riggs, 6 December 1951, Folder "Greenhouse," Box 2, Restoration Files, NLSGW.

20. Walter Mayo Macomber to General Glen E. Edgerton, 5 September 1951, Folder "Architect for Restoration, Buildings Committee Correspondence," PMVLA; MVLA AR 1952, 19–26; MVLA Minutes 1950, 101; MVLA Minutes 1951, 64.

21. MVLA Minutes 1950, 96; Charles Cecil Wall to Hope Powel, 3 June 1952, Superintendent's Monthly Reports, 1948–1952, NLSGW.

22. Sara Butler to Walter Mayo Macomber, 8 July 1952, Folder "Quarters," Box 4, Restoration Files, NLSGW.

23. See undated memo from Asst. Curator Morse to Charles Cecil Wall on Quarters, Folder "Quarters," Box 4, Restoration Files, PMVLA.

24. E. John Long, "Mount Vernon's New-Old Greenhouse," *Nature Magazine* 46 (October 1953): 405–8; MVLA Minutes 1953, 60; Gerald W. Johnson, "How the Girls Saved Mount Vernon," *Saturday Evening Post*, 21 February 1953, 102.

25. Four of the members of the MVLA's board in this period were also on that of the Robert E. Lee Memorial Association that oversaw Robert E. Lee's birthplace: Stratford Hall.

26. See MVLA Minutes 1962, 5–6.

27. Frank E. Morse, "Special Report on the Quarters for the Regent and the Vice-Regent for Illinois," October 1959, Box 4, Restoration Files, NLSGW.

28. Charles Cecil Wall to Hope Powel, 4 August 1952 and 3 December 1952, Superintendent's Monthly Reports, 1948–1952, NLSGW; MVLA Minutes 1953, 56.

29. "Special Summary Report on Negro Quarters" and memo from Asst. Curator Morse to Charles Cecil Wall on Quarters, both undated, Folder "Quarters," Box 4, Restoration Files, NLSGW.

30. MVLA Minutes 1958, 61–63; MVLA Minutes 1959, 78; MVLA Minutes 1960, 59; MVLA AR 1961, 32–33.

31. MVLA Minutes 1954, 60; memo on consultation with Mr. Chapelle and Mr. Terry of

the Division of Transportation, Smithsonian, on Meaning of Berths, 12 October 1960, Folder "Quarters," Box 4, Restoration Files, NLSGW.

32. Morse, "Special Report on the Quarters."

33. Memo on consultation with Mr. Chapelle and Mr. Terry of the Division of Transportation, Smithsonian, on Meaning of Berths, 12 October 1960, Folder "Quarters," Box 4, Restoration Files, NLSGW; Charles Cecil Wall to Rosamond Beirne, 5 October 1960, Superintendent's Monthly Reports, 1960–1963, NLSGW.

34. Charles Cecil Wall to Rosamond Beirne, 4 January 1961, Superintendent's Monthly Reports, 1960–1963, NLSGW.

35. MVLA Minutes 1961, 8.

36. Charles Cecil Wall to Rosamond Beirne, 2 February 1962, Superintendent's Monthly Reports, 1960–1963, NLSGW.

37. MVLA AR 1962, 24–25.

38. MVLA Minutes 1962, 26. See also Charles Cecil Wall to Rosamond Beirne, 2 March 1962, Superintendent's Monthly Reports, 1960–1963, NLSGW.

39. Charles Cecil Wall, "Observations on Planning," 29 April 1950, Folder "Buildings Committee–General," PMVLA.

40. Walter C. Dinsmore to Richard L. Berman, 5 March 1965, Folder "Solocast," PMVLA.

41. Current List of Acoustiguide Users, 1 October 1965, Folder "Solocast," PMVLA.

42. The Solocast Company, "Tourdisc Service Research at Mount Vernon, Virginia, December 1965," Folder "Solocast," PMVLA; "Tour of Mount Vernon," script for Solocast Tourdisc, p. 49, Folder "Solocast," PMVLA.

43. The Solocast Company, "Tourdisc Service Research at Mount Vernon."

44. MVLA AR 1985, 12.

45. "Tour of Mount Vernon," script for Solocast Tourdisc, Folder "Solocast," PMVLA.

46. Ibid.

47. William Herow to W. S. Robson, 22 November 1965, Folder "Solocast," PMVLA; The Solocast Company, "Tourdisc Service Research at Mount Vernon, Virginia, December 1965," Folder "Solocast," PMVLA.

48. James Marston Fitch, "How to Merge What You've Got (the Past) with What You Want (the Future)," *House Beautiful* 94 (February 1952): 60–61.

49. Robert Venturi and Denise Scott Brown, *Learning from Las Vegas* (Cambridge: MIT Press, 1972).

50. See Chester H. Liebs, *Main Street to Miracle Mile: American Roadside Architecture* (Boston: Little, Brown, 1985); and Richard Longstreth, *The Drive-In, the Supermarket, and the Transformation of Commercial Space in Los Angeles, 1914–1941* (Cambridge: MIT Press, 1999), 57–68.

51. See Timothy Davis, "The Miracle Mile Revisited: Recycling, Renovation, and Simulation along the Commercial Strip," *Perspectives in Vernacular Architecture* 7 (1997): 105–6.

52. See John A. Jakle, Keith A. Schulle, and Jefferson S. Rogers, *The Motel in America* (Baltimore: Johns Hopkins University Press, 1996), 72–73; A. K. Sandoval-Strausz, *Hotel: An American History* (New Haven: Yale University Press, 2007), 284–311.

53. See Suzanne E. Smith, *To Serve the Living: Funeral Directors and the African American Way of Death* (Cambridge: Belknap Press of Harvard University Press, 2010).

54. Jakle, Schulle, and Rogers, *The Motel in America,* 103.

55. "Roadside Cabins for Tourists," *Architectural Record* 74 (December 1933): 457. See also Lisa Michele Church, "Early Roadside Motels and Motor Courts of St. George," *Utah Historical Quarterly* 80, no. 1 (Winter 2012): 22–43.

56. Geoffrey Baker and Bruno Funaro, *Motels* (New York: Reinhold, 1955), 1–5.

57. See Jakle, Schulle, and Rogers, *The Motel in America,* 23–56.

58. Baker and Funaro, *Motels,* 6–7.

59. Richard A. Miller, "The Odds on Motels," *Architectural Forum* 107 (August 1957): 111; Jakle, Schulle, and Rogers, *The Motel in America,* 20.

60. "Carolina Inn Now Ready to Welcome Alumni," *Alumni Review,* qtd. in Kenneth Joel Zogry, *The University's Living Room: A History of the Carolina Inn* (Chapel Hill: University of North Carolina Press, 1999), 18.

61. See Kenneth Joel Zogry, "The Carolina Inn, Chapel Hill, North Carolina," National Register of Historic Places nomination, passed 1999.

62. See City of Stillwater, Minnesota, "10 Lowell Inn," www.youtube.com/watch?v=p9 UHSYGWFjU.

63. Louis Hatchett, *Duncan Hines: The Man behind the Cake Mix* (Macon, GA: Mercer University Press, 2001), 70–71. See also Patricia Condon Johnston, "Nelle Palmer of Stillwater: Entertainer and Innkeeper," *Minnesota History* (Spring 1983): 207–12.

64. See "The Howard Johnson's Restaurants," *Fortune* 2 (September 1940): 82–87; Anthony Mitchell Sammarco, *A History of Howard Johnson's: How a Massachusetts Soda Fountain Became an American Icon* (Charleston, SC: American Palate, 2013); Highway Host, "Queens, New York, AKA Rego Park," www.highwayhost.org/NewYork/Restaurants /RegoPark/regopark1.htm. The building was demolished in 1974.

65. On postcards, see Keith A. Schulle, "The Best of Both Worlds: Home and Mobility in Motel Postcard Iconography," *Material Culture* 31, no. 3 (Fall 1999): 21–52.

66. See Harold Whittington, *Starting and Managing a Small . . . Motel* (Washington, DC: Office of Information Services, 1963), 45.

67. Jakle, Schulle, and Rogers, *The Motel in America,* 90–119. See also Keith A. Schulle, "Traveling in Style: The Park Plaza Motel Chain," *Journal of the West* 41, no. 4 (Fall 2002): 63–70; and Keith A. Schulle, "When Texas Went East," *Journal of the West* 50, no. 2 (Spring 2011): 51–59.

68. Sammarco, *A History of Howard Johnson's,* n.p.

69. Postcard by A. W. Ashworth for Dale's Mt. Vernon Motel in Canandaigua, New York, author's collection. The postmark indicates that the motel was built by 1957. It has likely since been demolished.

70. Postcard by Curteich for Colony Motor Lodge, Strongsville, Ohio, author's collection.

71. Postcard by Colourpicture, Mt. Vernon Motor Lodge, Springfield, Missouri, author's collection.

72. Baker and Funaro, *Motels,* 149.

73. William B. Taylor, "The Economic Facts of Life about Hotel Design," *Architectural Record* 123 (April 1958): 204.

74. Baker and Funaro, *Motels,* 140–41.

75. C. Vernon Kane, "Motel Trends: Bigger and Better, but at What Kind of a Risk?," *Architectural Forum* 100 (February 1954): 108.

76. "Lodgings for Travelers," *Architectural Record* 119 (January 1956): 178.

77. See Whittington, *Starting and Managing a Small . . . Motel,* 45–47; Jakle, Schulle, and Rogers, *The Motel in America,* 76–78.

78. Rick Frazee, former owner of the Mt. Vernon Motor Lodge, conversation with author, 3 January 2015.

79. Postcard by Bill Bard Associates for Martha Washington Motel, Waldorf, Maryland, author's collection.

80. See Baker and Funaro, *Motels,* 225.

81. "Motor Hotels," *Architectural Record* 128 (July 1960): 145; "Hotels and Motels Reflect a Changing World," *Architectural Record* 140, no. 2 (August 1966): 137–38. See also Church, "Early Roadside Motels and Motor Courts of St. George"; Heyward D. Schrock, "A Room for the Night: Evolution of Roadside Lodging in Wyoming," *Annals of Wyoming: The Wyoming History Journal* 75, no. 4 (Autumn 2003): 36–39; Kevin J. Patrick and Keith A. Schulle, "The Lincoln Motor Court: Heritage Tourism and the Rise, Fall, and Resurrection of a Lincoln Highway Landmark," *Pioneer America Society Transactions* 25 (2002): 5–7; Jakle, Schulle, and Rogers, *The Motel in America.*

82. C. John Main, "The Motel Concept," *Architect & Building News,* 16 April 1970, 42.

83. Dean George Lampros, "Like a Real Home: The Residential Funeral Home and America's Changing Vernacular Landscape, 1910–1960" (Ph.D. diss., Boston University, 2013), 30–81, ProQuest (1500435705).

84. James J. Farrell, *Inventing the American Way of Death, 1830–1920* (Philadelphia: Temple University Press, 1980), 146–83.

85. Lampros, "Like a Real Home"; Dean Lampros, "Mansions as Marketing: The Residential Funeral Home and American Consumer Culture, 1915–1965," in *Visual Merchandising: The Image of Selling,* ed. Louisa Iarocci (Surrey, England: Ashgate, 2013), 175–92; Ronald W. Johnson and Mary E. Franza, "An Unheralded Preservation Influence: The American

Funeral Industry," *Cultural Resource Management,* no. 2 (2001): 33–36. See also Gary Laderman, *Rest in Peace: A Cultural History of Death and the Funeral Home in Twentieth-Century America* (Oxford: Oxford University Press, 2003), 1–33.

86. Lampros, "Like a Real Home," 444–50; Lampros, "Mansions as Marketing," 185–89.

87. Laderman, *Rest in Peace,* 78.

88. See Paul Jacobs, "The Most Cheerful Graveyard in the World," *Reporter* 19 (18 September 1958): 26–30; and Marilyn Yalom, *The American Resting Place: Four Hundred Years of History through Our Cemeteries and Burial Grounds* (Boston: Houghton Mifflin, 2008), 225–27.

89. Forest Lawn Memorial-Park Association, *Art Guide of Forest Lawn* (1963), v. See also Kevin McNamara, "Cultural Anti-Modernism and 'The Modern Memorial Park': Hubert Eaton and the Creation of Forest Lawn," *Canadian Review of American Studies* 32, no. 3 (2002): 308; Laura Kath, *Forest Lawn: The First 100 Years* (Glendale, CA: Tropico Press, 2006), 37; and Leslie S. Hoagland, "Making a Cemetery a Civic Asset Instead of a Civic Liability," *American City* 35 (July 1926): 66–68.

90. Forest Lawn Memorial-Park Association, *Art Guide of Forest Lawn,* 29.

91. See Marc Treib, "The Landscape of Loved Ones," in *Places of Commemoration: Search for Identity and Landscape Design,* ed. Joachim Wolschke-Bulmahn (Washington, DC: Dumbarton Oaks, 2001), 81–106.

92. Adela Rogers St. Johns, *First Step up toward Heaven: Hubert Eaton and Forest Lawn* (Englewood Cliffs, NJ: Prentice-Hall, 1959), 177.

93. Ralph Hancock, *The Forest Lawn Story* (Los Angeles: Academy, 1955), 113.

94. Kath, *Forest Lawn,* 68–69.

95. Forest Lawn Memorial-Park Association, *Art Guide of Forest Lawn,* 13.

96. "Forest Lawn Joins Right-Wing Chorus," *Christian Century,* 4 May 1966, 595. The magazine focused especially on Eaton's replica of the ancient sculpture Laocoön and His Sons. On the serpent that strangles the figures of Laocoön and his two young sons, Eaton's sculptor inscribed the words "Liberalism-Socialism," "Taxes," "Bureaucracy," and "Evil" to symbolize "bureaucracy, throttling the free spirt of America" (Forest Lawn Memorial-Park Association, *Art Guide of Forest Lawn,* 278).

97. See Kath, *Forest Lawn,* 65.

98. Forest Lawn Memorial-Park Association, *Art Guide of Forest Lawn,* 104–7.

99. See "The Theology of Hope," *Newsweek,* 11 December 1967, 92.

100. Julian Wasser, "First Step up to Heaven," *Time* 88 (30 September 1966): 54; Horace Sutton, "Ever-Ever Land," *Saturday Review* 41 (5 April 1958): 23–25. See also "Forest Lawn," *Travel* 123 (January 1965): 41–43. Walt Disney was buried at Forest Lawn–Glendale in 1966 near Eaton's own grave.

101. See McNamara, "Cultural Anti-Modernism and 'The Modern Memorial Park,'" 312–14.

102. See Barbara Rubin, Robert Carlton, and Arnold Rubin, *LA in Installments: Forest Lawn* (Santa Monica, CA: Westside, 1979), 56–62.

103. Evelyn Waugh, *The Loved One: An Anglo-American Tragedy* (New York: Little, Brown, 1948).

104. Tom Paxton, "Forest Lawn," recorded 1970 on *Tom Paxton 6;* John Denver, vocal performance of "Forest Lawn," recorded by John Denver in 1974 on *An Evening with John Denver.*

105. Jessica Mitford, *The American Way of Death* (New York: Simon and Schuster, 1963).

106. See Laderman, *Rest in Peace,* 83–118.

107. For the fallout from Mitford's book, see Laderman, *Rest in Peace,* 119–69.

108. Karrer-Simpson Funeral Home, Inc., http://karrersimpson.com/about/karrer-simpson-history.

109. M. David DeMarco Funeral Home, Inc., www.demarcofuneralhome.com/_mgxroot/page_10793.php.

110. Thank you to Aaron Wunsch for bringing this building to my attention.

111. Toppitzer Funeral Home, Inc. at Arlington Cemetery, *The Museum of Mourning Art at Arlington,* promotional pamphlet, author's collection.

112. Toppitzer Funeral Home, Inc. at Arlington Cemetery, *The Mausoleums at Arlington,* promotional pamphlet, author's collection.

113. MVLA AR 1964, 5; MVLA AR 1976, 4; MVLA AR 1984, 7.

114. MVLA AR 1978, 5; MVLA AR 1977, 6; MVLA AR 1972, 5. See also "By George . . . and for the People," *Nation's Business* 61 (October 1973): 56–59.

115. Kammen, *Mystic Chords of Memory,* 618–54.

116. MVLA AR 1970, 7–8.

117. See MVLA AR 1971, 6.

118. MVLA AR 1961, 5–6. See also "New Effort to Protect Mount Vernon," *American Forests* 70 (June 1964): 5; "To the Ramparts," *American Forests* 67 (September 1961): 45.

119. MVLA AR 1973, 5. See also "Completing Pascataway Park," *Washington Post,* 26 October 1974; Darrell G. Morrison, "Protecting a Presidential View of the Potomac," *Landscape Architecture* 55 (April 1965): 176–79.

120. MVLA Minutes 1979, 24.

121. Matthew J. Mosca, "Paint Decoration at Mount Vernon: The Revival of Eighteenth-Century Techniques," in *Paint in America: The Colors of Historic Buildings,* ed. Roger W. Moss (New York: Wiley and Sons, 1994), 105; MVLA Minutes 1980, 2, 17.

122. MVLA Minutes 1980, 17. For a period explanation of paint-analysis techniques, see Frank S. Welsh, "Paint Analysis," *Bulletin of the Association for Preservation Technology* 14, no. 4 (1982): 29–30.

123. MVLA Minutes 1983, 29. See also MVLA Minutes 1979, 24.

124. John A. Castellani to Frances Guy, 5 January 1980, Superintendent's Letters to the Regent, NLSGW; MVLA AR 1980, 32–41; Mosca, "Paint Decoration at Mount Vernon," 105–27.

125. MVLA Minutes 1981, 41.

126. MVLA Minutes 1959, 5, 48.

127. MVLA Minutes 1981, 41; MVLA AR 1982, 8.

128. See Martin Fuller, "Home of Our Father's Pride," *House and Garden,* August 1985, 58–73, 162–63; MVLA Minutes 1979, 24–25; and MVLA AR 1982, 8.

129. See Thomas H. Taylor Jr. and Nicholas A. Pappas, "Colonial Williamsburg Colors: A Changing Spectrum," in *Paint in America: The Colors of Historic Buildings,* ed. Roger W. Moss (New York: Wiley and Sons, 1994), 87–108.

130. See the Papers of George Washington, "About: Project History," http://gwpapers .virginia.edu/about/project-history-awards; and Donald Jackson, "Starting in the Papers Game," *Scholarly Publishing,* October 1971, 28–38.

131. See Mitnick, "Parallel Visions," 63.

132. Lengel, *Inventing George Washington;* Marling, *George Washington Slept Here,* 325–90.

133. MVLA AR 1970, 8.

134. James Thomas Flexner, *Washington: The Indispensable Man* (Boston: Little, Brown, 1974); Lengel, *Inventing George Washington,* 171–81.

135. MVLA AR 1973, 6.

136. Ibid., 17; George Washington to Robert Cary & Co., 12 January 1769, *The Papers of George Washington Digital Edition,* ed. Theodore J. Crackel et al. (Charlottesville: University of Virginia Press, Rotunda, 2007–).

137. For the first volume, see Donald Jackson and Dorothy Twohig, eds., *The Diaries of George Washington* (Charlottesville: University Press of Virginia, 1976).

138. Wall had considered hosting a sound and light show in the 1960s but ultimately decided against it because it "would intrude on the authentic setting" (Charles C. Wall, "Mount Vernon: Landmark of the Revolution," 15 May 1967, NLSGW; Charles Cecil Wall, "A Thing of the Spirit," August 1967, NLSGW; MVLA Minutes 1972, 11).

139. MVLA Minutes 1974, 58.

140. MVLA AR 1977, 6; MVLA Minutes 1976, 57; MVLA Minutes 1978, 3.

141. White House staff apparently wrote the script, with James Thomas Flexner and Charles Cecil Wall helping to revise (MVLA Minutes 1973, 8; MVLA Minutes 1975, 46).

142. *The Father of Liberty* qtd. in "The Heritage," *House and Garden* 148, no. 7 (July 1976): 40.

143. MVLA Minutes 1974, 42, 58.

144. MVLA Minutes 1975, 44.

145. Charles Cecil Wall to Elizabeth Cooke, 3 March 1975 and 3 September 1975, Superintendent's Monthly Letters to the Regent, NLSGW.

146. The MVLA lost more than thirteen thousand dollars the second year of the show

(Harrison M. Symmes to Elizabeth Cooke, 3 October 1977, Superintendent's Monthly Letters to the Regent, NLSGW).

147. MVLA AR 1970, 5; MVLA AR 1977, 6; MVLA AR 1978, 5.

148. MVLA Minutes 1980, 6; MVLA AR 1980, 9.

149. MVLA AR 1979, 9; MVLA AR 1980, 61.

150. See MVLA AR 1980, 60.

151. MVLA AR 1979, 9.

152. MVLA AR 1980, 60–61.

153. MVLA AR 1985, 4, 53.

154. MVLA AR 1981, 50–53; MVLA AR 1982, 10–11, 53–54; MVLA AR 1983, 44–48; MVLA AR 1985, 54–55.

155. Gilliam, "Remembrance."

156. MVLA Minutes 1982, 16; John Castellani, monthly letter to the Regent, February 1982, 5, NLSGW.

157. Jube Shiver Jr., "A Memorial to Slaves," *Washington Post,* 23 February 1982.

158. Dorothy Gilliam, "Memorial," *Washington Post,* 28 February 1983; Frank Matthews to the MVLA, 16 February 1982, Folder "Slave Memorial: Correspondence–Staff Dedication Ceremony," Box "Slave Memorial," NLSGW.

159. MVLA Minutes 1983, 12.

160. List of Slave Burial Site Memorial Competition jury members, Folder "Slave Memorial: Howard University Design Competition Jury," Box "Slave Memorial," NLSGW.

161. Minutes of the meeting of the Slave Burial Site Memorial Dedication Committee, 7 September 1983, Folder "Slave Memorial: Howard University Design Competition Jury," Box "Slave Memorial," NLSGW.

162. Gilliam, "Memorial"; Harry G. Robinson III to John Castellani, 17 September 1982, and minutes of the meeting of the Slave Burial Site Memorial Dedication Committee, 7 September 1983, Folder "Slave Memorial: Howard University Design Competition Jury," Box "Slave Memorial," NLSGW.

163. MVLA Minutes 1982, 32. The student fund was a suggestion of the Howard University dean Harry Robinson (minutes of meeting concerning the Howard School of Architecture design competition for slave burial ground monument, 23 September 1982, Folder "Slavery Memorial–Committee Meetings, Minutes/Agendas," Box "Slave Memorial," NLSGW).

164. Summary minutes, Slave Burial Ground Project meeting, 13 July 1982, Folder "Slave Memorial: Committee Meetings Minutes/Agendas," Box "Slave Memorial," NLSGW; minutes of Slave Memorial Dedication Committee meeting, 25 April 1983, Folder "Slave Memorial: Correspondence–MVLA Regent, Committee," Box "Slave Memorial," NLSGW.

165. Summary minutes, Slave Burial Ground Project meeting, 13 July 1982, Folder "Slave Memorial: Committee Meetings Minutes/Agendas," Box "Slave Memorial," NLSGW.

166. MVLA, "The Mount Vernon Slave Burial Ground Memorial Competition Program,"

Folder "Slave Memorial: Howard University Design Competition Jury," Box "Slave Memorial," NLSGW (emphasis in original).

167. Minutes of Slave Memorial Dedication Committee meeting, 25 April 1983, Folder "Slave Memorial: Correspondence–MVLA Regent, Committee," Box "Slave Memorial," NLSGW; "Memorandum for Frances Guy by John H. Rhodehamel RE Archaeological survey of the slave burial ground," Folder "Slave Memorial: Howard University Design Competition Jury," Box "Slave Memorial," NLSGW.

168. Minutes of Slave Memorial Dedication Committee, 29 June 1983, Folder "Slave Memorial: Correspondence–MVLA Regent, Committee," Box "Slave Memorial," NLSGW.

169. Mike Sager, "30 Teams Vied for Design of Slave Memorial at Mt. Vernon," *Washington Post,* 3 November 1982; MVLA Minutes 1982, 32–33.

170. David Edge qtd. in Carla Hall, "Renewed Memorial," *Washington Post,* 5 September 1983.

171. Ibid.

172. MVLA Minutes 1983, 44; Minutes of Slave Memorial Dedication Committee, 29 June 1983, Folder "Slave Memorial: Correspondence–MVLA Regent, Committee," Box "Slave Memorial," NLSGW.

173. Gilliam, "Memorial."

174. MVLA AR 1982, 10. For an account of the controversy and its impact, see James C. Rees, "Looking Back, Moving Forward: The Changing Interpretation of Slave Life on the Mount Vernon Estate," in *Slavery at the Home of George Washington,* ed. Philip J. Schwarz (Mount Vernon, VA: Mount Vernon Ladies' Association, 2001), 166–69.

175. Summary of meeting on slave burial ground, 10 June 1982, Folder "Slave Memorial: Committee Meetings Minutes/Agendas," Box "Slave Memorial," NLSGW.

176. MVLA Minutes 1983, 29; MVLA, "The Slave Burial Ground and Slavery at Mount Vernon," pamphlet, 1982, Folder "Slave Memorial: Brochure," Box "Slave Memorial," NLSGW.

177. Helen Anderson to Frank Matthews, 19 January 1983, Folder "Slave Memorial: Correspondence-MVLA Regent, Committee," Box "Slave Memorial," NLSGW.

178. MVLA AR 1987, 12–13.

179. MVLA AR 1984, 23–25.

180. Charles Cecil Wall, "Observations on Planning," 29 April 1950, Folder "Buildings Committee–General," PMVLA.

Conclusion

1. MVLA, "About Mount Vernon," www.mountvernon.org/about/.

2. Garlinghouse, House Plan 20151, "Georgian Grace," www.garlinghouse.com/plan_details.cfm?PlanNumber=20151.

3. Heartland Homes, "The Mount Vernon by Heartland Homes," video, www.youtube
.com/watch?v=gCsuTrJQ6Mg.

4. June Kurt, "Let's Play George Washington," *House Beautiful* 142, no. 3 (March 2000):
118–21. This was not the first time Mount Vernon had inspired a children's playhouse (see
Ruth R. Blodgett, "Come Away and Play," *House Beautiful* [December 1917]: 36–37).

Bibliographic Essay

A few additional words about sources are necessary. The majority of the research I conducted for this book draws on a number of different archival repositories. The availability and limitations of these archival resources was a deciding factor in the selection and scope of the book's content. The inclusion and discussion of additional examples depended on published primary sources.

The archives of the Mount Vernon Ladies' Association at the Fred W. Smith National Library for the Study of George Washington at Mount Vernon produced special challenges and opportunities. The Early Records of the Association cover the initial efforts of Ann Pamela Cunningham in the 1850s, continue through the furnishing and restoration of the buildings and landscape in the 1860s and 1870s, and thin at the end of the nineteenth century. Most of these records consist of correspondence between the vice regents, although some scrapbooks, handwritten institutional histories, and ephemeral objects supplement the letters. Records from the early twentieth century onward are organized in folders by project, issue, or committee. These records typically include correspondence between the vice regents and staff at Mount Vernon, drawings, photographs, and newspaper or periodical clippings.

Gaps in the twentieth-century archival record obscured historical decisions and shaped my approach to this period. Because the vice regents were living in different locations across the country, materials are especially strong in the first half of the twentieth century; most issues were handled via letter. After 1950, it is clear that many discussions occurred over the telephone, and far fewer written sources exist to detail step-by-step decision making. Archival materials relating to the last thirty years are not available to any outside scholar. This fact determined the end point for my narrative in the early 1980s.

The Fred W. Smith National Library for the Study of George Washington at Mount Vernon houses a treasure trove of published materials on the organization and site's history. The printed minutes of the board's annual or semi-annual meetings are invaluable for framing the discussions and decisions of individual issues, understanding budgets and organizational priorities, and seeing how the Association organized itself and its staff over time. Like archival materials, minutes for board meetings from the last thirty years are unavailable to outside scholars. Annual reports distilled the minutes into an easily accessible format. After World War II, this document acted as a glossy publicity tool, and even the most recent forms are on the shelves at the Library. These are especially instructive for understanding how the MVLA wished to be seen from the outside. A set of the official guidebooks running from 1876 through the present day demonstrates the evolving interpretive narrative of the historic area. The library also houses immense collections of photographs, drawings, and postcards of Mount Vernon. These objects helped me to track the changing state of the physical landscape, mansion, and outbuildings.

The majority of the sources for the world's fair replicas reside in central repositories. The Bancroft Library at the University of California, Berkeley, houses the records of the Panama-Pacific International Exposition. Much of the official records (and a complete collection of clippings scrapbooks) for the 1926 Sesqui-Centennial are housed in the Sesqui-Centennial Exhibition Association Records at the City Archives of Philadelphia. As a government-funded project, the United States pavilion at the 1931 Paris Colonial and Overseas Exposition is documented at the National Archives and Records Administration in College Park, Maryland. Records for the 1933 Chicago Century of Progress are located in Special Collections at the University of Illinois at Chicago. The vast majority of archival materials for the 1893 World's Columbian Exposition in Chicago no longer exist.

Records in these groups typically include official correspondence between the fair and the groups constructing various pavilions and attractions, contracts, press releases and other official publicity materials, scrapbooks or newspaper clipping files, and photographs. Because world's fair buildings were intended to be ephemeral, architectural drawings are exceedingly rare.

Most of the buildings featured in this book were planned by groups unaffiliated with the central governing agency or entity running the world's fairs. To supplement the main bodies of records, I sought additional archival sources for each of the replicas. Records for the 1926 Mount Vernon House, for example, are located in the Records of the YWCA of Philadelphia in the Metropolitan Collection of the Urban Archives at Temple University, Philadelphia. I found no additional archival materials for the 1915 Virginia Building.

I discovered most of the published primary sources for each of the world's fair buildings, along with all of the prints and objects in chapter 1 and other examples throughout the book, through Web-based databases and old-fashioned shelf-browsing. The Avery Index to Architectural Periodicals, the American Periodical Series, WorldCat, ProQuest Historical Newspapers, Google Books, and the Readers' Guide to Periodical Literature were particularly valuable resources. I culled house-plan catalogues from the enormous Building Technology Heritage Library.

Many of these resources have improved exponentially in their breadth and searchability since I first began this project ten years ago. This greatly changed the scope of the book's narrative over time. There is no efficient way that I could have "flipped through" the hundreds of catalogues I looked at to find the versions of Mount Vernon discussed in this book without the Building Technology Heritage Library's online database, for example. I similarly discovered hundreds of books and periodicals from the early twentieth century on Google Books, the vast majority of which were not online as recently as three years ago.

I did find many published primary sources, especially advertisements, through shelf-browsing and page-turning. Most volumes of popular publications of the early twentieth century, including *House Beautiful* and many architecture magazines, are thankfully still on the shelves at the University of Virginia's libraries, begging to be explored.

Finally, a last word about Google. Over the past year, Google Image Search has improved dramatically. Searching with terms such as "Mount Vernon," "columns," and "tradition," along with "funeral home" or "motel," generated hundreds of thousands of images that I scrolled through looking for buildings that resembled Mount Vernon. The search engine drew these terms from businesses' websites or from the transcription of captions on the backs of postcards. Just as Mount Vernon's architecture was key to these businesses' marketing, so were the words to describe it. The Web makes both searchable. From there, I developed lists of potential examples and began reaching out to businesses and purchasing postcards from online retailers. The sheer quantity of visual material available on the Web gives me confidence that I have selected representative examples.

Illustration Credits

Figures not otherwise credited are from the author's collection.

Building Technology Heritage Library: figs. 34, 35

Chicago History Museum: fig. 38

Forest Lawn: fig. 46

Garlinghouse Company: fig. 35

Library of Congress, Prints and Photographs Division: fig. 12

Courtesy of Mount Vernon Ladies' Association: title page spread, figs. 2, 3, 4, 5, 6, 7, 9, 10, 13, 14, 15, 17, 18, 19, 20, 22, 23, 31, 36, 39, 40, 41, 42, 43, 48, 49

National Archives and Records Administration: figs. 32, 33

Emmet Collection, Miriam and Ira D. Wallach Division of Art, Prints and Photographs, The New York Public Library: fig. 8

Curtis Palmer: fig. 1

Quinn Evans Architects: figs. 2, 3

Steven Stewart: fig. 46

Toppitzer Funeral Home: fig. 47

James Wills Bollinger Papers, University of Iowa Libraries: fig. 16

University of Virginia Library: figs. 11, 21, 24, 25, 26, 27, 28

Index

donations, 67, 83; purchase, 46, 47–48, 49–50, 213n25, 214n36, 214n39, 214n41; restoration, 60

funeral homes and cemeteries, 162; development of industry, 180; elements of MV used, 185–86; Forest Lawn funeral homes and memorial parks, 180–84, *181,* 258n100; MV features to assure families, 185; patriotism and war dead, 180; with political slant, 182–83, 258n96; segregation, 174–75; slaves' cemetery, 164, 194–95; Toppitzer Funeral Home, 185–86, *187*

furnishings (MV): changes in interpretation, 75, 224n194; donations, 63–64; and Halsted, 63; increased knowledge about, 71–72, 74, 224n186; of MV replica at Colonial and Overseas Exposition in Paris, 135, *136,* 137; taken by Herbert, 63; use of antiques, 71–73, *72;* use of inventory, 70, 71, 84, 157, 189, 222n162, 223n181; using to evoke past, 57–58, 59; left by J. A. Washington III, 55–56

Garden & Home Builder, 81

gardens. *See* landscape (MV)

Garlinghouse Company, 143, 199–200; "Colonial Cottage," 142, *143*

General Washington's Resignation (Barralet), 23, *24,* 206n49

Geographies (Morse), 20

George Washington (Houdon), 23

George Washington Bicentennial Commission, 131–32

George Washington Parkway, 129

Georgian architecture, 148, 206n40

Georgian Period, The (volume 6, *American Architect and Building News*), 91, 103, 229n44

Gilliam, Dorothy, 161, 194–95, 197

Gillis, R. A., 4-H (Jackson's Mill, West Virginia) dining hall, 116–20, *117,* 239n179

Godey's Lady's Book: ability of MV to influence public, 58; formation of MVLA, 46;

as fund-raiser, 214n42; Great Hall, *29,* 29–30; New Room, 29

Good Housekeeping, 137

Gordon, Beverly, 59–60

Gordon, John B., 124, 125

Gordon–Van Tine Company, 143

Grady, Henry W., 124

Great Depression, 130, 131–32, 137, 151

Gréber, Jacques, 134

Green, Nancy, 100

Greenberg, Allan, 200

greenhouse (MV): construction by Washington, 164; construction of commercial, by MVLA, 62; reconstruction of Washington's, 163, *163,* 164–66, *166,* 167

Greenough, Horatio, 38

guidebooks to MV, 26, 68–69, 176, 222n160

Gutta Percha Company's "Barreled Sunlight" white paint, 129

Hale, Sarah J.: ability of MV to influence public, 58; MV as national symbol, 46–47; raising funds for purchase, 50; use of *Godey's Lady's Book* to promote causes, 214n42

Halsey, R. T., 113

Halsted, Nancy, *42;* porch reconstruction, 76, 225n199; relic house idea, 86; system of restoration devised, 63

Hamilton, Mary, 51, 57

Hamrick, Mike, 2

Harper's Weekly, 71

harpsichord (of Nelly Custis), *52,* 64, 73, *74,* 223n181

Harrison, Ellen, 228n27

Hartley, Charles H., 118

Hasbrouck House, 59

Heartland Luxury Homes, 200

Herbert, Upton, 55, 63, 225n199

Heth, Nannie Randolph, 102, *103,* 234nn114–16

Hilfiger, Susie, 200

Hill, Benjamin, 125

Learning from Las Vegas (Brown and Venturi), 173

Lee, Mary Custis: Nelly Custis objects, 75; and Lossing, 215n46; sideboard donated by, 70, *71*

Lee, Robert E., 124

Liberator, 37

Life of George Washington (Everett), 70

Life of George Washington—The Citizen (Régnier after Stearns), 33, *35*

Lippincott's Monthly Magazine, 91

Little, Arthur, 90

little parlor (MV), restoration of, 73–75, *74,* 223nn181–82

living-history interpretations, 102

Lossing, Benson J.: engravings in guidebook, 69, 222n160; harpsichord of Nelly Custis, *52,* 64; inventory of George Washington estate, 70; and Mary Custis Lee, 215n46; raising funds for purchase, 51; reconstructions using drawings of, 76, 216n52

Lost Cause. *See* "Old South" myth

Louisiana Purchase Exposition (St. Louis, Missouri, 1904), 100

Loved One, The: An Anglo-American Tragedy (Waugh), 184

Lowell Inn (Stillwater, Minnesota), 176

lower garden (MV), 159–60

Ludlow and Peabody, 240n203

Macomber, Walter Mayo, 159, 164–66, 167, 168

Marriage of Washington, The (Stearns), 33

Martha Washington's Motel (Waldorf, Maryland), 179

Martha Washington's sitting-room (first-floor bedroom, MV), restoration of, 70–71, 223n169

"Martha Washington teas," 60

Matthews, Frank, 195

McKim, Charles Follen, 106

McKim, Mead and White, 104, 105–8; Orchard house, 106-8, *107*

McMakin, Mary, 55

Meadows, Christine, 189

Medary, Milton Bennett, Jr., 86–87, 88, 89, 228n27

Meissner, Gustav, 135

Metropolitan Museum of Art, 85, *87,* 111, 157

Michler, Nathaniel, 62, 75, 76

Mills, Robert, 38–39

Mitchell, "Daddy" Jim, 63

Mitchell, Martha, 83

Mitford, Jessica, 184

Mobile Tribune, 45

Modern Homes (Sears catalogue), 134, 140, *141,* 142–43

Monongahela West Penn Public Service Company, 118

Monticello, 100, 124, 151, 185

Morris-Knowles Engineers, 118

Morse, Frank, 165, 167, 168

Morse, Jedidiah, 20

Mosca, Matthew, 188

motels, 162; adaptability of Palladian organization of MV to, 177; assorted MV features on, 173–75, *176,* 176–79, *178;* messages communicated with similarity to MV, 174–75; post–World War II development of, 175; segregation, 174; transition to chains and franchises, 179–80

Mount Vernon, *ii–iii, 12, 15, 16, 17, 19, 29, 53, 78;* appreciated for architectural significance, 91–92; conditions under owner-occupants, 41; as defining secular American culture and identity, 26; federal purchase attempt, 45; first-floor plan of, *10;* as ideal American house and home, 81; malleability of meanings, 3–4, 8, 81–83, 199, 200; as model of preservation, 79; original construction, 11; as prime example of American home, 30–31; second-floor plan of, *11;* George Washington's alterations to, 10–13. *See also* printed verbal depictions of MV; printed visual depictions rooms (MV)

Mount Vernon (*continued*)

—and George Washington: as access to private side of, 30, 170–71; as access to real, 191; greater realism in portrayal, 198; as manifestation of character, 21, 22, 47–48, 117, 132, 190, 191; MV as central to image as ideal leader, 7, 169; representing, as farmer/family man, 30–34, *35*, 38, 39; representing, as gentleman architect, 10–13, 20, 51, 92, 153–54, 157, 229n50; representing, as slaveholder, *35*, 163, 166–67, 168, 171, 190, 191; reverence for, inspired by MV, 82

Mount Vernon (Parkyns), *17*

Mount Vernon and Its Associations, Historical, Biographical, and Pictorial (Lossing), 51–52, *52*, 70, 215n50, 216n52, 222n162

Mount Vernon Brand Straight Rye Whiskey, 5, 127–29, *128*

"Mount Vernon House" (YWCA), 114–16, 119–20, 238n172

Mount Vernon Inn restaurant, 193, 195

Mount Vernon Ladies' Association (MVLA): Archaeology Study Committee, 198; attempts to improve interpretation accuracy, 150–51, 157–59; attempts to maintain relevancy of Washington, 187; Committee on Furnishings for Outbuildings, 165; formation of, 44, 45–46, 212n17; fundraising as primary role, 193–94, 195; goals of, 42–43; Grand Council (1873), *42*, 48, 67; gulf between perceived responsibilities of, and MV's image in popular culture, 200; historic "firsts" accomplished by, 43; objections of use of word "authentic" by design magazines, 145; opposition to women as leaders, 48–49; overview of, 4–5; ownership costs of MV, 54; Papers of George Washington project, 190–91; plan to deed MV to Virginia, 47; public opinion about, 64–65, 129–30; purchase and possession of MV, 41–43, 49, 202n8, 213n31, 216n61; resignation of Cunningham, 65–66, 221n138; scholarly-based

publicity, 153–57, *155;* slave memorial competition, 195–98, *197;* slavery as presented by, criticized, 161–62; sound and light show, 191–92, 260n138, 260n141, 260n146; structure of, 48–49, 66; use of outside consultants, 62, 77, 86–89, 157–58, 188

—attempts to control MV: message visitors left with, 170; photographed images, 78–79; public image, 5, 128–29; replicas, 101, 138–39, 172; visual and auditory intrusions to MV, 187

—expositions/fairs and: Colonial and Overseas Exposition (Paris, 1931), 138; Colonial Village (Century of Progress International Exposition, Chicago, 1934), 147–48, 149–50; Panama-Pacific International Exposition (San Francisco, 1915), 101, 234n107; World's Columbian Exposition (Chicago, 1893), 97–98

—restoration of MV by: federal money for, 61–62; inspirations for, 59–60, *61;* as pioneers in, 58, 167; plans, 52–53; professionalism of, 151–58; rooms assigned to vice regents, 69–75, *72, 74,* 222nn161-62, 223nn168-69, 223nn181-82, 224n186; strategy, 57–58

Mount Vernon Ladies' Association of the Union (MVLA). *See* Mount Vernon Ladies' Association (MVLA)

Mount Vernon Motel (Albany, New York), 177, *178*

Mount Vernon Motor Lodge (Springfield, Missouri), 177

Mount Vernon Motor Lodge (Winter Park, Florida), 179

"Mount Vernon of the West," 176

Mount Vernon Papers, The (Everett), 214n41

Mount Vernon Reader, The, 30–31

Mount Vernon Record, 49–50, 52, 214n39

Mount Vernon Rooms (*Ladies' Home Journal*), 144, *145*

"Mt. Vernon, The" (Aladdin Company), 142–43

music room (MV), restoration of, 73–75, *74*, 223nn181–82
Mussey, John, 67
Muttontown Meadows house (Delano and Aldrich), 109, *109*

Nash, Arthur C., 176
National Association for the Advancement of Colored People (NAACP), Fairfax chapter, 195
nationalism: democratization and commodification of history, 112–13; MV as symbol of, 7, 18, 46–47, 48; and MVLA, 46, 48, 49–50
National Origins Act (1924), 113
National Register, 25
"New England Farmer's Home" (Centennial Exposition in Philadelphia), 60
New Room (MV): early verbal depiction, 20; as furnished by George Washington, 25; in *Godey's Lady's Book*, 29; as museum within house, *72*, 72–73; MVLA preferences as trumping authenticity in, 159; named by George Washington, 205n31; protection of objects in, 68; restoration, 62; Venetian window, 15, *15*, 153
"New South" and MV, 94
New York City replicas of MV, 139–40
New York Ledger, 50
New York Times, 153–54
Nicolet, Tell W., 118
North-East View of Mount Vernon, Painted on the Spot, A (Savage), 15, *16*, 17

objects, depictions of MV on, 18–20, *19*, 144
"Old South" myth: MV as symbol of, 82, 93–95, 103; replicas of famous southern homes as symbols of, 124–25; replicas of MV as symbol of, 82, 96, 98, 99–102, 120–22; and slaves' cemetery, 164, 194–95; success of, 102–3
Orchard house (McKim, Mead and White), 106–8, *107*

outbuildings. *See* dependencies (MV)
owner-occupants of MV: condition of MV under, 36–37; maintenance by, 41–42, 75; as pilgrimage site under, 26–28; refusal to sell to women, 47
ownership. *See* owner-occupants of MV
Oyenusi, Adetunji, *197*

Paine, Thomas, 23
paintings of MV, 15–16. *See also specific artists and artworks by name/title*
Palladian organization, 106, 131, 144, 173–74, 177
Palladio, Andrea, 12
Panama-Pacific International Exposition (San Francisco, 1915), 95, 100–102, *103*, 132, 234n107
Papers of George Washington project, 190–91
Parkyns, George Isham, 17–18, 20, 21; *Mount Vernon*, *17*
patriotism, MV as symbol of, 82, 176–77, 180, 182–83, 185
Paxton, Tom, 184
Peale, Rembrandt, 72–73; *Washington before Yorktown*, *72*
Pemberton, Norman W., 176
period rooms, 85, *87*, 90, 101–2, 134
Perry, Shaw and Hepburn, 151, 159
Peterson's Magazine, 94–95
Philadelphia Art Museum, 157
Philadelphia Monthly Magazine, 20
Philadelphia Sesquicentennial Exposition (1926), 114–16, 238n172
photographed images, MVLA control of, 78–79
piazza (MV), 13, 76; Aladdin Company "Kingston," 142; chinoiserie balustrade, 76, 157, 174; in commercial structures, 176, 177, 185; dating of, 154; as favorite way to reference MV, 174; 4-H (West Virginia) dining hall, 116–17, *117*; Garlinghouse Company "Colonial Cottage," 142, *143*; Gordon–Van

remembering MV in twentieth century, 5–6; Prospect Park, Brooklyn, 139–40; Sears catalogue mail-order house, 130, 134, 140, *141,* 142; standardization in 1950s, 173–74; Wesleyan College, 114, 120–22; YWCA, 114–16

—at expositions/fairs: Colonial and Overseas Exposition (Paris, 1931), 130–32, *133,* 134–35, *136,* 137–38; "Colonial Village" (Century of Progress International Exposition in Chicago, 1934), 146–50, *147, 149;* Louisiana Purchase Exposition (St. Louis, 1904), 100; Panama-Pacific International Exposition (San Francisco, 1915), 100–102, 234n107; Virginia Buildings at world fairs, 95–100, *97,* World's Columbian Exposition (Chicago, 1893), 95

—funeral homes and cemeteries, 162; elements of MV used, 185–86; messages communicated with similarity to MV, 174–75; MV features to assure families, 185; patriotism and war dead, 180; with political slant, 182–83, 258n96; racial coding indicating segregation, 174–75

—motels, 162; adaptability of Palladian organization of MV to, 177; assorted MV features on, 173–75, *176,* 176–79, *178;* messages communicated with similarity to MV, 174–75; racial coding indicating segregation, 174

—symbolic meanings conveyed by: America as place for only "right" people, 119–20; civic-mindedness and leadership, 119, 122, 134, 137–38; hospitality, 94, 99, 121–22, 176; "Old South" myth, 82, 96, 98, 99–102, 120–22; segregation, 174–75; trustworthiness, 94, 99, 121–22, 174, 183

Republican Court, The (Huntington), 60

"Residences of the Presidents" (*Family Magazine*), 32–33

resident caretakers of MV, 55, 61, 217n75

Rest Hill house (Pope), 108

restoration of MV: concept of, 52; costs, 73; and Cunningham, 57, 62, 63; documentation used for, 76, 152–53, 155; exterior, *53;* federal funds, 61–62; fund-raising, 60; inspirations for, 59–60, *61;* methods and materials used, 62; outbuildings, 66, 158, 163–69; plans and strategy, 52–53, 57–58; repopulation of furnishings, 51; shift in approach, 77, 151, 225n205; sources of information for, 62–63; strategy of MVLA, 57–58; use of antiques, 71–73, *72;* use of printed visual depictions, 76, 216n52. *See also specific rooms by name*

Richards, Alice, 138, 139

Richmond Enquirer, 49

Riddle, Theodate Pope, 105–6

Riggs, George W., 67

riverfront room (MV), restoration of, 70–71, 223n169

Robertson, Alexander, 20, 21

Robinson, Harry G., *197*

Robinson, J. Randolph, 108

Robinson, Sarah, 99–100

Rogers, Edgerton Stewart, 97–98, 101, 233n105

Rogers, Thomas Mellon, 77

roof (MV), described, 12

rooms (MV): assigned to original states/vice regents, 63, 69–75, *72, 74,* 222nn161–62, 223nn168–69, 223nn181–82, 224n186; measures taken for visitors' safety and comfort, 84. *See also specific rooms and areas by name*

Rorie, Glen, *197*

Rossiter, Thomas Prichard, 41–42, 76, 211n2

salt house (MV), 87–88, 165, 228n34. *See also* relic house (MV)

sanitary fairs, 60, *61*

Sargent, Charles Sprague, 85

"saturated worlds," 59–60, *61*

Saturday Evening Post, 161

Savage, Edward, 13, 15–16, 18, 164; *A North-East View of Mount Vernon, Painted on the Spot,* 15, *16, 17, 19*

Schreeven, William J. Van, 190
Scott, Winfield, 54
Sears, Roebuck and Company: exhibition/
    fair replicas, 130–32, *133,* 134–35, *136;*
    influence of catalogue houses, 130, 142–43;
    Modern Homes catalogue, 134, 140, *141;*
    New York City replicas, 139–40
second floor (MV), plan of, *11*
sectionalism: and formation of MVLA, 43,
    44, 45–46, 212n17; and MV as symbol of
    national unity, 46–47; and raising funds
    for purchase, 48, 49–50; and structure of
    MVLA, 48–49; and Washington National
    Monument Society, 39
secular relics, 59
Shurcliff, Arthur, 151, 250n108
Simmons, William Joseph, 123, 124, 125,
    241n218
sitting-room (of Martha Washington, MV),
    restoration of, 70–71, 223n169
slaves and slavery at MV: cemetery, 164, 194–
    95; and commercial uses of MV elements,
    186, 200; construction of quarters, 164;
    inventory at death of George Washington,
    222n162; memorial, 164, 195–98, *197;* re-
    construction of quarters, 163, *163,* 164–69,
    166, 169; romanticized in "Old South"
    myth, 93, 94–95, 99–100; romanticized in
    paintings, 33, *35,* 100; in Solocast recorded
    tour, 171; study and collection of material
    culture of, 198; as tour guides, 27
—and MV narrative: criticized and changed
    in 1980s, 161–62, 197–98, 200; quarters as a
    manifestation of Washington's genius, 190;
    Washington as slaveholder, *35,* 163, 166–67,
    168, 171, 190, 191
Solocast recorded tour, 170, 171–72
Southern Literary Messenger, 46
south side porch (MV), 157; restoration of,
    76, *78,* 157, 225n199
Sparks, Jared, 190
spinning house (MV), 89, *89*
Stearns, Junius Brutus, 31, 33–34, 100

Stoke Poges (England), 182
study (of George Washington, MV), 28, 55,
    140, *141*
summerhouse (MV), 76, 158, 225n199
Sweat, Margaret, *42;* on changes after Cun-
    ningham's resignation, 65, 66; restoration
    philosophy, 63
symbolic roles of MV: agricultural past, 93,
    104; America as place for "right" people,
    20–21, 22, 119–20; "American Mecca,"
    25–26; civic-mindedness and leadership,
    119, 122; flexibility of, 3–4, 8, 81–83, 199,
    200; importance of domestic tranquil-
    ity, 7, 39; as manifestation of character of
    Washington, 21, 22, 47–48, 117, 132, 190,
    191; as mythical Old South, 82, 93–95,
    96, 98, 99–102, 103, 120–22, 164, 194–95;
    national unity, 7, 18, 46–47, 48; by 1920s
    divergent, 114; patriotism, 82, 176–77,
    180, 182–83, 185; as premier example of
    American domestic architecture, 108;
    republican values, 2, 20–21, 22, 48; U.S. to
    foreigners, 131
—replicas and reproductions: America as
    place for only "right" people, 119–20;
    civic-mindedness and leadership, 119, 122,
    134, 137–38; hospitality, 94, 99, 121–22,
    176; "Old South" myth, 82, 96, 98, 99–102,
    120–22; segregation, 174–75; trustworthi-
    ness, 174, 183

tableaux vivant, 60
Tallmadge, Thomas Eddy, 151; Mount
    Vernon replica at Century of Progress
    International Exposition in Chicago
    (1934), 146–50, *147, 149*
Taylor, Benjamin Van Campen, 76–77,
    225n199
"Texas Gate" (MV), construction of, 80
Thomas Jefferson Memorial Foundation, 151
Tiffey, Sarah, 62
tomb of George Washington (MV), 35–36,
    37, 217n82